This book is dedicated to three splendid gentlemen of translation, Joseph T. Malone I, Arcadius Avellanus, and Irwin K. Styles; and to all underrecognized and ill-paid translators everywhere.

CONTENTS

ACKNOWLEDGEMENTS

I am indebted to a number of people who in one fashion or another have helped make this book a reality: to Mark Aronoff, who urged me to write it; to Roberto Austerlitz, Ed Greenstein, and Marilyn Gaddis Rose, who read earlier versions of the manuscript and made invaluable suggestions for improvement (mine the burden if I have not always heeded them!); to John Delt, Paola di Mauro, Ernst A. Ebbinghaus, Brother Charles Quinn, and Fay Storch for information acknowledged at appropriate spots throughout; to Jennifer Christmann and Alison Otis for hunting down copyright permissions; and, last but by no means least, to my students at Barnard College and Columbia University, who over the years have helped me grapple with the issues treated throughout.

Acknowledgement is hereby gratefully extended to the following persons and agencies for permission to use copyrighted materials in various examples and figures as indicated, as well as in nearby portions of the text (fuller publication data are provided under indicated items in the Bibliography): The American Oriental Society, for portions of Malone 1983f (see example (8.13) in chapter 8); Richard Behm, for portions of Malone 1987a and 1987b (see (14.12) in chap. 14); Donna Brown, for portions of Brown 1982 (see (13.6b) in chap. 13); MIT Press, for portions of Malone 1982c (see (14.11) in chap. 14); Pantheon Books, a division of Random House, Inc., for portions of Hunt & Stern 1972 (see (1.10t) and (1.12t) in chap. 1, (2.1bt) and (2.3t) in chap. 2, (6.9t) in chap. 6, (5.2at) in chap. 5, (7.3t) in chap. 7, (9.6t) and (9.8t) in chap. 9, (15.4t–15.5t) and (15.7t) in chap. 15, (16.7t) in chap. 16).

INTRODUCTION

0.1 BASIC GOALS OF THE BOOK

One way to usher in the work of this book is to provide a few comments on the title and subtitle.

0.1.1 Linguistics and Translation

'The science of linguistics *in* the art of translation'. The use of the preposition 'in' is meant to convey that the linguistics is being put at the service of the translation, a point further specified by the subtitle, 'some tools from linguistics for the analysis and practice of translation'. It would be equally legitimate and important to study the interface of both on an equal basis or to subordinate translation to linguistics, for example in studying the impact on linguistic theory of attested translational equivalences across a variety of languages. In fact, publications are not hard to find incorporating both these approaches: e.g., Jäger (1975), Wilss (1977).

0.1.2 The Science of Linguistics

'The *science* of linguistics in the art of translation'. With one reservation (see §0.1.3), the title might be less catchily but more informatively rephrased as 'the pure-linguistic science of theoretical linguistics in the service of the applied-linguistic technology of translation'. What I have tried to do in this book, and what I would like to encourage others to carry forth and improve on, is to exploit the open-ended resources of pure-linguistic science for the fashioning of techniques and procedures (the 'tools' of the subtitle) to serve as applied-linguistic accessories in the analysis and practice of translation.

The crucial point in this dialectic is the significant degree of independence between pure linguistics and applied linguistics: not every discovery or formulation of the theoretician will be of equal value for translational purposes, and some of the most useful applied-linguistic distillates may, conversely, be of little theoretical interest per se.[1]

The question necessarily arises in this connection as to how much knowledge of linguistics a reader of this book is assumed to have. The answer is *none*, with the important qualification that the amount of linguistics that one does happen to command should entail a commensurate degree of facility in using and, particularly, developing techniques like those set forth in the book.[2]

0.1.3 The Art of Translation

'The science of linguistics in the *art* of translation'. The reservation mentioned at the outset of §0.1.2 is this disclaimer: the 'art of translation' must not be construed as simply shorthand for 'applied-linguistic technology of translation'. As all translators will aver, their business simply cannot be reduced to a branch of technology, linguistic or otherwise. Despite a certain amount of progress in automatizing the translation of scientific language over the past quarter century (see Hutchins (1984) for a survey), the prospects of most other text types following suit seem bleak indeed. In the case of religious texts, for example, the briefest glance at the distinguished work of Eugene Nida and his associates (see Bibliography) should quickly convince one that Bible translation of high quality would be out of the question without the human translator's unbounded intelligence and creative ingenuity.[3]

The quintessence of translation as art is, if anything, even more patent in the case of literary texts, which will comprise the majority of examples in this book.

0.1.4 The Analysis and Practice of Translation

'Some tools for the analysis and practice of translation'. The techniques and procedures outlined in this book are designed to serve either as tools for the study of completed translations (the ANALYTIC mode), or as helpmates in the act of translation (the OPERATIVE mode).

0.2 LINGUISTIC SCAFFOLDING

The science of linguistics is not monolithic but rather comprises a network of subdisciplines traversed by a variety of analytic perspectives. Moreover, not all facets of linguistics are equally applicable to translation. Thus, DIACHRONIC linguistics, whose goal is the study of language change, development, and history, is at best marginally and occasionally relevant. On the other hand, SYNCHRONIC linguistics, which views language function and structure in abstraction of change over time, is of paramount importance to the study of translation. Unless otherwise specified, all linguistic assumptions and principles to be adduced throughout are synchronic.

Another breakdown of linguistic labor involves the size of the language units taken as analytic objects. A case in point is DISCOURSE ANALYSIS (cf. Van Dijk (1985)), which considers the structure and function of large naturalistic units, such as a dialogue in the spoken mode or a sequence of paragraphs in the written mode. Since the great majority of examples throughout this book are excerpts from written texts of one sort or another, and since the adequacy of their translation characteristically depends at least in part on properties of their including text, many of the linguistic techniques and vantages employed will be discourse-analytic in nature, at least implicitly.[4]

All contemporary linguistic theories agree in recognizing language as being pervasively layered, such that its forms and functions relate to one another through a variety of systematically interdependent complexes. On the other hand, substantial disagreement exists as to the number and nature of such complexes. For the purposes of this book, three sorts of complexes will be recognized: ORGANIZATIONAL COMPONENTS (§0.2.1–§0.2.3), COMPOSITIONAL LEVELS (§0.2.4), and REPRESENTATIONAL STRATA (§0.2.5).

0.2.1 Primary Organizational Components

Four central components will be assumed. They are related approximately as portrayed in diagram (0.1) (cf. Malone (1980a)). For expository convenience, a component will often be referred to with the name of the linguistic discipline taking it as an object of study. In (0.1) the names of these disciplines are parenthesized.

(0.1)
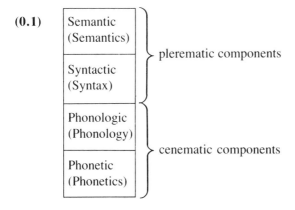

The SEMANTIC and PHONETIC components model LINGUISTIC MEANINGS and SPEECH SOUNDS (pronunciation) respectively, and so in a sense constitute the two major interfaces whereby language mediates to the nonlinguistic world: via the semantic component to the cognitive world of ideation and denotation and via the phonetic component to the world of articulation and audition (physiological production and perception of acoustic speech signals).

The mutual relations of meanings and speech sounds are mediated by a pair of 'service components': the SYNTACTIC, which organizes meanings into forms (e.g. words, phrases, sentences) and the PHONOLOGIC, which deploys a language's phonetic resources in the symbolization of the forms built up by the syntax.

It may be seen that this characterization of the four components of (0.1) suggests a fundamental binary organization, with semantics and syntax pairing off toward meaning and phonetics and phonology pairing off toward sound. Since this duality will play an important role throughout the book, the terms PLEREMATIC and CENEMATIC (Hockett (1958:575)) will often be used as generic labels for the pairs semantics-syntax and phonetics-phonology, respectively.

0.2.2 Secondary Organizational Components

In addition to the four central components of (0.1), various other componentlike facets of language may be posited. Four such facets will be of some importance in this book: MORPHOLOGY, LEXICOLOGY, PRAGMATICS, and ORTHOGRAPHY.

Morphology deals with the structure and function of words, while lexicology deals with lexical items, or LEXEMES—linguistic units that serve as fundamental building blocks for discourse, abstractive of any grammatical particulars that might accrue to them in specific contexts (e.g. tense markers in the case of verbs, or number markers in the case of nouns). Since lexemes are often coterminous with words, there is considerable overlap in the concerns of lexicology and morphology. Furthermore, both these disciplines crosscut the components of (0.1), since both words and lexemes have semantic, syntactic, phonologic, and phonetic properties (cf. Aronoff (1983)). For most purposes throughout this book, it will be convenient to consider words and lexemes as plearematic units. Moreover, the overlap between morphological and syntactic patterning will at times be so close as to justify use of the portmanteau term MORPHOSYNTAX.

Pragmatics and orthography are more accurately viewed as PARALINGUISTIC areas than as fields within linguistics proper.

Pragmatics deals with the conventional uses of linguistic units not accounted for directly as functions of (other) linguistic components. Since pragmatics characteristically overlaps with semantics and syntax to a considerable extent, it will be convenient to treat it in what follows largely as a plerematic area.

Because a writing system constitutes a representational accessory to a language in terms of an inventory of graphic symbols taking linguistic units as arguments (cf. Gelb and Whiting (1980)), the concerns of orthography will be closest to the components housing the linguistic units so symbolized. Though a survey of writing systems will show the involvement of all linguistic components in one fashion or another, by far the most pervasive and important components for orthographic representation are phonology and phonetics. Hence, it will be feasible and convenient in what follows to construe orthography largely as a cenematic component.[5]

The preceding discussion suggests that (0.1) be supplemented approximately as in (0.2), where the arrows mark interfaces of particular importance (at least for purposes of this book).

(0.2)

P		M	Semantics	L		O	plerematic components
r	→	o	→	← e		r	
a		r	Syntax	x		t	
--- g ---		p	-----------	i	--	h	------------
m		h	Phonology	c		o	cenematic components
a		o		o	←	g	
t		l	Phonetics	l		r	
i		o		o		a	
c		g		g		p	
s		y		y		h	
						y	

0.2.3 An Extended Illustration

Some of the points covered in §0.2.1–§0.2.2 may be illustrated by means of the Turkish joke and its translation given in (0.3). Following conventions to be used throughout, *s* marks the source text (0.3s), and *t* the target text (0.3t). The label *an.* prefaces an ANALYTIC TRANSLATION, i.e., an expository target rendition whose exact nature, ranging from quite free to extremely literalistic (as here), will depend on the analytic focus at hand.

One way of appreciating the distinction between semantics and morphosyntax is to isolate cases where a meaning stays more or less constant while the formal apparatus conveying that meaning varies. Such situations abound in translation between languages as dissimilar as Turkish and English, and the example in (0.3) contains several cases in point. While the meaning of the question asked by the judge (0.3c) is (approximately) identical in both texts, in Turkish the interrogative function (symbolized by *Q* in the analytic translation) is expressed MORPHEMICALLY, by the particle *mı-* in *mısın* ('Q' in the analytic translation 'Q-you'), while in English the function is expressed TAGMEMICALLY, by preposing the subject *you* to the verb *drink* with the help of the auxiliary verb *do*. (For a definition of the above terms, cf. Bloomfield (1933:161–68; cf. also below in this section, and §11.2 in chapter 11).

The joke also contains a few illustrations of pragmatic force, ranging from the patent to the subtle. On the patent side are religious-cultural milieu conditions

(0.3) **sa**. İçki içerken yakalanmıştı. Hem de Ramazanda . . .
sb.Derhal şeriat mahkemesine götürüldü, kadının huzuruna
çıkarıldı. Kadı sordu:
sc. —Erenler, içki kullanır mısın? . . .
Bektaşi, mest ve mahmur, kadıya şu haklı suali sordu:
sd. —Eyvallah . . . İkram mı edeceksin? . . . (Anonymous:71)
an.**a**. Drink drinking he-was-seized. Even and on-Ramadan . . .
b. Immediately Moslem-religious-law into-its-court
he-was-taken, Moslem-religious-judge into-his-presence
he-was-brought. Judge asked:
c. —Holy-one drink use Q-you?
Bektashi, drunk and besotten, to-judge this reasonable question
asked:
d. —Thank you . . . Kind-offer will-you-be-making? . . .
ta. A Bektashi was caught drinking, and during Ramadan at that.
tb. So he was hauled into religious court where the judge asked him;
tc. 'Sir, do you drink?'
td. 'Why thank you, Your Honor! What are you offering?'
(M1985a:26)

for understanding that in traditionally strict Moslem countries (in this case, Ottoman Turkey) imbibing alcohol is a crime, particularly during the holy month of Ramadan. On the subtler side is the fact that the success of the joke depends upon Turkish and English sharing a pattern of CONVERSATIONAL IMPLICATURE (Grice (1975)): a regularity whereby, in this case, an utterance that is semantically a request for simple information ((sc) *içki kullanır mısın?* = (tc) *do you drink?*) may be pragmatically understood as a vehicle conveying a polite offer ('May I offer you a drink?'). If source and target languages did not share this implicature—as often they do not—the translator would be hard put indeed to provide a naturalistic (as opposed to philological) target rendition.

The difference between morphology and lexicology may be illustrated handily with two examples from (0.3td): though the units *thank, you*, and *offering* are morphological objects, qua words, the corresponding lexemes are the two words *thank* and *you* taken as units, the supra-word group *thank you* taken as a set expression, and the infra-word units (morphemes) *offer* and *-ing*.

Even as a one-to-many relation from function to form was used to bring out a difference between the pleremic components of semantics and syntax, so an analogous discrepancy may be appealed to in the cenematic area. The Turkish words *mahkemesine* (an. 'into-its-court') and *huzuruna* (an. 'into-his-presence') (0.3sa) end in the morphologically identical element *-ne* = *-na* 'into', the phonetic difference between the front vowel [e] and the back vowel [a] following as a consequence of ASSIMILATION to the nearest preceding vowel in each case: front [i] and back [u], respectively (for these properties, cf. the chart in §13.). Thus, though the suffixes are phonetically distinct, they are phonologically identical. In this case one would say that a minimal morphosyntactic unit, or MOR-

PHEME, having a unitary phonological representation /-nE/, is manifested phonetically by either of two ALLOMORPHS, [-ne]~ [-na], depending on the environment (cf. immediately below and §13.4 in chapter 13).

While English orthography is quite opaque in relation to its cenematic structure, Turkish orthography is quite transparent in this regard—so much so that its letters *e, a, i, u*, and *n* could be used directly as the phonetic symbols [e], [a], [i], [u], and [n] in the preceding example. (Cf. the chart in §13.) In cases where orthographic-cenematic differences assume a focal role, angle brackets (<   >) will set off spellings, while cenematic representations will be marked as either phonetic ([   ]) or phonological (/   /; more accurately, as applied-linguistic distillates of phonological representations called 'ABSTRACT PHONETIC REPRESENTATIONS' (APRs)—see §13.4).

0.2.4 Compositional Levels

Substantial agreement exists among linguists that the units of at least some organizational components occur in hierarchical arrangements instantiating part-whole relations. Such organization is clearest in the area of morphosyntax, where it has traditionally been studied under the label of PARSING.

In what follows, structuring of this type will be indicated by curly brackets, in a way that may be made clear with an example from (0.3ta). The bracketing 0{ 1{he}1 1{ 2{was hauled}2 2{ 3{into}3 3{religious court}3 }2 }1 }0 analyzes this string into four COMPOSITIONAL LEVELS, that of sentence 0{   }0; that of subject and predicate 1{   }1 1{   }1; that of verb and complement 2{   }2 2{   }2; and that of preposition and complement 3{   }3 3{   }3.

The bracketing may be varied and brought to any desired degree of precision or sketchiness. Morphosyntactic labels may replace numerical tags (e.g., NP {he}NP would mark the subject as a noun phrase), or both may be omitted, as may the brackets around a singleton constituent whose role is clarified by the overall structure (e.g. {he {was hauled} . . . } in lieu of { {he} {was hauled} . . . }).

'Flat' bracketing may be useful when analytic interest focuses on a unit of just one sort. For instance, a bracketing like {he} {was} {hauled} {into} . . . brings the word level into focus, while {he} {was} {haul} {ed} {in} {to} . . . provides an analysis at the level of the morpheme (minimal morphosyntactic unit). Cf. §6.1 in chapter 6.

0.2.5 Representational Strata

Roughly speaking, the analysis of a linguistic string in a given component into REPRESENTATIONAL STRATA provides a set of representations for that string whose extreme members, i.e., those representations closest to either end of the component, are in some sense structurally akin to the adjacent components, with adjacency reckoned as in chart (0.1). Thus, in the syntactic component, a representation on the stratum adjacent to semantics will in some sense be 'semanticlike', while the stratum at the opposite extreme of the syntax will contain representations with certain 'phonologylike' properties.

The affiliation of extreme strata for adjacent components has sometimes led theoreticians to 'collapse' specific pairs of such adjacent components into one complex analytic object. In fact, such uniformization is so widespread in cenematics as to be virtually standard practice; and one could accordingly modify the charts of (0.1) and (0.2) by collapsing phonology and phonetics into one supercomponent, with phonetics reanalyzed as the stratum at the opposite end from syntax.

Since the notion of representational strata will receive considerable discussion and illustration in chapters 11 through 14, examples will be foregone here.

0.3 FORMAT OF TRANSLATIONAL EXAMPLES AND BIBLIOGRAPHICAL REFERENCES

0.3.1 Translational Examples

Most translational examples throughout will appear in the format of (0.3), with the exception of analytic translations, which will normally appear on line in the main text, if and as needed.

Examples from languages employing Latin-based orthography will normally be presented in that orthography (as (0.3s)). Non–Latin-based orthographies have, for the most part, been retranscribed according to the conventions given in the Chicago Manual of Style (Chicago (1982)). Exceptions are Hebrew, Arabic, and Yiddish, which are transcribed in accordance with a phonetic notation explained at the outset of chapter 13 (§13.0).

As in (0.3), source and target portions of an example are prefaced by s and t, respectively. These portions in turn are frequently broken down into smaller sections marked a,b,c, and so on. Such smaller sections are calibrated across source and target in either of two ways, according to convenience: sa,sb,sc, . . . ; ta,tb,tc, . . . (as in (0.3)), or as,bs,cs, . . . ; at,bt,ct, . . .

Units within examples are frequently tagged for discussion within the body of the text. Such units are usually set off by brackets ([   ]), supplemented where necessary by double brackets ([[   ]]) (e.g. (1.1) in chapter 1). Other marking techniques will either be mentioned at the time (e.g. italics in (11.1) of chapter 11) or be clear from the context (e.g. referential indices in (5.3) of chapter 5).

0.3.2 Bibliographical References

All bibliographical citations refer to the Bibliography at the end of the book. See there also for the form of references given within the text of the book.

0.4 OVERVIEW OF THE BOOK'S STRUCTURE

The sixteen chapters of the book are divided into three sections: Part One (chapters 1 through 7), Part Two (chapters 8 through 12), and Part Three (chapters 13 through 16).

Part One is devoted to the presentation and illustration of TRAJECTIONS, an informal analytic system whereby a pair of source and target texts may be resolved into elementary plerematic (§0.2.1) translational patterns. In addition to analytic work of their own, trajections will provide a basic scaffolding for the study of translational situations throughout the book, especially in Part Two.

Part Two is given over to the development of a variety of techniques and procedures informed by either or both of two analytic perspectives, the SYSTEMIC and the FORMALISTIC (definitions to be provided in §8.0). Most of the notions and tools of Part Two are distillates of plerematic theoretic-linguistic concepts.

Part Three deals with a range of translational situations where, in one sense or another, knowledge of the intended extralinguistic message of the source text is insufficient for replication of that message in the target text, even when the translator's competence in both languages is unimpeachable. Since such insufficiency stems primarily from phonetic or phonological discrepancies between source and target languages, most of Part Three will be cenematic (§0.2.1) in nature.

0.5 LIST OF TERMS AND SYMBOLS NOT DEFINED ELSEWHERE

There follows a list of terms and symbols either not defined elsewhere or having multiple usages. (For others, see the Index). Analphabetic entries are given last.

A Adjective (e.g. §8.1 (8.2)).

boundary A structural point marking the transition from one constituent to another. In this book only WORD BOUNDARY is used, symbolized by '#' (e.g. §14.1).

C Consonant (e.g. §8.1).

C_0 A series of zero or more consonants (e.g. §14.1).

case In the grammatical sense, a form of a noun or adjective marking some aspect of its plerematic relations to other elements in the sentence. The following multiple example illustrates the phenomenon for Russian, each of the six tokens of the noun *Nataša* 'Natasha' instantiating a distinct function, respectively: DATIVE (indirect object), PREPOSITIONAL and INSTRUMENTAL (constructed with the prepositions *o* 'of' and *meždu* 'between', respectively), NOMINATIVE (subject), ACCUSATIVE (direct object), and GENITIVE (possessive).

> *s.* [Nataše] prixodilo inogda . . . Vospominanije [o Nataše] . . . [meždu nim i Natašej].[Nataša] byla v svojej komnate. . . . Boris pomnil tu [Natašu] . . . sijajuščije glaza [Nataši] (Tolstoy i:442f)
>
> *t.* It sometimes occurred [to Natasha] . . . memories [of Natasha] . . . [between himself and Natasha] . . . [Natasha] was in her own room . . . Boris remembered [Natasha] . . . [Natasha's] laughing eyes (Edmonds i:525f)

(Cf. also §1.5 for Greek, §11 for Latin, §16.2 for German, etc.)

CONJ Conjunction (e.g. §10.1).

contentive   A word belonging to a major part-of-speech class (e.g. noun, verb, adjective) characterized by relatively rich semantic content. Antonym, **functor** (Cf. Hockett 1958:264f) (e.g. §8.3).

functor   A word belonging to a minor part-of-speech class (e.g. preposition, pronoun) characterized by relatively impoverished semantic content but wide syntactic ('grammatical') function. Antonym, **contentive** (e.g. §8.1).

NP   Noun phrase; a noun together with any modifiers constructed with it (e.g. §2.1).

P   Preposition (e.g. §10.1).

performer   Speaker or writer (e.g. §7.2).

PP   Prepositional phrase; a constituent consisting of a preposition and the NP in construction with it (e.g. §10.1).

PRN   Pronoun (e.g. §10.1).

S,S′   Sentence or clause (e.g. §1.1, §12.3 with example (12.9) and note 6). S is also used in trajectional schemata for *Substitution* (e.g. §1.1).

segment   A vowel or a consonant (e.g. §13.2).

V   Vowel   (e.g.§8.1).

VB   Verb   (e.g. §8.1).

X,Y   Variable or unknown element or group of elements. (In addition to numerous occurrences throughout the book (e.g. §13.2), several examples incidentally follow here in this list).

*X   A form or interpretation nonoccurring (incorrect, meaningless, ungrammatical) in a given language (e.g. §1.2).

X-,-X,-X-   An element that occurs bound to some other element, whether prepositively (X-), postpositively (-X), or medially (-X-) (e.g. §7.4, §13).

X/Y   Source X and target Y (e.g. §0.3.2(v)); trajectionally, X and Y as translational alternatives in Zigzagging (§1.1.2(b)) or Matching (§1.4).

Boundary (See above).

[X] X is phonetic (pronounced) (e.g. §0.2.3); or featural (in which case it will normally appear as $[+X]$ or $[-X]$—e.g. (6.5)—and multiple specifications are given per either $[+X, -Y, \ldots]$ or $\begin{bmatrix} +X \\ -Y \\ . \\ . \\ . \end{bmatrix}$).

p[X] X is phonetic (pronounced), Used instead of plain [X] in contexts where there may be confusion with brackets functioning to set off translational elements (§0.3.1); e.g. examples (1.12), (13.9).

<X> X is a link in a chain (e.g. (2.2)); or orthographic (e.g. (13.14)).

CAPITAL LETTERS   mark grammatical elements (e.g. A, CONJ, etc. above), including analytic translations of functors (e.g. PASSIVE-PAST in (14.1)); trajectional schemata (e.g. AB → A in §1.1); fortis consonants (e.g. [kóRax] in §13.0); abstracted elements in abstract syntactic representations (e.g. §11.2).

lower-case letters   mark rhyme schemes (e.g. §1.3, §14.1) or other orthometric (poetic) patterns (e.g. parallelistic *ababcc* in §8.1).

0.6   A NOTE ON TERMINOLOGY

This book contains a great deal of terminology, for the most part in the form of ordinary-English terms redefined specifically for translational purposes. It is to be hoped, however, that the reader will not be unduly disconcerted by this terminological abundance. Four points might be made in its defense:

i. Each term has a clear and specific function. If the term were to be dispensed with, discussion of the function would be unduly protracted, needlessly blunted, or even rendered virtually impossible.

ii. All new terms are clearly defined upon their introduction and listed in the index with cross-references to their major occurrences.

iii. An effort has been made to use terms with some natural mnemonic relationship to their stipulated sense. For instance, the fact that the term DIVERGENCE suggests fanning out ($<$) while CONVERGENCE suggests zeroing in ($>$) will be seen in chapter 2 to be quite consonant with the technical meanings of these terms. Moreover, the generic over these two terms, ZIGZAGGING, itself suggests a composite of these two gestalts, $\gtrless$ or $\lessgtr$—a point actually brought to analytic fruition in chapter 8 (§8.1).

iv. In presenting terms for trajections, by far the largest subsystem in the book (see chapter 1), capitalization is used (e.g. DIVERGENCE, CONVERGENCE, and ZIGZAGGING in the foregoing point). This convention is intended to relieve the reader from the burden of keeping constantly in mind which ordinary-language words have been expropriated as technical terms. That is to say, an innocuous typographical usage (capitalization) makes it possible to have one's cake and eat it too, in a manner of speaking: one reaps the benefits of a motivated systematization by virtue of a sufficiently rich terminology; but at the same time the terms are tagged as such (by being capitalized) and so help the reader to distinguish them from ordinary-language terms of similar form or content.

NOTES

1. Important in this connection is the necessary relativization of the analyst's findings to the work at hand: formulations developed in the applied-linguistic service of translation must not be evaluated as if they purported to be contributions to pure-linguistic theory. See §6.3 for discussion.

2. A useful survey of the rudiments of linguistic theory can be provided in any number of recent introductory textbooks, e.g., Akmajian, Demers and Harnish (1984). Occasional references to more specialized linguistic works will be provided at relevant spots throughout.

3. This position is revealed with special clarity in the primacy that Nida and Taber (1974: chapter 2) invest in what they call 'Dynamic Equivalence' in translation, as opposed to 'Formal Correspondence'.

4. Despite this primacy, it will be convenient throughout to extend the term TEXT to spoken language as well.

5. Although this construal best serves the plan of this book, Robert Austerlitz correctly points out that orthography sometimes does evince plerematic functions. For instance, the lexical distinctiveness of the words *bear* and *bare* is cued by their distinct spelling but not at all by their pronunciation, which is identical.

PART ONE

Chapter *1*

TRAJECTIONS; MATCHING (EQUATION AND SUBSTITUTION)

1.1 TRAJECTIONS IN GENERAL

1.1.1 Basic Characterization

A TRAJECTION may be characterized as any of a number of basic plerematic (§0.2.1) translational patterns into which a given source-target pairing may partially be resolved.

Nine SIMPLE trajections are posited, eight of which pair off under GENERIC trajections, for a total of thirteen:

MATCHING (subsuming EQUATION and SUBSTITUTION);
ZIGZAGGING (DIVERGENCE and CONVERGENCE);
RECRESCENCE (AMPLIFICATION and REDUCTION);
REPACKAGING (DIFFUSION and CONDENSATION); and unpaired
REORDERING

One COMPLEX trajection, RECODING, will be briefly discussed in §6.1(iii), and some patterns involving MULTIPLE trajections will be considered in §6.2.

In this section, preliminary illustrations will be provided for the nine simple trajections. Detailed treatment of both simple and generic trajections will begin in section §1.2 and continue through chapter 5.[1]

Each trajection will be introduced with a formulaic schema, using capital letters as variables for linguistic elements and an arrow going from the source (text or language) to the target (text or language). With the exception of E,S, and M (§1.2–§1.4), a letter occurring on both sides of an arrow marks the elements in question as respective source and target COUNTERPARTS, without regard to the specific disposition of those counterparts. Thus, while the schema for Reduction, AB → A, might be used to register the fact that in translating a German imperative like *Hören Sie!* (an. 'listen you!') into either English *Listen!* or Spanish *¡Escuche!*, the pronoun (B) is dropped, yet at the same time the graphic identity of the As does not imply that the English and Spanish verbs are identical in structure. (In fact, while *Listen!* is a bare stem, *¡Escuche!* ends in a suffix inflected for the singular subjunctive.)[2]

In most cases, trajectional schemata will be presented in 'stylized' rather than 'tailored' form. Thus, AB → BA for Reordering is not meant to denote exclusively cases of two elements switching positions (like English to Spanish *red glass* → *vaso rojo* (an. 'glass red')), but rather stands for any translational nexus characterized by positional differences of source and target counterparts. ('Tailored' schemata may, of course, be pressed into service when needed, as in (6.10)).

Two sorts of disambiguating subscripts will occasionally be used, per these examples: (i) A_s = 'some source element A'; B_t = 'some target element B'; (ii) E_a = 'target Equation of source A'; S_b = 'target Substitution of source B' (cf. (6.10c)).

It will also be useful to have three-letter abbreviations of the trajections. These will be provided as each trajection is introduced.

1.1.2 Preliminary Examples

(a) *Matching* (Mat). Equation (Equ) obtains when an element of the source text (A_s) is rendered by a target text element deemed the most straightforward counterpart available (E_a); schematically $A_s → E_a$, or more simply, $A → E$.

Substitution (Sub) obtains when a source text element (A_s) is rendered by a target element deemed as being other than the most straightforward counterpart available (S_a); $A → S$.

Examples may be provided from a line of Old Irish verse. In her English rendition of the anonymous poem 'The Woman Who Reaps the Watercress', Ruth Lehmann translates (1.1s) as (1.1t). The trajection *uisci* → *water* is Equation while *mid* → *wine* is Substitution. Referentially, *uisci* is 'water' while *mid* refers to a beverage with the physical and cultural properties of 'mead', not 'wine'. (Note that the ancient Irish did have a beverage with the properties of wine, one which they named *fíon*. Thus *fíon* → *wine* would be Equation, as would *mid* → *mead*.)

(1.1) s. Is é mo [mid] m'[[uisci]] fúar. (Lehmann:113)
an. 'My cold [[water]] is my [mead].
   t. The cold [[water]] is my [wine]. (Lehmann:75)

(b) *Zigzagging* (Zig). Divergence (Div) holds where an element of the source text (A_s) may be mapped onto any of two or more alternatives in the target text (B_t, C_t); A → B/C.

Convergence (Cnv), as the inverse of Divergence, is the trajection whereby two or more distinct source text elements (B_s, C_s) may each be mapped onto one and the same target element (A_t); B/C → A.

Examples may be provided with translations from and to English, which stands apart from most modern European languages in having only one undifferentiated second person singular pronoun *you*, corresponding to familiar-formal doublets in French (*tu-vous*), Spanish (*tú-Usted*), Russian (*ty-vy*), German (*du-Sie*), etc. Thus, translation from English to such languages will normally require Divergent trajection of *you*, while translation in the opposite direction will often occasion Convergence. So in an American mystery novel, a detective is first addressed by a socially close fellow detective with the statement in (1.2sa) and then by his socially distant employer with (1.2sb), statements whose undifferentiated pronoun *you* Steinbach has appropriately Diverged in her German translation to *Du* and *Sie* in (1.2ta) and (1.2tb), respectively. Conversely, when in the German original of Heinrich Böll's novel *Billiards at Half Past Nine*, a seasoned inmate of a mental hospital first addresses a new inmate formally with *Sie* (1.3sa), then, as familiarity grows, switches to *du* (1.3sb), the translator simply Converges into English *you* in both cases (1.3ta,b).[3]

(1.2) **sa**. [You] must have brought the wrong package. (Stout:89)
    sb. [You] might as well leave and report in the morning. (Stout:90)
    ta. [Du] muβt das falsche Paket erwischt haben. (Steinbach:122)
    tb. Können [Sie] meinetwegen gehen und morgen früh
        Bericht erstatten. (Steinbach:122)

(1.3) **sa**. Nun hören Sie einmal zu, Neuer, sind [Sie] katolisch? (Böll:201)
    sb. Friedlich, Alter, das weiβt [du] also noch. (Böll:203)
    ta. Listen, new one, tell me, are [you] a Catholic? (X:216)
    tb. Quietly now, old man, [you] know what to do. (X:218)

(c) *Recrescence* (Rcr). Amplification (Amp) obtains when the target text picks up an element (B_t) in addition to a counterpart (A_t) of some source element (A_s); A → AB. In the inverse trajection Reduction (Red), a source expression (AB_s) is partially mapped onto a target counterpart (A_t) and partially omitted from the translation; AB → A.

Examples of both types of Recrescence are given in (1.4), an excerpt from Kobo Abe's Japanese novel *The Woman in the Dunes*, where the woman of the title yells up from her house in the sand pit to tell an old man at the top of the dune where to find the rope ladder by which the novel's hero will, in a moment, climb down to his fate. The Amplification consists in translator Saunders's expanding *Koko* 'Here!' to 'Here I am!', while the Reduction involves nontranslation of the conjunction *kara* (roughly a pragmatic (§0.2.2) analogue of 'because' whereby *S kara* conveys 'I say S because of its relevance to what you mean to do'—in this case, lower the ladder into the sand pit).[4] Note the role of 'Ø', the linguistic symbol for zero (null), in calibrating source-target Recrescental pairs. Zeroes will be the subject of chapter 10.

(1.4) **s.** Koko [Ø], koko . . . Sono tawara no waki ni, hasigo ga aru
[[kara]] . . . (Abe 1962:20)

　　t. Here [I am]! Here! There's a ladder over by the sandbags. [[Ø]]
(Saunders 1964:22)

(d) *Repackaging* (Rpk). Diffusion (Dif) is the trajection whereby a source group AB is, in any of a variety of ways, unpacked or spread out into a more loosely organized target counterpart, a situation to be symbolized A⌢B → A|B. The inverse trajection is Condensation (Cnd), whereby a source string is, again in any of variety of ways, more tightly bound or packed together in the target; A|B → A⌢B.

An example of both types of Repackaging may be provided from the Bible, with Moses's words to God (given in (1.5s)). The King James translation (1.5ta) is Diffusional: while the original Hebrew strings each consist of two tightly bound words (an. 'mouth-heavy' and 'tongue-heavy'), the English translations consist of loosely bound phrases comprised of several words each. On the other hand, the Greek translations in (1.5tb) are Condensational, each Hebrew string being rendered by one complex word (an. 'poorvoiced' and 'heavytongued').

(1.5) **s.** kii [xəvađ-pɛɛ] u[[xvađ lɔɔšoon]]
　　　　ʔɔɔnooxii (K:Exodus 4,10)

　　ta. but I am [slow of speech], and [[of a slow tongue]] (KJ)

　　tb. [iskhnophōnos] kai [[braduglōssos]] egō eimi (Rahlfs)

(e) *Reordering* (Rrd). This is the only unpaired trajection, and hence it also lacks a generic. Reordering involves a difference in positioning between source and target elements; AB → BA.

An example is provided in (1.6), where Don Quixote prophesies an elysian portrayal of the future to Sancho Panza. In Cervantes' original Spanish the products (first column) each precede their origins (second column), e.g. *asiento* 'seat' precedes *los troncos de los durísimos acornoques* 'the trunks of the hard cork-trees'. In his English translation, however, Ormsby Reorders this arrangement CHIASTICALLY, to place the origins before their products.

Each of the simple and generic trajections will now receive more protracted attention, whereby discussion of paired simplices will precede that of their generic. The rest of this chapter will be devoted to the set Equation, Substitution, and Matching. The remaining sets, including the maverick Reordering, will be covered in chapters 2 through 5, one set per chapter. (The treatment of complex and multiple trajections will be deferred until chapter 6.)[5]

(1.6) **s**. Daránnos con abundantísima mano de su dulcísimo
fruto las encinas

asiento	los troncos de los durísimos alcornoques
sombra	los sauces
olor	las rosas
alfombras de mil	los extendidos prados
colores matizados	(Cervantes:680[II 67])

    t. The oaks will yield us their sweet fruit with bountiful hand

the trunks of the hard cork-trees	a seat
the willows	shade
the roses	perfume
the wide-spread meadows	a thousand dyes (Ormsby:411)

1.2 EQUATION

Equation (Equ; A → E) represents a limiting case of translation—sort of a null case, in fact, since ideal Equation would, if it existed (cf. §6.3), involve just that minimal symbolic transference symptomatic of any passage from one language to another.

Even when slackly interpreted, Equation is rarely or never found to obtain between source and target texts for long, continuous stretches—and most cases involving any more than two or three contiguous words can be expected to involve languages closely related both typologically and genetically. Thus, in my translation of André Bjerke's Norwegian poem 'The Grown-ups' Party', I was barely able to squeak past the first couplet using Equation; see (1.7). Had the second couplet been forced to a similar treatment, the result would have been the non-English *For hours ago, were you sent‖in to sleep* ← *For timer siden var du sendt ‖ inn i søvenen.* (My actual translation is *Hours before you were sent ‖ up to bed*).

(1.7) **s**. Hva var det some foregikk
på de voksnes fest? (Bjerke:36)

    t. What was it that happened
at the grown-ups' party? (M1981a)

The very fact that Equation is something of a translational null case makes it different from other trajections in a number of ways.[6] Useful in this regard is the rule of thumb in (1.8), whereby Equation is effectively characterized as the default trajection.

(1.8) After a pair of source and target texts has been analyzed to the point
of usefulness in terms of Substitution, Zigzagging, Recrescence, Re-

packaging, and Reordering, any residual source-target relations may be trajectionally considered as Equational.

1.3 SUBSTITUTION

As the most clearly antipodal trajection to Equation, Substitution (Sub; A → S) may be largely characterized by studying the circumstances under which Equation is thwarted and preempted. Of such circumstances, the following rather haphazard list comprises some frequently occurring types: (i) lack of an Equational target-language counterpart; (ii) grammatical constraints; (iii) discrepancies in idioms or other set expressions; (iv) cultural differences; (v) what might be called 'intermodular' pressure, i.e. feedback from one linguistic or textual component onto another.

Numerous examples of factor (i) in Bible translation can be found in the important work of Eugene Nida, who documents cases where a Hebrew, Aramaic, or Greek source lexeme must be Substituted in translating the Holy Scriptures into various New World languages lacking an Equational target term. See, for example, Nida (1945).

A few examples of factors ii through v will be provided here.

Example (1.9), an excerpt from Glaucos's prayer to Apollo in the sixteenth book of the *Iliad*, provides a good illustration of Substitution triggered by grammatical constraints. In the original Greek, the object of the verb *akouein* 'hear' appears in the dative case, as signaled by the suffixes *-i* and *-ōi* in *aneri kēdomenōi* '(an)afflicted man', a verb-case signal 'only used in prayer to a god— doubtless to indicate that the hearing is a favor to the suppliant' (Monro ii:317). Since English's lack of a case system precludes anything remotely approaching replication of this signal in the target text, Rouse neatly Substitutes an expedient specific to English for signaling prayer: the archaic pronoun *thou* (plus its concomitant verb suffix *-st*).

(1.9) s. dunasai de su pantōs akouein aner[i] kēdomen[ōi]. (H ii:85[XVI 515f])

   t. [Thou] ha[st] power everywhere to hear an afflicted man. (R:196)

Substitution attendant on translinguistic differences in idioms or other set expressions is illustrated in (1.10), on the basis of several examples from Grimm's fairy tales. (A literal reading of the German expressions may be synthesized in each case by replacing the target Substitute by the analytic translation listed beneath or beside the source Substituend; e.g. for case (a), 'the air was clear' versus English 'the way was clear'.)[7]

Substitution motivated by cultural differences is nicely exemplified by Kroll's observation on the reaction by Occidental translators to a renowned in-

(1.10) **sa**. Als der Hase merkte, daß die [Luft] rein war (G:238)
an.'air'

sb. mit einem [blauen] Auge davongekommen war (G:285)
an.'blue'

sc. [Zuckererbsen[an. 'sugar peas' (G:373)

sd. [blaue Bohnen] an. 'blue beans' (G:351)

se. du bist einer, der [blau pfeifen] kann (G:379)
an.'whistle blue'

sf. eine [steinalte] Frau (G:422)
an.'old as a stone'

ta. As soon as he saw that [the way] was clear (HS:301)

tb. escaped from it with a [black] eye (HS:377)

tc. [sweetmeats] (HS:496)

td. [bullets] (HS:467)

te. you are one of those who can [work wonders] (HS:504)

tf. a [very aged] woman (HS:565)

stance of poetic embodiment of the Classical Chinese belief that a person could whistle

(1.11) to put himself and his breath . . . 'in tune' with the sonance of the natural world. Such whistling could also summon up spirits, wind, rain, and other phenomena. . . . It is [thus] odd that . . . it has never been noticed that in [the] celebrated quatrain [of the T'ang poet Wang Wei] 'A Lodging in the Bamboo' . . . the 'luminous moon' that appears in the final line of the poem has in fact shown itself in consequence of the poet's 'long whistling' in line two. . . . Most translators are apparently so embarrassed to have Wang Wei 'whistling' in that bamboo grove that they regularly change his action to 'humming' . . . (Kroll:244)

Consider finally a commonplace manifestation of Substitution due to inter-modular pressure, that of replacement of source-language elements by semantically distinct target elements in order to replicate a source-text rhyme scheme. This phenomenon, particularly widespread in translating verse within certain poetic traditions (e.g. medieval to early modern European, Classical Arabic and derivatives), is illustrated in (1.12) with three samples from the numerous cases of the incantational verse that pervades Grimm's fairy tales. While the Substitutions in (1.12a) and (1.12b) are relatively rare for their simplicity, the more intricate (1.12c) is more representative. Note that in addition to the focal Substitution (*unter der Brücke* an. 'beneath the bridge' → *beside the water*), the original sestet with rhyme-assonance scheme *aabbcc* has been Reduced to a quatrain with scheme *abab*; and the Substitute *beside the water* has been Reordered to rhyme

with *daughter* (-*b-b*). (For the phonetic representation of the rhyming syllables at the end of (1.12bs), see the chart in §13.0)

(**1.12**) **as**. Der Wind, der [Wind]
          Das himmlische [Kind] ('child') (G:70)
     at. The wind, the [wind]
          The heaven-born [wind] (HS:90)
     bs. Kikeri[ki] (p[kii])
          Unsere schmutzige Jungfrau ist wieder[hie] (p[hii]'here') (G:104f)
     bt. Cock-a-doodle-[doo]
          Your dirty girl's come back to [you] (HS:135f)
     cs. Ach, du liebes [Hirtelein],
          Du bläst auf meinem [Knöchelein],
          Mein Bruder hat mich [erschlagen],
          [[Unter der Brücke]] [begraben]
          Um das wilde [Schwein]
          Für des Königs [Töchterlein] (G:114)
     an. 'Ah my dear little shepherd,
          Thou blowest upon my bone,
          My brother hath slain me,
          Buried me [[beneath the bridge]]
          For the wild pig
          For the King's young daughter'
     ct. Ah, friend, thou blowest upon my [bone]!
          Long have I lain [[beside the water]];
          My brother slew me for the [boar],
          And took for his wife the King's young [daughter] (HS:150)

1.4 MATCHING

Matching (Mat; A → E/S or A → M) is the trajection subsuming Equation and Substitution and by dint of that status provides a convenient repository for certain trajection types not satisfactorily characterizable as either Equation or Substitution to the exclusion of the other. Moreover, anticipating that not all Matching phenomena will relate to Equation and Substitution in the same way formally, it will be useful to provide two schemata for Matching: A → E/S when analytic emphasis is on A as GENERIC to E and S, e.g. a trajection manifested by some sort of interplay between Equation and Substitution; or A → M when the analysis focuses on A as COMMON DENOMINATOR to M—that is, to state the same point negatively, a trajection whereby A is mapped onto a target counterpart M not obviously (or usefully) characterizable in terms of Zigzagging, Recrescence, Repackaging, or Reordering.

Cases of the first type are common as ploys for introducing stylistic variation into a COREFERENCE CHAIN, i.e. a series of noun phrases referring to the same person, thing, or other denotatum. Thus, if the source text contains a series of pronouns (A), and the translator breaks the monotony by interweaving coreferent proper names (S), the result may be a coreference chain schematizable as AAAA . . . → ESES . . . Trajectionally, this result can be neatly characterized generically as Matching (A → E/S), since the translator has introduced variation by alternating Equation (A → E) and Substitution (A → S). (This ploy is frequently used by Rouse in his translation of the *Iliad*; an example will be given in (§16.8). This in turn may be contrasted with another common strategy for coreference chains, that of Recrescence, an example of which will be provided in (§3.13)).

Most special applications of Matching, however, are of the common-denominator variety A → M, where M cannot be satisfactorily understood as either Equation or Substitution though it shares properties of both. Perhaps the simplest case is that in which a target language simply has no sufficiently similar counterpart of a source lexeme to pass as Equation, yet the translator is able to choose an approximant too close to be rightly labeled Substitution. Thus, the translation of Montaigne's sixteenth-century French term *astrologie* into modern English *astrology* is not precisely Equation, since the Renaissance discipline of *astrologie* was in certain important regards closer to modern *astronomy*, though not close enough to render this alternative Equational either. On the other hand, *astrology* may arguably be the closest modern English lexeme available despite the qualifications, so that out-and-out Substitution does not seem to be involved either. And yet *astrologie → astrology* may usefully be labeled Matching, as opposed to Zigzagging, Recrescence, etc.; see M1982a:24f for discussion.[8]

Matching of type A → M provides a useful perspective for looking at various special nexuses, among them (i) carry-over Matching, (ii) calque Matching, (iii) prefab Matching, and (iv) false friendship. Only carry-over Matching will be discussed in any detail here (§1.4.1). The three remaining types of Matching will be considered summarily (§1.4.2), with cross-references to M1982a and M1986a.

1.4.1 Carry-over Matching

CARRY-OVER MATCHING obtains when the source element A is not translated into the target language but merely carried over as such into the target text, so that M = A.

At first blush it might seem that carry-over Matching is the purest form of Equation, since identity is obviously the absolute upper limit of equatability. And yet carry-over very rarely constitutes Equation, because when A leaves the source text for the target, it thereby totally changes the language of its context, a change which, as will be seen, almost always affects the function of A in the target text.

The most common and analytically interesting cases of carry-over are those in which A, as a linguistic element, belongs either to the source language (SOURCE-BIASED carry-over) or to the target language (TARGET-BIASED carry-over). An example of the source-biased type appears in (1.13), where the English appellatives *Mr.* and *Mrs.* are taken intact into the German translation. Moreover, by very dint of their being carried over, the *Mr.* and *Mrs.*—here and throughout Steinbach's translation—lend the German version of the novel a special American flavor which, crucially, would not have surfaced had Steinbach Equated the appellatives to their German counterparts *Herr* and *Frau*. Furthermore, this effect of source-biased carry-over is so commonplace as to warrant a rule of thumb (1.14).

(1.13) s. 'Go ahead. [Mrs.] Molloy's interest runs with ours.
[Mrs.] Molloy, this is [Mr.] Panzer'. (Stout:60)

t. 'Schießen Sie los. [Mrs.] Molloys Interessen sind
auch die unseren. [Mrs.] Molloy, das ist [Mr.] Panzer'. (Steinbach:84)

(1.14) All else being equal, source-biased carry-over Matching will lend the target text a flavor of source-language correlates (e.g. culture).

While source-biased carry-over normally induces an increment in the target text (source flavor), target-biased carry-over often induces a decrement, since any special effect occasioned by target-language elements in the source text bids fair to be lost when those elements are repatriated to their own language. Thus, while the English locutions *blue devils* and *groom* in (1.15s) impart a special British flavor to the original French passages, that flavor is neutralized when the locutions blend into the all-English context of the target (1.15t). Thus, we have rule of thumb (1.16), as a counterpart of (1.14).

(1.15) as. —Nous avons tous nos [*blue devils*], répondit-elle. (Balzac:238)

at. 'We all have our [*blue devils*], she replied'. (Waring:199)

bs. —. . . Mon [*groom*] vient par la voiture de Chinon,
il le pansera. (Balzac:239)

bt. '. . . My [groom] is coming from Chinon by coach,
and he will rub him down'. (Waring:199)

(1.16) Target-biased Matching will often deprive the target text of any special flavor imparted to the source text by the pressence of target-language elements.

And yet account must be taken of another rule of thumb, one that tends to counteract (1.14) and (1.16):

(1.17) The frequency of elements of language L within a text of language N will often be proportional to the importance of L-correlates in the message of the N-composed text.

Principle (1.17)'s counterforce to (1.14) is operative in cases where L = N, in the sense that any source-correlative flavor in a target text will tend to be minimal as a source-target difference in instances where the source text is itself source-correlative. Thus, it may be true that carry-over of *Mr.* and *Mrs.* in (1.11) imparts an American flavor to the dialogue, but American flavor is hardly missing from the English-language source text either.

The counteraction of (1.17) to (1.16) is more probabilistic and normally depends on the survival into the target text of other specific source-correlative symptoms than the carry-over elements whose force is in question. And yet (1.17) virtually predicts the presence of at least some such symptoms in cases where the importance of L-correlates in the source text is strong, it being reasonable to assume that a message about L-correlates (e.g. English culture) will not be limited to the mere expedient of sprinkling elements of language L (e.g. English words). And indeed, this prediction is clearly borne out for (1.15) (not surprisingly, since *Le Lys dans la Vallée* is a novel in which English persons and culture play a very significant role). In the specific cases of (1.15), moreover, the English flavor threatened with loss by *blue devils* and *groom* being flooded in the all-English context of the target text is counteracted in the immediate context, as may be seen in the fuller excerpts provided in (1.18). Thus, in (1.18a), the English-language status of *blue devils* is explicitly tagged as such by the speaker, and the import of that tagging is not neutralized in the target text ('That, I think, is the English word?') despite repatriation of *blue devils* to its own language. Example (1.18b) is similar for the word *groom*, though in this case the textual reference is not direct to the language but indirect to the country ('Is the groom from England too?').

(1.18) (= (1.15) with context)

    as. —Nous avons tous nos [*blue devils*], répondit-elle.
        N'est-ce pas le mot anglais? (Balzac:238)

    at. 'We all have our [*blue devils*]', she replied. 'That, I think, is the
        English word?' (Waring:199)

    bs. —. . . Mon [*groom*] vient par la voiture de Chinon, il le pansera.
        —Le [*groom*] arrive-t-il aussi d'Angleterre?
        dit-elle. (Balzac:239)

    bt. '. . . My [groom] is coming from Chinon by coach, and he will
        rub him down'.
        'Is the [groom] from England too?' said she. (Waring:199)

The foregoing considerations suggest a specifically trajectional rule of thumb:[9]

(1.19) A gain or loss in flavor occasioned by carry-over Matching will often
    be counteracted in the context through principle (1.17).

1.4.2 Calque Matching, Prefab Matching, and False Friendship

CALQUE MATCHING is similar to carry-over Matching in that a source element is taken into the target text, but while carry-over involves SUBSTANTIVE elements (normally words), calque Matching involves RELATIONAL elements, whereby a source pattern is taken into the target text but fleshed out with target forms. Vinay and Darbelnet (1972) discuss several cases of English-to-Canadian French calque Matching; e.g., the road sign *Slippery when wet* → *Glissant si humide* (an. 'Slippery if wet'), to which may be contrasted noncalqued European French *Chaussée glissante* (an. 'Slippery roadway') (1972:19,22,256). In M1986a an analysis is provided of Saunders's (1964:111) calque-Matching trajection of the Japanese idiomatic compound *arizigoku*, an. 'ant hell', into English in the form of neologistic *ant hell* rather than conventional *ant lion*, which Webster's Third International dictionary defines as 'an insect having larva that digs a small conical pit in sandy soil in the bottom of which it lies buried with its long jaws protruding to catch any insects (as ants) which fall into pit' (Webster's 1961:97). Given the specific nightmarish details of this larva's activity from the point of view of an ant, it is not surprising that Abe uses *arizigoku* metaphorically for the plight of the hero, Jumpei Niki, caught at the bottom of his sandpit prison. Saunders then successfully replicates the power of this metaphor by calque-Matching into *ant hell*. Had he rather chosen automatic lexical Equation to *ant lion*, the metaphor (of being locked into a horrible place) would have been compromised.

PREFAB MATCHING occurs when the translator renders a source element into the target text not de novo but by employment of some already conventionalized (prefabricated) counterpart. Like all trajections, prefab Matching may be well used or abused. Thus, while Lefevere (1975:50f) criticizes the excesses of appeal to 'set expressions' in translating Latin poetry, in M1986a I try to show the merits of using a traditional English-language Catholic bible for the translation of scriptural allusions in an Irish poem ('Ní Dhomhnaill' 1981/M1985e).[10]

FALSE FRIENDSHIP, a notion originally conceived by a scholar named Vuibert in 1928 (Vinay and Darbelnet [*faux amis* an. 'false friends']:70), may be viewed trajectionally as an erroneous Matching triggered by some perceived but spurious similarity between an element of the source text and some presumed equivalent in the target language. Since the properties and occasions of this phenomenon receive considerable attention in M1982a, illustration will be limited here to two cases of false friendship incurred by myself in published translations from Irish.

The starker but in a sense less harmful of the two was my misrendition of the noun *péileacán* 'butterfly' as *pelican* in the title of a poem; see (1.20a). The saving irony of this case is that my translation of the poem itself was commended by its author as capturing the *brí* ('meaning and power') of the original despite my outrageous reidentification of its winged protagonist.[11] (The error itself, by the way, was due to my overlooking the crucial accent mark on the *é* of *péileacán*, the Irish word for 'pelican' being *peileacán*).

The second case is subtler but more ominous in that it bespeaks a general problem of some magnitude for translating texts composed under certain linguistic-cultural circumstances. The infelicity in question consisted in my translating the Irish word *Daidí* as *Daddy* (1.20b), a technically correct rendition which, moreover, is etymologically accurate, since *Daidí* is historically the Irish adaptation of the English word *Daddy*. However, as Brother Charles Quinn pointed out to me after the translation was published, it is indeed questionable whether an Irishman of this speaker's age and social circumstances "would ever say anything like 'Daddy'; something like 'the ould lad' or 'the ould man' would be more likely."[12]

The special linguistic-cultural circumstances that make this matter problematic may now be appreciated. Since modern Ireland is, for better or worse, a largely English-speaking country, and has been for more than a century, a person intending to translate an Ireland-based narrative from Irish Gaelic into English is under most circumstances virtually forced, for the sake of realism, to translate the narrative into ANGLO-IRISH, the variety of English spoken natively in Ireland. This catch can have very significant repercussions for a translator, like myself, whose native language is some non-Irish variety of English: dialect differences between the ideal target language and the actual target language commanded by the translator may be of such magnitude as to require the translator to learn the ideal dialect as if it were virtually a third language.[13]

(1.20) **as**. Radharc-chathair thromluíoch le [péileacán]
ar strae (Hutton:11)

      at. A nightmarish city-vision of a wandering [pelican] (M1983a:16)

      bs. 'Neil an tSaorsaigh, bhís fada go maith ina teannta san mhuis agus níor phósais í mar sin fhéin—'
'Bíodh a mhilleán ar a [Daidí] aici, má sea; ba bheag leis an gabháltas' (Ní Shúilleabháin 1977:5)

      bt. 'Nelly Sears. Yes, you went with her quite a spell, and yet you never married her after all'.
'It was her [Daddy's] fault, then; he didn't think I had enough land'. (M1983b:98)

NOTES

1. Much of Part One of this book was set down in preliminary form in M1981b.

2. This example is based on the German and Spanish FORMAL (or POLITE) imperatives.

3. Incidentally, the patterns of usage of the familiar-formal pronouns are by no means uniform from language to language. A telling symptom of this variation may be seen in Tolstoy's Russian footnotes to the copious French passages in *War and Peace*, where he quite frequently translates formal French *vous* with familiar Russian *ty* (e.g. Tolstoy i:50,97,104,382,386,468,548).

4. Cf. Horn's 'metalinguistic' usages (1985:150).

5. In view of the fundamental nature of the translational nexus, it is not surprising that virtually all authors writing on the general nature of translation recognize at least some analogs of trajection. By way of illustration just four cases will be mentioned here: (i) Nida's 'techniques of adjustment' (additions, subtractions, alterations) (1964:chap.10); (ii) Kade's modes of 'Äquivalenz' (totale, fakultative, approximative, Null; cf. resp. Equ, Div, Cnv, Sub)(1968); (iii) a panoply of categories set up by

Vinay and Darbelnet, several paired off similarly to trajections under their generics: e.g. 'amplification' and 'économie' (cf. Recrescence) (1972:5), 'concentration' and 'dilution' (cf. Repackaging)(1972:7); (iv) Guillemin-Flescher's categories of 'agencement syntaxique' (1981: 107ff). Various specific trajectional analogues of other authors will be mentioned in appropriate spots throughout.

6. Similar in this respect is Jäger's opposition of 'Translation' (cf. Equation) to 'koomunikativ heterovalente Sprachmittlung' (cf. other trajections, in particular Reduction [Referierung] and Amplification ['Expandierung']) (1975:31).

7. Hunt and Stern do not always employ Substitution in rendering idiomatic expressions, however. Equational examples are frequently encountered, including nonce renditions of German locutions having no conventional counterparts in English; e.g. *stumm wie ein Fisch* (G:179) → *mute as a fish* (HS:235), *maüschenstill* → *as still as a mouse* (HS:579).

8. To be sure, such cases of anachronism also pose unilinguistic problems of interpretation, quite apart from translational questions. Thus, one might ponder how best to interpret the term *philosopher* in the following excerpt from Joseph Conrad's novel *Victory*, now that almost a century has passed since the book was written:

> He paused to reflect on this psychological phenomenon, . . . as no [philosopher] was at hand to tell him that there is no strong sentiment without terror (Conrad:134 — written in 1912–1914).

9. A nexus akin to carry-over Matching may arise when a source text contains elements of two languages (or dialects) whose differences are then neutralized under translation to a third language. Thus, in one of Grimm's fairy tales composed in the Low German dialect ('*Ferenand getrü und Ferenand ungetrü*'/'Ferdinand the faithful and Ferdinand the unfaithful'), utterances addressed to and by the king are in standard High German (G:427). This distinction is lost in Hunt and Stern's English version (571). (In regard to dialect as a problem for translation, some interesting cases are adduced by Skvorecky (1985)).

10. E.g., *I am not worthy that thou shouldst enter*, the Douay Bible's rendition of the words of the humble centurion to Jesus (Luke 7:6), rather than a more literal rendering of the source-text Irish like *I am not worthy that you should come to me*. (Note incidentally that, in a sense, run-of-the-mill lexical Equation is simply an extreme case of prefab Matching.) Cf. the rule of thumb, 'Search for the standard translation, if one exists' (Rose:91).

11. 'is maith liom é agus is dóigh liom go dtugann tú brí an dáin leat go dílis' (letter of 20 May 1983) = 'I like it, and you seem to bring across the *brí* of the poem quite faithfully' (JLM).

12. 'N'fheadar an ndéarfadh sean-duine rud mar "Daddy's"—the ould lad' nó 'the ould man' is túisce a thiocfadh chuige' (letter of 30 May 1984).

13. False friendship is in one way or the other recognized by many writers on translation; see e.g. chapter 1 of Chukovsky (1984), and McMillan (1982).

Chapter *2*

ZIGZAGGING (DIVERGENCE AND CONVERGENCE)

2.1 DIVERGENCE

Divergence (Div; A → B/C), whereby an element of the source text may be mapped onto any of two or more alternatives in the target text, is a translational nexus reflecting relative paradigmatic richness of the target resources compared with the source—with no prejudice as to whether such richness holds for the languages at large (e.g. if the target lexicon has more potential lexemes for encoding some referent) or merely for the specific text.

Divergence crops up as a problem for translation with notorious frequency, because there is almost never any advance guarantee that the source text will contain sufficient cues as to whether B or C is the better rendition of A in a given case. This problem arises simply because B and C do not pertain to the source language in the first place and so are normally of no concern to the source author, who virtually by definition of the medium must make do with A alone.

In view of this fact, perhaps the most useful general STRATEGICAL advice for coping with Divergence is to develop skill and cunning in teasing out of an apparently unpromising context cues for choosing between two or more potential target renditions (B or C) of one source element (A). A few examples will be presented here (§ 2.1.1–§2.1.3), representing three focal types of contextual cue: (i) linguistic, (ii) situational, (iii) stylistic.

2.1.1 Linguistic Cues

While linguistic cues for guiding translation under Divergence are per se as common as grass, most of them tend to be of more service to people still developing their skills in the source language than to fully accomplished translators for whom the linguistic facts of the source language rarely require conscious pondering. Thus, H.M. Jones's correct translation of the verse *Über die brandende [See]* from Heine's poem 'The North Sea' as *Over the breaking [sea]* rather than **Over the breaking [lake]* would, even had the context been insufficient, follow from the fact that the German noun *See* is feminine in the sense of 'sea' but masculine in the sense of 'lake' and from the fact that the intended sense is signaled here by the feminine form of the definite article *die*, rather than masculine *den*. (Cf. (2.1a), and the converse situation for the correct sense of 'lake' clued by the masculine form of the indefinite article in the example from Grimm's fairy tales (2.1b).) However, translators competent in German, as Jones and Hunt & Stern certainly are, would know these gender-sense correlations immediately and react correspondingly without further ado.

(2.1) **as**. Über [die] brandende [See] (Heine:69[I,8])
    at. Over [the] breaking [sea] (H.M.Jones:68)
    bs. kam an [einen][See] (G:574)
    bt. come to [a][lake] (HS:781)

There are circumstances, however, where pertinent linguistic facts may not prove so salient; where in one way or another their disposition within the source text is subtle or submerged enough to elude even seasoned translators not fully on their guard. Cogent, natural-state examples are rarely found, partially because contextual factors tend to far outstrip purely linguistic factors as cues in many types of text, but the few plausible cases I have encountered are marked by one or both of two properties: INTRICACY of linguistic pattern and OPTIONALITY (VARIABILITY) of linguistic rule. Two examples will be presented here, both involving COREFERENCE CHAINS where a series of two or more noun phrases (NPs) are used to denote the same extralinguistic element (cf. (1.15)). In what follows, coreference (identity of denotation) will be indicated by tagging members of a coreference chain with an identifying letter within angle-brackets; e.g. in a series of NPs symbolized by the numerals 1 through 6, the sequence 1<a> 2<b> 3<a> 4<b> 5<a> 6<b> represents the interlacing of two simple chains (1 . . . 3 . . . 5 and 2 . . . 4 . . . 6) into one complex chain.

The first example involves a pair of Ancient Greek morphemes, *men* and *de*, which have several tagging properties making them useful for keeping referential relations straight in complex coreference chains. The property of interest here is that *men* and *de* form a SWITCH-REFERENCE SET, such that an NP tagged with one of them is interpreted as referentially disjoint from a next-following NP tagged with the other. Thus, in (2.2a) the first token of *ho* 'he' is tagged with *de* while the second is tagged with *men*, a distribution conveying that the two *ho*s should not refer to the same individual, an effect that Rouse (2.2b) accurately captures by Diverging to *he* first and then to *who*. But now there is yet a third *ho*, and since it is tagged by *d'* (an allomorph of *de*) it may not be taken as coreferential with the preceding *ho* (tagged with *men*), though it may be so taken with the lead-off *ho*, itself marked by *de*. At this point Rouse wisely reacts, since English has no syntactic device with the tagging power of *men* and *de*, by Diverging *ho* yet a third time, to the proper name *Patroclos*.

(2.2) **as.** [ho de]⟨a⟩ Thespora⟨b⟩, Ēnopos huion, deuteron
    hormētheis—[ho men]⟨b⟩ euksestōi eni diphrōi
    hēsto aleis˙ ek gar plēgē phrenas, ek d'ara
    kheirōn hēnia ēikhthēsan—[ho d']⟨a⟩ eghkeï
    nukse parastas (H ii:81[XVI,401–404])

   t. Next [he]⟨a⟩ drove at Thespor⟨b⟩, [who]⟨b⟩ was
    crouching down in his chariot dazed with terror, the
    reins dropped from his hands. [Patroclos]⟨a⟩ came
    quite close and stabbed him (R:194f)

The second example of a linguistic cue for guiding Divergence involves a special property of German pronouns having as antecedents a noun designating a human referent. In a coreference chain such a noun may be picked up by a pronoun having either the syntactic gender required by the antecedent as a linguistic object or the semantic gender dictated by the sex of the referent. Thus, in (2.3s) the noun *Mütterchen*, an. 'little mother', is syntactically neuter, as are all German nouns ending in the diminutive suffix *-chen*, but semantically feminine, referring as it does to a female human.

Now it turns out that the source coreference chain in (2.3s) is mixed in terms of gender, the first four pronominal links (<a3>–<a6>) being neuter and the last two (<a7> and <a8>) feminine—a switch of a type frequently encountered in Grimm's fairy tales, probably for the sake of stylistic variation.[1] The problem for Hunt and Stern in translating passages like this is to determine whether a neuter pronoun should be taken into the target text by an English neuter pronoun like 'it, its', as opposed to a human-referential pronoun like 'she, her, hers'—a problem trajectionally involving Divergence, since any given German neuter (e.g. *es*<a5>) could in isolation correspond in English to either a neuter (e.g. *it*) or a feminine (e.g. *she*).

It will be well to summarize here how cases (2.2) and (2.3) illustrate the ways that grammatical cues may serve even a seasoned translator in guiding Divergence. Both situations involve coreference chains containing pronouns which, in isolation, might Diverge into English in a variety of ways, depending on their intended reference—a reference which, though given by the respective rules of the Greek and German languages no less than the elementary case of German *See* → *sea/lake* in (2.1), nevertheless requires a certain amount of COMPUTATION on the part of the translator. This INTRICACY factor is moreover compounded in the case of (2.3) by the OPTIONALITY of the switch from neuter to

(2.3) s. Es war einmal [ein steinaltes Mütterchen]⟨a1⟩. . . .
Da war aber [das Mütterchen]⟨a2⟩ ganz
geschäftig, mehr als man ihm
bei [seinen]⟨a3⟩ hohen Jahren zugetraut hätte, sammelte
Gras für [seine]⟨a4⟩Gänse, brach sich das wilde Obst
ab, soweit [es]⟨a5⟩ mit den Händen reichen konnte, und
trug alles auf [seinem]⟨a6⟩ Rücken heim. Man hätte
meinen sollen, die schwere Last müßte [sie]⟨a7⟩ zu
Boden drücken, aber [sie]⟨a8⟩ brachte sie immer
glücklich nach Haus (G:532)

    t. There was once upon a time [a very old woman]⟨a1⟩. . . .
There, however, [she]⟨a2⟩ was quite active, more so than
anyone would have thought, considering [her]⟨a3⟩ age,
and collected grass for [her]⟨a4⟩ geese, picked all the
wild fruit [she]⟨a5⟩ could reach, and carried everything
home on [her]⟨a6⟩ back. Anyone would have
thought that the heavy load would have weighed [her]⟨7⟩
to the ground, but [she]⟨a8⟩ always brought it safely
home (HS:725)

feminine gender with the source text coreference chain, since in addition to knowledge of the language and its rules, the translator must also deduce or guess when the source author is in fact exercising the option rather than deploying the morphosyntactic elements in question for some other reason (in this case, for example, to refer to some other character than the old woman).

2.1.2 Situational Cues

A situational resolution to Divergence is illustrated in (2.4). Homeric Greek is like many languages in evincing a common sort of polysemy in its vocabulary for spatial directions (cf. Brown 1983), whereby a term for 'right(hand)' (*deksia*, appearing here in its elided form *deksi'*) is also a term for 'east', and a term with the sense 'left(hand)' (*aristera*) may also mean 'west'. This sets up potential Divergence with English as target language, *deksia* → *right/east* and *aristera* → *left/west*, a trajectional choice-point that Rouse has ostensibly solved in (2.4t) by appeal to the situation portrayed in the context: *deksi'* → *east* for congruity with *pros ēō t'ēelion te* 'to the rising sun', and in parallel fashion *aristera* → *west* as most compatible with *poti zophon ēeroenta* 'to the darksome gloom'.

(2.4) s. tōn ou ti metatrepom' oud' alegizō, eit' epi [deksi']
iōsi pros ēō t' ēelion te, eit' ep' [aristera]
toi ge poti zophon ēeroenta (H i:238[XII,238–240[)

    t. What is a bird to me? I care nothing for birds,
whether they fly [east] to the rising sun, or whether
they fly [west] to the darksome gloom (R:145)

Another example of situational resolution to Divergence appears in (2.5) and hinges on the fact that the Norwegian noun *ekteseng(en)* can denote either a bed when first put at the disposal of a newly wedded couple (English *marriage bed*), or the same object at a later date, or a functional replacement (English *double bed*). Since the scenario of Mykle's story was years after the father's wedding, and the context involved only the suitability of the bed as a cushion for jumping from the rope ladder, I had no problem in solving this Divergence in favor of *double bed*.

(2.5) s. Ikke slik at taustigen skulle henge inne i
stuen. Nei, på soveværelset måtte de være. Så
kunne den henge ned, tett ved siden av [ektesengen] (Mykle:29)

    t. The rope ladder couldn't hang in this room. No, it
would have to be in the bedroom. So it could hang
down right beside [the double bed] (M1980b:95)

2.1.3 Stylistic Cues

A stylistic cue for Divergence, in the broad sense taken here, will involve a language pattern (or usage) dictated neither by linguistic rule (or convention) nor by the situational requirements of the text. Stylistic patterns are relatively easy to recognize when they have become conventionalized, as, for example, various rhyme and metrical schemes in classical Occidental poetry (cf. chapters 13 and 14). However, conventionalization is neither a prerequisite for stylistic patterning nor itself an all-or-none phenomenon, and it is possible for what is (in pertinent respects) the same stylistic pattern to be strictly conventionalized in one tradition and yet quite protean and freewheeling in another. Thus, while certain types of MORPHOSYNTACTIC PARALLELISM are nearly definitional for both ancient Canaanite (cf. §10.1) and traditional Finnish poetry, the same general device is by and large an optional accessory to modern Occidental prose. But despite its generally will-o'-the-wisp distribution in contemporary Western prose, there are texts where parallelism is so strongly represented as to be unmistakable—and a case in point from an Italian novel, kindly provided by Paola di Mauro, furnishes an excellent example of stylistic resolution to Divergence. In the passage in question, the description of a dream ends with a burst of nouns, *viottole, rupi, fughe, inseguimenti, [grida], schioppettate!* (2.6s), rendered into English by Colquhoun as *paths, cliffs, escapes, pursuits, [edicts], musket-shots!* (2.6t). But while the Italian noun *grida* as a SINGULAR answers to English *edict*, as a PLURAL (of *grido*) it answers to English *screams*. And in fact, di Mauro astutely analyzes the trajection *grida* → *edict(s)* as a mistranslation for correct *grida* → *screams*, because only in the latter interpretation is the morphological parallelism of *grida* with the six other plural nouns in the series respected.[2]

(2.6) s. viottole, rupi, fughe, inseguimenti, [grida],
schioppettate! (Manzoni:17)

    t. paths, cliffs, escapes, pursuits, [edicts],
musket-shots! (Colquhoun:17)

2.1.4 Artistic Suspense; Stylistically Induced Divergence

The preceding examples were geared to situations in which the Divergence was both resolvable in principle and a desideratum of the translation. But though such cases clearly predominate, there are situations where resolution of Divergence is either undesirable, or precluded in principle, or both. One such case type might be called that of ARTISTIC SUSPENSE, where the semantic vagueness or indeterminacy of source A relative to the fuller specificity of target B/C (assuming A → B/C) itself plays an organic role in the source text, and where accordingly, fidelity of translation counterindicates resolving that vagueness or indeterminacy in the target rendition. Thus, the movie *Killer on Board*[3] concludes with the hero and heroine standing on the deck of a plague-racked cruise ship as it docks in San Francisco, and the heroine's old boy friend waiting at the base of the gangplank bearing a bouquet of posies. The hero, who during the plague-haunted cruise had himself become the de facto boy friend of the heroine, now turns to her with an unspoken question in his eyes. 'Everything's okay with us,' she says. But whom does she mean by 'us'? (a) Herself and the hero? (c) Herself and the old boy friend with the posies? (c) Everyone on board, who had hopefully just escaped death by the plague? We aren't told—we are left in artistic suspense to decide the matter for ourselves. But now, how would one translate this movie into a language like Samoan, where in lieu of a referentially undifferentiated first person nonsingular pronoun like *us* (A), a choice must be made between dual inclusive *taua* (good only for situation (a) above), dual exclusive *maua* (only for situation (b)), plural inclusive *tatou* (only for (c)), and plural exclusive *matou*? Presumably the effect of the heroine's final words would have to be REVAMPED rather than translated—just because Divergence in this case could not be resolved without damaging the artistic integrity of the original text (script).[4]

Finally, while the question of *stylistic variation* arose in connection with the source-text deployment of German neuter and feminine pronouns in (2.3), both that example and all others considered so far have turned on differences of COGNITIVE MEANING on the target side. But in fact there are a great many cases in which the Divergence is at the service of stylistic variation in the target text as well. For example, American sportscasting language tolerates and indeed considerably abets more synonyms per meaning than many other English-language registers, a fancy well illustrated in the cartoon sports report appearing in (2.7) (MacNelly 1982), where the reporter is de facto engaged in a unilinguistic strategy of Divergence (cf. §7.6), looking for synonyms to the verb *beat*. Nor is American English alone in this penchant for variation in sports terminology. If anything, the phenomenon is even more freewheeling in Latin-American Spanish. Thus, a brief newspaper report (300 words in all) on two baseball games contained the list of synonyms given in (2.8), a distribution all the more striking in view of the fact that the report was chosen totally at random.[5]

The translator's task with stylistic Divergence is, fundamentally, to know (or feel) when the target tradition allows (or likes, or requires) more synonyms

(**2.7**) **a**. And now for the latest sports news:
   b. Cincinnati [beat] the Jets 42–35,
   c. Seattle [smashed] Tamps 27–3,
   d. the Giants [wriggled past] the Eagles 28–27,
   e. Washington [blasted] Dallas 42–7,
   f. the Pats [blitzed] the Colts 31–3,
   g. Los Angeles [frazzled] the Dolphins 31–17,
   h. the Raiders [creamed] the 49ers,
   i. Houston [devastated] the Saints 51–6,
   j. Chicago [clobbered] Green Bay 27–10,
   k. Pittsburgh [pulverized] the Lions 42–19,
   l. Cleveland [annihilated] Kansas City 24–0,
   m. Buffalo [disemboweled] Atlanta 31–17,
   n. Saint Louis [discombobulated] Denver 10–7,
   o. and San Diego . . .
   p. . . . ? . . .
   q. . . . [dekrelnificated] the Vikings 19–14.
   r. Heck, even sportswriters run out of verbs sometimes! (MacNelly 1982)

(**2.8**) 'team':   *novena, club, equipo*
   'hit'(noun):   *imparable, hit, incogible*
   'hit'(verb):   *conectar, jitear, disparar*
   'inning':   *episodio, inning, entrada*
   'home run':   *carrera, cuadrangular, homer, jonrón*
   'game':   *partido, juego*
   'beat':   *vencer, apabullar* (*El Diario-La Prensa*, 1977)

per meaning than the source tradition, and what (if any) criteria are best employed in choosing among the synonyms. It must not be assumed, incidentally, that stylistic Divergence will always involve major lexical items (contentives) like verbs, nouns, and adjectives. The phenomenon may equally involve differential deployment of syntactic resources. Thus, in Biblical Hebrew narrative, it is considered fine style to connect a long series of clauses with the proclitic conjunction basically corresponding to English *and*, a morpheme that may show up in several allomorphic shapes including wə-, and u-; see the example in (2.9s). In English, however, such prolix repetition runs against the grain of the tradition, as may be gauged by the King James translators' five-point Divergence in (2.9t).[6]

(**2.9**) **s**. [wə]huu yašqiiṭ [u]mii yaršiaʕ [wə]yaster
      pɔɔniim [u]mii yəšuurɛnnuu ‖ [wə]ʕal-goy [wə]ʕal-ʔɔɔdɔɔm
      yɔɔḥaḏ (K:Job 34,29)
   t. [When] he giveth quietness, who [then] can make trouble?
      [And when] he hideth his face, who [then] can behold him?
      [Whether] it be done against a nation, [or] against
      a man only (KJ)

2.2 CONVERGENCE

Convergence (Cnv; B/C → A), as the mirror image to Divergence, at times provides a moment of respite to the translator since a paradigmatic opposition in the source language (B ≠ C) has no direct (or ready-made) counterpart in the target language, and so the translational 'strategy' may often simply be the mechanical null case of following the path of least resistance to a uniquely determined target counterpart (A). But the existence of such facile situations should never lull the translator into sloth, because Convergence provides its own ordeals. Most notorious is probably the PREGNANT use of the B ≠ C opposition within the source text, whereby B and C are semantically opposed to one another without the redundancy of covarying with other non-Convergent signals. An example turning on the opposition between the formal and familiar German pronouns *Sie* and *du* (cf. (1.2)–(1.3)) is given in (2.10s), where a bellhop shocks and insults a pompous stranger by suddenly addressing him with the familiar pronoun *du*. Had the translator merely reacted automatically to the bare linguistic fact that English has only the one counterpart *you* to both German *Sie* and *du*, and correspondingly Converged in translation with no compensation, the resulting '*Have I got it right? You want to talk with the manager?*' would leave the reader rather puzzled at the stranger's vehement reaction and its consequences to the bellhop, which are detailed over several following pages. In fact however, the translator does not allow the Convergence *Sie/du* → *you* to dilute the force of the original German but rather attempts to redeem the effect of the source text through Amplification, by addition of the familiar-flavored appellative *sonny* (2.10t).

(2.10) s. 'Hab ich recht gehört? [Du] willst den
Geschäftsführer sprechen?' (B:26)

t. 'Have I got it right? [You] want to talk with
the manager, [sonny]?' (X:31)

As was the case with Divergence, Convergence may also involve stylistic problems, in addition to semantic pitfalls like that of pregnant usage. I ran across a case in point in translating the Danish word *udvey* an. 'out-way' in the excerpt from a short story by Tove Ditlevsen given in (2.11s). The most straightforward English counterpart of *udvey* would be *way out*, but to have so translated would to my sensibilities have incurred an awkward repetition of the Danish word *måd(en)* in the title of the story and as an important refrain throughout the text itself. That is, the offensive Convergence *-vey/måd* → *way* would not so much have impaired the meaning of the target text as it would have damaged its style —a result that I attempted to evade by Substituting *recourse* (2.11t).

(2.11) s. Den sidste [udvey] var at åbne alle porer og
ånde hele personen ind (Ditlevsen:7)

t. The last [recourse] was to open all the pores
and breathe the whole person inside (M1985:5)

2.3   ZIGZAGGING

Zigzagging (Zig; A ↔ B/C), the generic trajection to Divergence and Convergence, can be expected to have certain special properties deriving from the fact
that the trajections that it subsumes are mutual mirror images. Important in this
regard is the observation that one and the same translational nexus can be Divergent or Convergent depending upon which of the languages is source and which
target—a sort of reversibility that makes Zigzagging a convenient rubric for considering certain types of resource differences between languages, irrespective of
the direction of translation.

To be sure, resource differences among languages are strictly speaking virtually endless in variety and scope, and an attempt at presenting anything like a
balanced sampling of possibilities (not to speak of an exhaustive cataloguing)
would rapidly collapse under its own weight. Only one type of case will be illustrated here, in fact, but it is a type encountered with some frequency, particularly
in literary language (in the broad sense), and one to which the translator must respond with skill and feeling. I refer to resource differences with respect to a semantic domain that one of the translational languages subdivides along some
special parameter, while the other language treats it monolithically. Frequently
enough, the parameter investing the subdivision is EMBLEMATIC; i.e. symbolically charged, (cultural) ingroup-oriented, affective-subjective, or the like (cf.
M1985d), which can make it all the more tricky to model in the target text. Thus,
various languages have pairs of LEXICAL DOUBLETS whose choice depends upon
the value of the referent on a parameter like subjective-objective, royal-common,
sacred-profane. Yiddish, for example, has large numbers of Hebrew- (or Ara-
maic-) Germanic doublets distinguished in accordance with the sacred-profane
dichotomy: so in the bilingual notice on a box of Manischewitz matzo farfel
(2.12), the Hebrew-Aramaic nouns *hašgoxə* 'supervision' and *xaverəm* 'members' are religious-referent doublets for what might in a lay context appear as
Germanic *oyfzəxt* and *mitglidər* or the like.[7]

(**2.12**)   s. Gebokən untər štrengə [hašgoxə] fun barimtə
                rabonəm [xaverəm] fun 'Agudəs haRabonəm'
            t. Produced under the strict [supervision] of
                prominent rabbis, [members] of 'Agudas haRabbonim'
                (Union of Orthodox Rabbis of the United States
                and Canada)

In Irish, the religious intersects with the patriotic in prefixing the names of
non-Irish saints with *san* (from Latin *sanctus*), while the native Gaelic form
naomh is reserved for the names of Irish saints—and, of course, for the genetically non-Irish but emblematically ideal-Irish Saint Patrick (Naomh Pádraig)
(Dinneen:939). Traditional Malay evidenced a large list of royal(courtly)-com-
moner lexemes such as *bĕrangkat-bĕrjalan* 'walk', *bĕradu-tidor* 'sleep', *hulu-
kĕpala* 'head', etc. (Lewis:294); A public(objective)-private(subjective) distinc-

tion is conveyed by cases like Norwegian *pipe* '(smoker's)pipe' – *snadde* 'smoker's pipe, having usually a personal character' (Jorgenson & Galdal:314).

Strategically, there are cases where Zigzagging encapsulates alternative solutions to a translational nexus. Thus, in chapter 22 of Voltaire's *Candide*, one encounters the phrase *cette illustre Westphalienne* (Voltaire:142), a description that defies part-for-part recapitulation in English due to its lack of an adjective-marking gender system. The purely referential information conveyed by this phrase, with no regard to connotations, would dictate an English counterpart like *that illustrious Westphalian female one*, an aesthetic monstrosity that would simply be unacceptable as a serious translation. What might be done? Zigzagging provides antithetical solutions to try out in cases of this sort: Convergence would dictate that the French gender-opposition *cette illustre Westphalienne* (feminine) ≠ *cet illustre Westphalien* (masculine) be neutralized into (Converge upon) the genderless English *that illustrious Westphalian*; while Divergence would dictate that the general-female-conveying *cette illustre Westphalienne* be enriched (Diverge) into whatever is judged the most appropriate of various specific-female-conveying lexicalizations like *that illustrious Westphalian woman/girl/damsel/lady/* . . . All contextual and stylistic factors considered, Lowell Bair's Divergent translation, *that illustrious Westphalian lady*, seems just right (Bair: 143). The Zigzagging and its resolution in this case may be portrayed as in (2.13), where the boxed pair represent's Bair's actual translation.

(2.13) s (Voltaire:142)

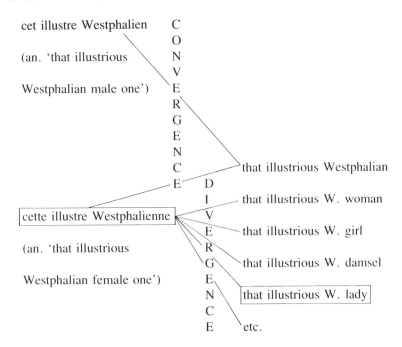

NOTES

1. Such switching is not always purely stylistic, however. Thus, the availability of neuter-gender diminutives at times provides a handy device for differentiating references to two denotata that would normally be referenced by pronouns of the same gender. A case in point occurs in the fairy tale 'Die wahre Braut' (G:553–58), in which two female denotata, a girl and her stepmother, are in the first half of the story referenced by neuter and feminine pronouns respectively, the former justified by the formally diminutive noun *Mädchen* (an. 'maid-little'). In the second half of the tale, however, feminine pronouns begin to be used to denote the girl, at the moment when the death of the stepmother immunizes this switch against referential ambiguity. (G:556).

2. Di Mauro's translation is supported by that of Y (1876:22): *pathways, rocks, flight, chase, [cries], muskets.*

3. Shown on metropolitan New York City-area TV channel 4, 10 October 1977.

4. Situations sometimes arise where Divergence is *necessary* though *not* desirable. A case in point will be discussed in (9.13).

5. This Latin American penchant for prolix sports terminology has apparently borne literary fruit at least once; see Dorfman (1985).

6. Similar in spirit but analytically falling within the pale of variational Reduction (§3.2) was my whittling away many instances of sentence-initial *Og* . . . 'And . . .' in translating Mykle (1968) (see M1980b). Mykle used twenty-eight sentence-initial tokens of *Og*, which I Reduced on the basis of stylistic feel to eighteen of English *And*.

7. Thanks to Fay Storch for suggesting *oyfzəxt* (replacing my guess *oyfzeyung*) and for pointing out that while the Hebrew-Aramaic doublets may also appear in secular contexts, the Germanic doublets may not appear in religious contexts. (Note also Russian *Čermnoje More* 'Red Sea' in ecclesiastical usage, versus *Krasnoje More* in secular usage (Malkiel:12); and the Classical Greek distinction between *ikhōr* 'blood of Gods' and *haima* 'blood of people or animals' (Flagg:10,149)).

Chapter *3*

RECRESCENCE (AMPLIFICATION AND REDUCTION)

3.1 AMPLIFICATION

Amplification (Amp; A → AB), whereby the target text picks up a translational element (B) in addition to a counterpart (A_t) of a source element (A_s), is probably the single most important STRATEGIC trajection for bridging anticipated gaps in the knowledge of the target audience—that is, for providing the target audience with extra explicit information not required by the source audience. To be sure, there are other functions and types of Amplification as well, but the importance and variety of the type described—which will be referred to as COMPENSATORY Amplification—suggests that it be discussed first.

3.1.1 Compensatory Amplification—Glossing

A good example of compensatory Amplification was provided without comment in (2.12), where, it will be recalled, the bilingual notice on the Manischewitz matzo farfel box ended in . . . *xaverəm fun "Agudəs HaRabonəm"* = . . . *members of "Agudas HaRabbonim" (Union of Orthodox Rabbis of the United States and Canada)*. Here, the parenthesized material in the English version has no counterpart in the Yiddish source but rather has presumably been added as a DESCRIPTION of *Agudas HaRabbonim*, in the expectation that people able to read only the English version of the notice might not know what the *Agudas HaRab-*

bonim actually is. In cases like this, the description answers to B of the Amplificational schema A → AB. A rather similar instance, taken from a bilingual French-English editorial in a Haitian newspaper published in New York, appears in (3.1), where in (3.1t) 'Negro Guerrilla', which by itself would pass as the Equational counterpart of 'Nègre Marron', is further clarified through comparison to a United States cultural equivalent, viz. the Unknown Soldier. This Amplification is presumably designed to fill out the sense of the French original for English-speaking readers insufficiently familiar with Haitian history.

(3.1) **s.** 'Nègre Marron' (*Haiti-Observateur*, 13–20 mai 1977,p.16)

    t. 'Negro Guerrilla', [Haiti's equivalent of the Unknown Soldier] (loc.cit.)

The reader will have noticed that the extra target element (B) in these examples of compensatory Amplification is not evoked so much by linguistic considerations of the target language as by extralinguistic considerations of the target audience. This being, moreover, the disposition of things in most cases of compensatory Amplification, one might predict that this sort of trajection will tend to be structurally quite whimsical—and indeed, this is so. To mention only two symptoms of this structural slack: (i) A given text may traject into the same target language with or without Amplification, subject to extralinguistic audience conditions; (ii) The descriptive part (B) of the target trajection need not be in the same language as the base part (A_t).

Point (i) may be illustrated with excerpts from translations of two Irish short stories destined for a largely American readership. Had these translations been published in Ireland, I would have judged it both unnecessary and in poor taste to presume to supply Irish readers with reasons either for cutting peat (viz. *for the fire* (3.2at)) or for spreading out seaweed (vis. *to dry* (3.2bt)).

(3.2) **as.** 'Allas fir an mhóin sin bíodh fhios agat,

       a chailín,ceart í spáráil . . .' (Ní Shúilleabháin 1977:3)

    at. 'Men have sweated to cut that peat [for the fire],

       keep that in mind, girl. Use it sparingly.' (M1983b:83)

    bs. I ngarraí uainn síos bhí fear ag leathadh

       feamainne. (Ní Shúilleabháin 1968:5)

    bt. In a little field nearby a man was spreading out

       seaweed [to dry]. (M1983d:11)

As for point (ii), note the phrases in (3.3a) from an article in a Haitian-American newspaper, and assume for the moment that they have been translated from English as indicated. In each case, an English Amplification accompanies the French target rendition, presumably because the target audience—Haitians seeking to purchase a house in the United States—will be encountering exactly these English locutions (*mortgage, closing*) in their negotiations, and the newspaper article accordingly provides them with both name (in English) and function (in French) at the same time. But a moment's reflection will show that the same

effect could be achieved by reversing the languages involved in the Amplification on the target end—and indeed, this is evidenced in the selfsame article;
(3.3b). Note finally that in a situation of this type it would make equal sense to
assume that the source language itself may have been French, in which event the
target text is given by pervasive carry-over Matching (§1.4.1), modified by English compensatory Amplification.

(3.3) as. the government mortgages . . . without closing expenses
    at. les hypothèques du gouvernement [(mortgages)] . . . sans
       frais supplémentaires [(closings)] (*Haiti-Observateur*, 13–20
       1977,p.13)
    bs. a service for securing mortgage
    bt. un service pour l'obtention de 'mortgage' [(hypothèque)] (loc.cit.)

Most of the preceding cases of compensatory Amplification are akin to, if
not out-and-out instances of, what philologists call GLOSSING: i.e., the annotation
of a text with elucidatory material, which may range in length from single words
(often but not necessarily in a language different from that of the text itself) to
complex paraphrases or definitions. While it may be debatable whether all cases
of compensatory Amplification constitute glossing, I would claim that the converse does hold: that glossing is a special and important case of compensatory
Amplification. And largely for that reason the discussion of this sort of Amplification will close with a sampling of cases in point.

First of all, in view of its function, glossing may be correctly predicted to
occur with special frequency in certain types of text. For example:

(a) *Philosophical treatises*, because the source language is often pressed into
special, even strained service in order to convey novel ideas, and the resulting
neologism predictably compounds translational difficulties. In the Occident, the
source language is frequently Latin, which then carries over into the target text
glosses as well e.g. (3.4):[1]

(3.4) a. once we have taken the different movements of the
    stars [(*orbium*)] into account (Nicholas of Cusa, apud Santillana:63)
    b. Kepler excogitates the exterior movement of the thing
    once brought forth [(*naturata*)], it diffuses its light
    [(*lumen*)] from every part of itself . . . since light [(*lux*)]
    is the perfection of the first body (Robert Grosseteste, apud
    Fremantle:137)

(b) *Texts in developing languages*, whether the development is specific to a
particular register—e.g., French in response to developments in American linguistic theory (source language English), as in (3.5a), or whether the development is quite general—e.g., Irish (Gaelic) in its attempted comeback against
English as a general-culture language in Ireland, as in (3.5b).

(3.5) a. domaines non-bornés [(*unbounded*)] . . .
la règle de mouvement est polycatégorielle
[(*cross-categorial*)] (Milner 1978)
  b. caomhnaithe agus inniúlachta fuinnimh
[(energy conservation and efficiency)] (Ó Muircheartaigh 1978)

(c) *Texts modified for language learners*, e.g. the excerpt in (3.6) from the youth section of a German-American newspaper, where presumably the glosses are intended to help young American readers learn German.

(3.6) lm allgemeinen wird über die Höhe des Verdienstes
[(earnings)] in Deutschland nicht geredet und Freunde
wie Nachbarn beurteilen [(judge)] die Höhe des Bankkontos
nach den üblichen Aushängeschildern [(pretense[s])]
wie Haus, Auto, Farbefernseher [(color TV)] (*Aufbau*, 20 May 1977)

(d) A grab-bag of cases involving *texts conveying information not (readily) available to the audience in the language (or dialect) of the text at large*, e.g., an advertisement for a New York fish store in a Haitian-American newspaper, where down-home Creole-French equivalents are given as glosses for English or Standard French (3.7a); or from a German-American newspaper with a large Jewish-German readership who have not been in Europe since the 1930s, a letter in which a Czech place name is glossed by its pre–World War II German equivalent (3.7b).

(3.7) a. RED SNAPPER [(Sarde rose ou grise)], KING FISH
[(Capitaine), (Béquine), (Cong)], CREVETTE
[(Cribiche, Cyrique)], et tous les autres poissons
et fruits de mer que les Haïtiens mangent et
connaissent (op.cit. in (3.3a))
  b. Ich bin soeben von einer langen Kur in Karlovy Váry
[(Karlsbad)] zurückgekehrt (op.cit. in (3.6))

Observe finally that glosses do not always occur in canonical parenthesized form. Linkage by a conjunction like *or* is a common alternative, either just so (3.8a) or in embellished form (3.8b). It may be that the further compensatory Amplification slides from parenthesized form toward syntactic integration into the text, the less it will be felt as an instance of glossing in the narrow sense. Note just one case, from a bilingual English-Spanish editorial (3.9), where the English idiom *throw in the towel* is calque-Matched (§1.4.2) into Spanish literally as *tirar la toalla*, but then provided with the glosslike qualifier *de la rendición* 'of surrender' to clinch the intended sense.[2]

(3.8) a. vital impulses [or *élan vital*] (White:67)
Fragebogen [or questionnaire] (Puzo:40)
  b. it is evident that the essences of the sorts,
[or if the Latin word pleases better, species,]
are nothing else but these abstract ideas (Berlin:72)

(3.9) s. it looked like . . . Reagan . . . would throw in
the (towel) (*El Diario-La Prensa*, 26 March 1976)
   t. Parecía que Reagan tendría que tirar la toalla
[de la rendición] (loc.cit.)

3.1.2 Classificatory Amplification

It may be possible to glimpse something common to a medley of apparently disparate trajectories and posit what will be called CLASSIFICATORY Amplification
(as distinct from compensatory Amplification) in two tendential if not absolute
ways: (i) while the function of the latter has been seen to be largely STRATEGIC,
classificatory Amplification is largely STRUCTURAL; (ii) while the description (or
gloss) of compensatory Amplification is characteristically motivated by extralinguistic conditions of the target audience, the corresponding added part (B
of the schema A → AB) under classificatory Amplification—to be called the
CLASSIFIER—is normally evoked by linguistic conditions of the target language.

Classificatory Amplification comprises Matching plus an added element
conveying particular semantic or syntactic information concerning the Matched
element which, from the vantage of the source language, is normally redundant
or irrelevant. The term 'classifier' was suggested for such added elements by
similarity to CLASSIFIER CONSTRUCTIONS in various East Asian languages, where,
under various syntactic circumstances, a noun is accompanied by a formative
marking the noun's membership in a given semantic-syntactic class. In fact,
translation into a classifier language may often be construed as involving classificatory Amplification in the sense of this book, perhaps especially when the classifier rules in the target language are semantically productive. This seems to be
the case for Cantonese, for instance, as evidenced by the fact that various En-
glish-borrowed nouns are fitted out with semantically appropriate native classifi-
ers. Thus, the following English-to-Cantonese trajectories probably constitute
genuine classificatory Amplification: *beer* → *bē-jaú* (where *jaú* is the classifier
for alcoholic beverages (root sense 'wine')); *(calling)card* → *kāat-pín* (*pín* classifies small flat objects, etc.) (T'sou 1975).[3]

Moving away from examples involving classifier systems in the nontrans-
lational sense, consider in (3.10a) Robert Graves's translation of the Latin nickname *Cedo Alteram* (an. 'Hand [me] another') with the help of *Old* in the spirit
of what might be called a 'classifier of nickname status' in English;[4] and in a

(3.10) as. (centurio Lucilius interficitur, cui militaribus
facetiis vocabulum) 'Cedo Alteram' (indiderant,
quia fracta vite in tergo militis alteram clara voce
ac rursus aliam poscebat) (Tacitus: 56[I,23])
   at. (that Heaven was angry with them for their murder of)
[Old]Give-me-Another (and for their defiance
of authority) (Graves:174)

(3.10) *continued*

   bs. Has så med forundring på de store taljene og blokkene
   som hang under taket (Mykle:29)

   bt. He gazed with astonishment at the huge [array] of
   block and tackle hanging from the ceiling (M1980b:95)

somewhat similar vein (3.10b), where I fitted out my English rendition of the Norwegian phrase *de store taljene og blokkene*, an. 'the large tackles and blocks', with the noun *array* as what might be called a 'classifier of mass-noun status' since, to my feeling, the English binomial *block and tackle* resists pluralization.

3.2 REDUCTION

Reduction (Red; AB $\rightarrow$ A), as the inverse of Amplification, is a pattern whereby a source expression (AB) is partially trajected onto a target counterpart (A) and partially omitted from the trajection (B).

   Since Reduction is the mirror image of Amplification, it is predictable that various of its properties will fall into place simply by reversing the direction of translation; i.e., by studying instances where source and target are effectively interchanged, at least in relevant respects. Thus, in translating the French phrase of (3.11a) into English, the omission of the glosslike comment *comme disent les Anglais* 'as the English say' would constitute a sort of Reduction that is effectively the mirror image of compensatory Amplification: a description (*comme disent les Anglais*) has been omitted rather than supplied—in this case because the language homogeneity of the target text would deprive the gloss of its function.[5]

   The case in (3.11b) is similar, except that the Amplification it mirrors is classificatory rather than compensatory: Since Irish is less tolerant than English in employing metonymy for the coinage of expressions directly referring to people in terms of characteristic items of apparel and the like, the noun *lucht* 'people' is pressed into service as a foil—in which case it effectively classifies the phrase *(na b)peiticótaí dearga*, an. '(of the) red petticoats', as attributive rather than referential.

(3.11) **as**. un phénomène naturel, un 'act of God',
   [comme disent les Anglais] (op.cit. in (3.3a))

   at. a natural phenomenon, an act of God (JM)

   bs. '[Lucht] na bpeiticótaí dearga a thugtaí ar
   na mrá Connachtacha (M.MacNeill, apud Hartmann:48)

   bt. 'The red petticoats' they used to call the
   Connacht women (M.MacNeill, apud Hartmann:50)

3.2.1 Compensatory Reduction

Such anti-Amplificational cases aside, it is perhaps noteworthy that there are genuine instances of what might be called COMPENSATORY REDUCTION, where the strategy of omission functions much like the strategy of addition in compensatory Amplification, as a device to bridge gaps of knowledge between a relatively knowledgeable source audience and a relatively ignorant target audience. Two examples from Ralph Manheim's translation of Günter Grass's novel *The Tin Drum* are given in (3.12). In both cases, the Reductive strategy consists in omitting source-text information interpretable as *both* circumstantial or tangential to the story *and* unlikely to make much sense, at least without inordinate glossing, to the average American reader. In (3.12a) the source text mentions not merely a crowded *(street)car*, as does the target text, but in fact a hook-up of *two* streetcars, one *(Triebwagen)* pulling the other *(Anhänger)*, much in the fashion of a subway train. But since streetcars are not (or in their heyday were not) thus connected in most American cities, Manheim cleverly evades the specifics of German streetcar assemblage altogether. Somewhat similarly in (3.12b), the original text mentions not just posting bills but specifically posting them on *Litfaßsaülen*, that is, on fat cylindrical posts specially designed for bill-posting —artifacts which until quite recently were rare or nonexistent in the United States.[6]

(3.12) as. der [Triebwagen mit Anhänger] . . . vollbesetzt mit
müden und dennoch lauten Badegästen des Seebades
Bösen (Grass:176)

at. the [car] filled up with weary but vociferous
bathers from the beach at Bösen (Manheim:206)

bs. hätte er Plakate [an Litfaßsaülen] kleben
können (Grass:418)

bt. might have been fine for posting bills (Manheim:486)

3.2.2 Variational Reduction

As was intimated in discussing the Biblical Hebrew stylistic penchant for long series of clauses connected by $w\vartheta$- ~ u- 'and' (2.9), literary traditions may differ widely in their relative tolerance of (morphological) REPETITION, and when the target tradition is less tolerant than the source tradition, Divergence may sometimes be employed to break up the monotony. Schematizing the actual Biblical example adduced in (2.9), we might portray the King James translators as employing Divergence to diversify what might be called a six-point RECURRENCE CHAIN: *A A A A A A* to *B C AB C D E* (*A* = 'and', *B* = 'when', *C* = 'then', *D* = 'whether', *E* = 'or'). But if the links in the source chain are complex, sometimes it is possible to break up the monotony with Reduction, in any of a variety of ways. Thus, a source chain schematized as *AB AB AB AB AB AB* may be Reduced in STEP-DOWN fashion to *AB AB AB A A A*, or CHIASTICALLY to *A A A AB AB AB*, or PERIODICALLY to *A AB A AB A AB*, or by a medley of techniques to a MIXED chain like *AB A B A AB A* or the like.[7]

A particularly interesting case of such VARIATIONAL REDUCTION was analyzed in M1986a, centering on the mixed recurrence chain of the Japanese noun

ootosanrin throughout Kobo Abe's novel *The Woman in the Dunes*, and its translation into English by E. Dale Saunders. The chain, reproduced in (3.13), revealed the following properties:

(i) The initial trajection (3.13a) is DEFINITIONAL DIFFUSION (chapter 4), involving explicitation for the target audience of the criterial properties of an unfa-
miliar referent, in this case of the commonplace Japanese utility vehicle called
ootosanrin (an. 'auto-three-wheel'), which Saunders aptly chacterizes as a truck
(C in the schema) functionally a pickup (B), and formally having three wheels
(A);

(ii) Subsequent links in the chain (3.13b−l) represent various Reductions of
the initial Diffusion;

(iii) There are two magnitudes of Reduction in evidence, WEAK ABC → AC
(e.g. at link (b)), and STRONG ABC → A (e.g. at (c)) or → C (only at (j));

(iv) In those sections of the chain where the links are closest together, strong
Reduction is used; e.g. from weak AC to strong A at (b-c) and from AC to the
subsequence C-A-A at (i-j-k-l);

(v) Almost conversely to (iv), the strategy goes from strong A to weak AC
only after major gaps between links, at (d) and (i).

(3.13) Variational Reduction in the recurrence chain of *ootosanrin*
(Abe (1962)/Saunders (1964))

pages	translation	schema
a. (30/32)	three-wheeled pickup truck	ABC
b. (35/38)	three-wheeled truck	AC
c. (36/38)	three-wheeler	A
d. (70/79)	three-wheeled truck	AC
e. (86/95)	three-wheeled truck	AC
f. (112/122)	three-wheeled truck	AC
g. (177/194)	three-wheeler	A
h. (178/197)	three-wheeler	A
i. (215/238)	three-wheeled truck	AC
j. (215/238)	truck	C
k. (215/238)	three-wheeler	A
l. (216/239)	three-wheeler	A

With one prima facie disturbing exception, points (i−v) suggest the following principle for recurrence chains:

(3.14) All else being equal, the closer together (farther apart) two adjacent
links in a recurrence chain, the less (more) identifying information the
second link should bear.

The exception is link-gap (f-g), which, despite constituting the widest gap in
the novel, is bridged by weak-to-strong linkage (AC-A) rather than the strong-to-
weak variety expected by point (v). As is detailed in M1986a, however, of all the
links in the chain only (g) occurs in a slot where the immediately preceding con-

text IMPLICATES (re)identification of the referent as a motor vehicle—hence the dispensability of the English word *truck* despite the long absence of any mention of *ootosanrin*. Thus, principle (3.14) is not really violated, the apparent anomaly being genuinely dispensed by the 'all else being equal' clause.

3.3 RECRESCENCE

Recrescence (Rcr; A ↔ AB), the trajection generic to Amplification and Reduction, at times provides a vantage on certain aspects of translation less easily accommodated by either of the specific trajections taken singly. Just three types of example will be treated (§3.3.1–§3.3.3). Examples are listed, as may be seen, in increasing order of semantic impact on the source-target text relation.

3.3.1   Minimax Size Adjustments for Metrical Fit

In my translation of André Bjerke's Norwegian poem 'The grown-ups' party', I rendered the couplet in (3.15s) as *Ah, it's a long way still! | A long way still!* (3.15t). Since *(det er) lenge til!* is analytically '(it's) long till!' (understand '[a] long [time] till [then]!'), the translation of this locution as *(it's) a long way still!* constitutes Amplification by addition of *still*, and probably also by the addition of *a . . . way* . But at the same time Reduction is involved, since in the second verse *A long way still!* appears only once, while Bjerke's original has *Lenge til!* twice.

(**3.15**) s. Å, det er lenge til!
    Lenge til! Lenge til! (Bjerke:37)
  t. Ah, it's a long way still!
    A long way still! (M1981a)

It is analytically useful to view a translational response like this holistically as Recrescence, not simply because Amplification and Reduction are both involved but because the strategy itself is fundamentally holistic. What was involved is a MINIMAX response to antithetical requirements of the emerging English version: on the one hand, the key Norwegian phrase *lenge til* could not be Equated into coherent English as *long till*; but on the other hand, the beefed-up (Amplified) version *a long way still* was, to my sensibilities, simply too long to bear repetition in the final line. Thus, I employed the minimax solution of Amplifying the phrase itself but Reducing the overlong result by dropping one of the phrase's occurrences. Since Bjerke's poem was composed in free verse, my reaction to the length factor was purely impressionistic-aesthetic—not any less genuine for that, I hope, but it is true that free verse affords the translator relatively wide berth in such matters. Thus, I felt no particular compunction that the Recrescent strategy resulted in a bobbed syllable count for the English couplet (6:4), as opposed to Bjerke's perfect balance in the Norwegian original (6:6).

However, when dealing with more rigid verse traditions, translators normally respond with more scruples toward form, and in 'such cases it is wise to study the target-language resources for their Recrescence-potential in order to do justice to the stricter size requirements imposed by the source tradition. In this enterprise it is usually rewarding, at least in a general way, to study various traditions of versification UNILINGUISTICALLY in their own right, outside of the TRANSLINGUISTIC translational paradigm, because quite often the poets within such traditions will have developed unilinguistic analogues of Recrescence (and other trajections) in order to increase their own versatility within the requirements of their own tradition. To cite just one especially interesting example, the bards of the Finnish folk epic *Kalevala* helped meet the OCTOSYLLABIC metrical requirements of their tradition (Kiparsky 1970) by extending the resources of Finnish derivational morphology to expand nouns by addition of the adjectivizing suffix *-(i)nen* (genitive *-(i)sen*). Thus, in verse 227 of runo 9, *kuuen kukkasen nenästä* 'from the tips of six blooms', the required eight syllables are in part provided by the artifice of using the trisyllabic 'adjectivized' noun form *kukkasen* 'of bloom(s)' rather than the normal noun form *kukan*, which would fall short by one syllable. Interestingly, this special Amplificationlike strategy also has a Reductionlike counterpart: e.g., the normal adjective form *suloinen* 'sweet' drops its suffix and shows up looking like a noun as *sula* at 7:187. This ambidirectionality clinches the Recrescencelike nature of the strategy.[8]

3.3.2 Global Preferences for Larger or Smaller Units

When one compares the excerpt in (3.16s) from the first page of Günter Grass's German novel *The Tin Drum* with Ralph Manheim's translation in (3.16t), one may note two innocuous-looking instances of Reduction, which I have marked off with brackets: simplification of the source compound-noun *Anstaltsleitung*, an. 'institution-management', to the simplex *management* in English, and in parallel fashion simplification of *Bettgitter*, an. 'bed-bars', to *bars*. I qualify these Reductions as innocuous-looking, but I think it may be predicted with some confidence that a page-by-page search through the rest of the Grass-Manheim text pair would reveal scores of analogous cases, where morphologically complex German words are trajected into morphologically simplex English counterparts by Reduction—even though the corresponding complex formations would pass strict muster as technically correct English (. . . *to have the [bed bars] built up higher* . . .), just as the simplex formations would mutatis mutandis result in technically correct German (. . . *das [Gitter] möchte ich erhöhen lassen* . . .).

What is at issue is that German seems to evidence a GLOBAL PREFERENCE for morphological complexity, relative to English, in lexical word-building. Or it might rather be that English, relative to German, evidences a corresponding global preference for simplicity, at least in the Germanic component of its lexicon. In either event, a commensurate amount of GLOBAL RECRESCENCE is called for when translating between two such languages. Failure to do so could easily result in an aura of lexical-semantic unnaturalness in the target text, whether it be a feeling of clutter in an English target text (*bed bars*), or of sparseness in a corresponding German target text (*Gitter*).

(3.16) s. mein Bett ist das endlich erreichte Ziel, mein
Trost ist es und könnte mein Glaube werden, wenn
mir die[Anstalts]leitung erlaubte, einige
Änderungen vorzunehmen: das [Bett]gitter möchte
ich erhöhen lassen (Grass:9)

t. my bed is a goal attained at last, it is my
consolation and might become my faith if the
[Ø]management allowed me to make a few changes:
I should like, for instance, to have the [Ø]bars
built up higher (Manheim:10)

3.3.3 Japanese *kureru-yaru* and Author's Empathy

In M1981b I speculated on the implications for Recrescence of the Japanese phenomenon described by Kuno and Kaburaki in (3.17) and provisionally concluded that the real problem would be one of Amplification (and Divergence): how to go about translating English texts characterized by sentences like [*23*] (below) differentially into a Japanese target text requiring any of [*24a*], [*24b*], or [*24c*]?[9]

(3.17) Consider a situation that can be described as follows:
[*23*] Taroo helped Hanako.
The same situation can be described in Japanese in at least the following three ways:
]*24a*] Taroo ga Hanako o tasuketa.
                      helped
[*24b*] Taroo ga Hanako o tasukete
                      helping *yatta*.
                               gave
[*24c*] Taroo ga Hanako o tasukete
                      helping *kureta*.
                               gave
Example [*24a*] represents an objective description of the situation, and because of this, it is seldom used in colloquial speech. In [*24b*], *yatta* (subject-centered) is used as the matrix verb, coupled with the continuative form *tasukete* 'helping, help and' of *tasukeru* 'help'. This sentence represents the speaker's empathy with Taroo: namely, it shows that the speaker is describing the event by placing himself closer to Taroo than to Hanako. On the other hand, in [*24c*], the nonsubject-centered giving verb *kureta* is used. This sentence represents the speaker's empathy with Hanako: it shows that the speaker is describing the event from Hanako's angle. (Kuno and Kaburaki:634)

But while this question still looms as an important one for English-to-Japanese translation, I gave short shrift to the inverse question of Reduction (and Convergence) involved in translating Japanese sentences like [*24a,b,c*] into English sentences like [*23*]. Subsequently, however, study of Saunders's translation (1964) of Abe's novel *The Woman in the Dunes* (1962) revealed the simplemindedness of that conclusion. Since full results of the study are reported elsewhere (M1986a), just two cardinal points will be adduced here:[10]

(3.18) a. Reduction from Japanese to English through trajectional loss of *yaru* and *kureru* incurs the risk of losing information conveyed PREGNANTLY (cf. §2.2) by those forms, in particular

    b. loss of information conveying the PROTAGONIST'S EMPATHY, which in narrative is often tacitly manifested through the author's (narrator's, speaker's) descriptions and statements.

The cogency of these points comes through in those cases where differential use of *yaru* or *kureru* identifies the protagonist's empathy (3.18b) by isolating the narrator's empathy (3.17) when there are no other textual cues to the same effect (3.18a). Thus, on the occasion of a symbolically important and deadly confrontation between a spider and a moth, Abe uses this device to convey identification of the novel's hero, Jumpei Nikki, with the killing spider rather than with the victim moth (M1986a: example (12)).

NOTES

1. Note that the gloss in (3.4b) effectively forestalls undesirable Convergence of the Latin terms *lumen* and *lux* into undiffentiated English *light*. (Cf. also §7.5).

2. I have parenthesized (*towel*) on the English side because the actual version had *sponge*, which I took the liberty of normalizing to enhance comparability with Spanish *toalla* for expository reasons. (I don't think this *sponge* ≠ *towel* discrepancy vitiates the example, but there may be some factor I'm overlooking.)

3. The case of a 'wine'-morpheme classifying 'beer' bears comparison to the Homeric Greek verb *oinokhoein*, an. 'to wine-pour', in its extension to other beverages; see the comments of Monro in 1,598 of the *Iliad* (1958i:260).

4. Parentheses in (3.10a) are used to set off contextual material, since Graves' passage is a derivative from rather than translation of Tacitus's original. For comparison, here is an actual translation of (3.10as): (The company-commander Lucilius lost his life. In joking army talk his nickname was) 'Another-please' (because every time he broke a stick over a soldier's back he used to shout loudly for another and then another) (Grant:46).

5. If we assume that news dispatches of *general* content on New York City Spanish-language radio programs have been translated from English, then the report over station WADO (Spring 1978, date lost) that Irish nationalist hunger-striker Francis Hughes, just before his death, *recibió los últimos sacramentos*, an. 'received the last sacraments/rites', might reconstructively constitute Reduction from something like *received the last rites [of the Roman Catholic Church]*, the tail-end of which could safely be bobbed in the Spanish version, since the overwhelming majority of WADO listeners

would know without further ado that *los últimos sacramentos* are a specifically Roman Catholic insti-
tution. (Conversely, one frequently hears over WADO an Amplificationlike reference to President
Reagan as *el presidente [norte]americano*, an. 'the [North] American president', a qualification that
would be jarring on an English-language station in the same region.)

6. To the extent that language usage may itself become cultural habit, the frequent simplification of
Russian names by omission of the partonymic when translated into French also smacks of compensatory Reduction; see Maillot (1979).

7. RECURRENCE CHAINS evidence considerable overlap with COREFERENCE CHAINS (§1.4, §2.1.1),
the latter normally being special cases of the former where the stuff of the recurrence is reference-
independent of its linguistic vehicle. The converse relation does not hold, however, since linguistically identical elements may be referentially disjoint, or even incapable of bearing reference in the
technical sense. This is true of the chain in (2.9), for example, while the chain to be adduced in (3.13)
is both recurrential and coreferential. (For a case of philological equivocation as to whether the parallelistic recurrence chain in the Biblical verse Judges 5,26 is also coreferential, see O'Connor
(1980:51f).)

8. For analogous reasons (vis-à-vis iambic pentameter), Shakespeare at times uses longer and shorter
doublets of the same name: e.g. from *Troilus and Cressida, Cressida ~ Cressid, Pandarus ~ Pandar,
Diomedes ~ Diomed* (1864:769–808). (For the use of similar deformations in classical antiquity, see
Curtius(288).)

9. The reader may have noticed that the type forms given in (3.13) are *kureta-yatta*, while those
given in the section-heading to §3.3.3 (and in (3.18) below) are *kureru-yaru*. The former are past
tense forms; the latter are nonpast citation forms.

10. An example of these points will incidentally be provided in (8.9at), where *tomatte kureta* (an.
'stopping *kure*-PAST') in lieu of simple *tomatta* (an. 'stopped') conveys that cessation of the danger-
ous stretching of the rope ladder was to the benefit of the protagonist. Though Saunders Reduces this
specific effect out of his translation (8.9as), the general force of the empathy still goes through by virtue of the Equation *Saiwai* → *Fortunately*.

Chapter *4*

REPACKAGING (DIFFUSION AND CONDENSATION)

4.1 DIFFUSION

Diffusion (Dif; $A^\frown B \to A|B$), whereby a source element or construction is in some sense rendered by a more loosely or expansively organized target counterpart, will be illustrated with four different types of example (§4.1.1–§4.1.4).

4.1.1 Diffusion versus Amplification

It is important to distinguish Diffusion from Amplification, a caution nicely illustrated with the King James translation of Proverb 8,19 in (4.1). The close succession of target nominals *gold . . . fine gold* may lure the analyst into viewing the translation here as being Equational *hɔɔruuṣ* → *gold* gollowed by Amplificational *pɔɔz* → *fine gold*, but this is inaccurate for the latter trajection. In order for the translation *fine gold* to constitute an actual case of Amplification, the source *pɔɔz* would have to be cross-identified with part of the target *fine gold*, the remainder constituting the added description; that is, to take the error most likely to be made in this case, the Amplificational schema $A \to AB$ would have to be assigned the values $A = pɔɔz = gold$, $B = fine$. But this is incorrect, since the word *pɔɔz* encapsulates within itself the semantic features corresponding to both *fine* and *gold*; thus, we are actually faced with Diffusion, whereby in the target language these features are, so to speak, segmentalized out into the independent words *fine* and *gold*.

(4.1) s. ṭoov piryii mee[ḥɔɔruuṣ] umip[pɔɔz]
uθvuuʔɔɔθii mikkɛsɛf nivḥɔɔr (K:Proverbs 8,19)

t. My fruit is better than [gold], yea, than [fine gold];
and my revenue than choice silver (KJ)

It may be instructive to contrast this example of Diffusion with a superficially similar case of true Amplification and take the occasion to introduce the conventional notation for FEATURE ANALYSIS by modeling both examples accordingly. The Amplification is F.C.W. Hiley's translation, in line 100 of Catullus's poem 64, of the Latin word *auri*, an. '(of)gold', as *burnisht gold*, where addition of the adjective *burnisht* instantiates what Lefevere analyzes as infusing the target text with elements 'not warranted by the source text' (112f). Using the conventional notation for features, these Hebrew (4.1) and Latin trajections may be portrayed as in (4.2). The letters F,G, and R represent CORE FEATURES standing in for hypothesized semantic properties roughly corresponding to 'fine', 'gold', and 'burnisht', respectively, while the plus sign is a COEFFICIENT indicating positive values of the features in question. (Negative values, signaled by the minus sign, will be illustrated in chapter 6 (6.5).) Note how these examples pair off with the respective schemata for Diffusion and Amplification. In (4.2a) [+ F] and [+ G], Condensed in one source word *pɔɔz* ($F_s \frown G_s$), are Diffusionally spread out into two target words ($F_t | G_t$). In (4.2b), however, the one source word *auri*, with its feature (G_s), is per se in a one-to-one (Equational) relation with target counterpart *gold* and its feature (G_t), while the Amplification consists in the addition of the adjective *burnisht*; hence G → RG.

(4.2) a. pɔɔz → fine   gold
[+ F]   [+ F] [+ G]
[+ G]

b. auri   → burnisht gold
[+ G]   [+ R]   [+ G]

4.1.2 Definitional Diffusion

It is a fact of ethnolinguistics that differentiation of lexical meaning tends to be proportional to cultural saliency of the referent—as in the well-known cases of Eskimo having words for several types of snow (Whorf:208), or Classical Arabic with its specialized terminology for camels. A few examples of this phenomenon are given in (4.3), with English lexicographical definitions provided from bilingual dictionaries:

(4.3) a. Irish *scolb* 'the crack or break in an egg caused by the emerging bird' (Dinneen:980)

b. Norwegian *morild* 'phosphorescence of the sea' (Jorgenson and Galdal:206)

c. Russian *protalina* 'place where the snow has melted' (O'Brien:234)

d. Japanese *ootosanrin* 'an auto-tricycle; a three-wheeler motor van' (Katsumata:1323)

e. Turkish *sünnet* '1. Sunnah (practices and rules not laid down in the Quran but derived from the Prophet's own habits and words); 2. ritual circumcision' (Alkım et al.:1040)

The point about such cases is that the entry:definition format constitutes a *virtual recipe for Diffusion*, all else being equal. This is so because, in a standard bilingual dictionary, it is precisely the lack of any true lexical counterpart of the entry in the (lexicographical) target language that necessitates the provision of a definition in lieu—a definition which, in a good dictionary, will reconstruct in spread-out fashion the semantic features and relations implicit in the entry lexeme.

To make the same point more concisely from a somewhat different vantage point, a good entry:definition pair may per se be taken as an instance of Diffusion *geared to the null context*—to be used, that is, when there is no feedback from the surrounding text. Such a trajection will be called DEFINITIONAL DIFFUSION.[1]

It will immediately be appreciated that translation rarely occurs in a null context, so that normally some appeal to the context will be possible, and often necessary to boot. A few examples of this effect appear in (4.4), where in each case but (c) the actual contextualized translation is shorter than the corresponding definitional Diffusion in (4.3): by Reduction of the latter in (4.4a) and by Substitution in (4.4b).[2] (This general phenomenon will receive further attention in §4.3, where contextualizations of (4.3d–e) will also be adduced (note 5).)

(4.4) **as**. Bhí gé ar gor aici agus bhí tuairim láidir aici
go raibh [scolb] ar na huibhe (Ua Maoileoin:12)

at. She had a goose hatching the eggs, and there was
every indication that the [cracks] were already
appearing on them (JM)

bs. Men du là med øyne ‖ some [morild] i mørket (Bjerke:36)

bt. But you lay with eyes ‖ like [sea-glow] in the dark (M1981a)

cs. Nad nami navislo seroje nebo, sploš' pokrytoje tučami,
vokrug rasprosterlis' luga v tëmnyx pjatnax
[protalin] (Gorky:500)

ct. Above us hung a heavy, grey, clouded sky. Around us
stretched enormous snow-covered fields, dotted with
black spaces, [showing where the snow was thawing]
(Montefiore and Jakowleff:110)

4.1.3 Diffusion of Grammatical Inflections

As has just been seen Diffusion may be evoked when the target language has no straightforward counterpart to a source lexical item. However, it need not be a source lexical item that triggers the Diffusion; it is not infrequently a source

GRAMMATICAL INFLECTION that the target language is unable to Match. Thus, French may inflect its verbs in the CONDITIONAL MOOD to convey the hearsay or reported nature of past actions, and since English lacks any corresponding inflection, Diffusion by circumlocution is called for. An illustration of this is provided in (4.5a), followed by a similar example from German, which inflects its verbs in the SUBJUNCTIVE MOOD to similar effect (4.5b).

(**4.5**) **as**. En Éthiopie, principalement à Addis-Abéba, la
capitale, plusieurs centaines d'étudiants [auraient
été regroupés] par l'armée [et fusillés] (op.cit.in(3.3a),p.5)

　at. In Ethiopia, especially in the capital Addis Ababa,
[[it is reported that]] several hundred students [were
rounded up] by the Army [and shot] (JM)

　bs. So[sei]nunmehr klar, daß der Atlantikboden vor etwa 100
Millionen Jahren noch auf dem Niveau des heutigen
Meeresspiegels gestanden habe. (op.cit.in(3.6),p.16)

　bt. An so [it is] now clear, [[according to Professor Emmermann]]
that the floor of the Atlantic approximately 100 million
years ago was at what is today sea-level. (JM)

4.1.4　Diffusion of Sentences

The kinds of Diffusion dealt with so far have all involved trajectional relations between groups of words in the target text and single words, or even smaller units (inflections), in the source text. But the notion of Diffusion need not be thus limited and is usefully extended to cover any of a variety of size and density factors beyond the morpholexical, where the target is organizationally looser or more expansive than the source. Often of importance, for example, are differences in permissible (or desirable) SENTENCE SIZE.[3] Thus, the German prose of Thomas Mann constitutes a distinguished and notorious case of sesquipedalian sentences, which English translators often wisely resolve by Diffusion into two or more sentences in the target text. An example of this is provided in (4.6), where it will be seen that Lowe-Porter has Diffused Mann's one sentence into three (if only periods are counted) or four (if the semicolon on the second-to-last line is counted).

(**4.6**) **s**. (with sublinear analytic translation)
　a. Sich selbst legte　er solche Fragen　　eben nur vor,
to himself posed he such　questions　　just

　b. weil　　er keine Antwort darauf wußte, [Joachim]⟨a⟩
because he no　　answer to-it　knew　　Joachim

　c. seinerseits war zur Teilnahme　daran fast　　gar nicht
for his part was to　participation in-it almost not at all

　d. zu gewinnen, da　[er]⟨a⟩,, wie Hans Castorp es eines
to win over　since he　　as　Hans Castorp it one

　e. Abends auf französisch gesagt hatte, an　　nichts
evening in　French　　had said　about nothing

   f. dachte als daran, im   Flachlande Soldat zu sein
       thought except   in-the lowlands to be a soldier
   g. und mit der bald sich nähernden, bald foppend
       and with the now approaching   now mockingly
   h. wieder ins Weite   schwindenden Hoffnung darauf
       again in the distance disappearing hope   for it
    i. in einem nachgerade erbitterten [[Kampfe]] ⟨b⟩ lag,
       in an   ever more bitter   struggle   was-engaged
    j. [[den]] ⟨b⟩ durch   einen Gewaltstreich zu beenden
       which by means of   bold action   to end
   k. [er]⟨a⟩ sich neuerdings geneigt zeigte (Mann:316)
       he   was showing himself ever more inclined
    t. For himself, it was precisely because he did not know the answers
       that he put the questions. For [Joachim]⟨a⟩, it was hardly possible to
       get [him]⟨a⟩ even to consider them, [he]⟨a⟩having, as Hans Castorp had
       said, in French, on a certain evening, nothing else in his head but
       the idea of being a soldier down below. [Joachim]⟨a⟩ [[wrestled]]⟨b⟩
       with these hopes of his, that now seemed almost within his grasp, now
       receded into the distance and mocked [him]⟨a⟩ there; the [[struggle]]⟨b⟩
       grew daily more embittered,[he]⟨a⟩ even threatened to end [[it]]⟨b⟩
       once for all by a single bold bid for liberty. (Lowe-Porter:345)

As a partial corollary of its Diffusion into several sentences, moreover, (4.6t) shows COREFERENCE CHAIN AMPLIFICATION: thus, where Mann's original has the three-link chain *Joachim*⟨a⟩ . . . *er*⟨a⟩ . . . *er*⟨a⟩, Lowe-Porter's English text shows the six-link *Joachim*⟨a⟩ . . . *him*⟨a⟩ . . . *he*⟨a⟩ . . . *Joachim*⟨a⟩ . . . *him*⟨a⟩ . . . *he*⟨a⟩. (In §12.5 this Amplificational effect will be seen to follow from the requirement of marking target-reassembled clauses for their mutual semantic relations. The other chain, tagged in ⟨b⟩, will be discussed in §5.2.)

4.2 CONDENSATION

Condensation (Cnd; A|B → A⌒ B), whereby a source element or construction corresponds to a tighter or more compact target counterpart, is, all else being equal, a less frequent translational phenomenon than its mirror-image Diffusion, for reasons to be adduced a bit later (§4.3.3). Two examples will be provided here (§4.2.1–§4.2.2).

4.2.1 Condensation in Response to Poetic Requirements

As will be discussed in chapter 14, Old Irish poetry prizes ALLITERATION, and hence in translating a versed prophecy by Saint Bearcan, I replicated the *b*-initial set of the original (4.7s), an. 'two thirty years in power', with the *s*-initial set in (4.7ta); contrast O'Kearney's more prosaic translation in (4.7tb), with no alliterative effect.

(4.7) **s**. Dha triochatt *b*liadain gu m-*b*rí (Bearcan:106)
    ta. Full *s*ixty years in *s*way (M1982b:20)
    tb. Twice thirty years will his might last (O'Kearney:107)

In its trajection of the numerical expression, O'Kearney's translation is more conservative than mine, however, since he takes the two-word original into a two-word target counterpart, *twice thirty*. I, however, Condensed *dha triochatt* into the one word *sixty*, in order to have an *s*-initial alliterative partner for *sway* (translating *brí*, an. 'power', which O'Kearney renders as *might*).

If we look at the internal structure of the word *sixty*, on the other hand, something above and beyond Condensation seems to emerge. Even as *-ty* can arguably be viewed as an allomorph of *ten*, since *six-ty* = *6* × *10* (just as *seven-ty* = *7* × *10*, etc.), Old Irish *dha triochatt* is manifestly *2* × *30*. Thus, though both source and target expressions are BIPARTITE, the translation has brought with it a TRADE-OFF RELATION: *dha* (*2*) trades 'upward' for *six-* (*6*), while *triochatt* (*30*) trades 'downward' for *-ty* (*10*). The question of how this trade-off fits in, trajectionally speaking, will be discussed in more detail in §6.1(iii).

4.2.2 Condensation to Compensate for Syntactic Deficiency

As is effectively expressed by Monro in his commentary (1958 i:345), interpretation of line 230 in the ninth book of the Iliad is strained by the fact that two infinitives with unexpressed subjects, *saōsemen* 'to save' and *apolesthai* 'to be lost', must be understood as having *different* subjects, respectively the Greeks and their ships. Thus, (4.8s), an. 'in doubt . . . to-save or to-be-lost ships-fine-decked', means roughly 'it is uncertain whether *we* (*Greeks*) will save our ships or whether *they* (*the ships*) will be lost'.

Above and beyond its interpretive difficulty within Greek itself, this line resists anything like Equational translation into English, a language that simply lacks the resources of Homeric Greek to deploy intricate syntactic patterns where subject reference of verbs must be computed (cf. also (2.2)). With this in mind, it is not surprising that Rouse's translation of this line involves wholesale renovation (4.8t). And yet the multiple differences between source and target do not obscure his focal use of Condensation in responding to the crux of the problem: by packing the subjects of the 'saving' and 'being lost' into one constituent *our whole fleet*, Rouse effectively sidesteps unwanted syntactic problems and yet comes away with a target version arguably as lean as the original.

(4.8) **s**. en doiēi de saōsemen ē apolesthai nēas eüselmous (H i: 169[IX,230])
    t. Life or death is in question for our whole fleet (R:106)

4.3 REPACKAGING

Repackaging (A⌐ B ↔ A|B), the generic for Diffusion and Condensation, is like the other generic trajections in providing useful analytic vantages unavailable in terms of the specific trajections taken individually. In this regard Repackaging is perhaps most similar to Recrescence. In fact, the first point of discussion below (§4.3.1) will deal with Repackaging analogues of two of the three Recrescental points treated in chapter 3.

4.3.1 Size Adjustments and Preferences

As was illustrated in §3.3, Recrescence may provide a minimax analytic procedure (or strategical tool) for dealing with constraints of size requirements across source and target texts, especially in translating poetry (§3.3.1). Recrescence was also shown to be a useful gauge of certain source-target differences of optimal size level for translational units (§3.3.2).

Since both of these facets have as a common denominator SIZE, it is not surprising that analogues of both are commonplace in Repackaging as well. This seems likely because many or most cases of trajection type will directly or indirectly involve size differences of translational units, the tendency being for Amplification and Diffusion to increase size (seen in fact in § 4.1.4 under Diffusion) and Reduction and Condensation to decrease it.[4]

Ample discussion of what is effectively Repackaging as a minimax technique in translating Latin poetry is provided by Lefevere, whose excerpt in (4.9) is particularly apposite:

(4.9) Expanding the line [Amplifying—JM] is not the only means of ensuring a relatively strict adherence to a metrical scheme. The blank-verse translator can also take the opposite approach: he can choose to compress [Condense—JM) what the source text says, provided the compression is either warranted by or in keeping with certain elements in that source text. Most blank-verse translators use the two techniques simultaneously [Repackaging—JM].

If one has chosen to compress a part of the original message, the most obvious technique appears to be more or less systematic use of compounds. 'Testis erit magnis virtutibus unda Scamandri' ('the water of Scamander will be a witness to his great deeds of valor') becomes 'Scamander's witness-waves his fame shall spread' [MacNaghten], telescoping the source text's 'water' and 'witness' into one iamb-saving compound. (Lefevere:69)

Even as languages may differ Recrescentally with respect to optimal size units, as was seen in the German/English example in (3.16), languages may also have varying size preferences involving Repackaging. A good unilinguistic example is provided by Onondaga which, like other Iroquoian languages, evinces the phenomenon of NOUN INCORPORATION, whereby a noun subject or object may form part of its verb or adjective rather than constituting an independent word. Within certain limits, moreover, noun incorporation is optional, and in such cases the Onondaga stylistic preference is for the incorporated (Condensed) variety rather than for the unincorporated (Diffused); see the respective examples in (4.10):

(**4.10**) **a**. ʔonǫhsaká·yǫh 'the house is old' (Chafe:50)
     b. ʔokayǫ́ neʔ kanǫ́hsaʔ 'the house is old' (Chafe:50)

4.3.2 Repackaging and Recurrence Chains

The discussion in chapter 3 of Saunders's Reductional strategy in translating Abe's coreference chain of *ootosanrin* (3.13) skirted an important question. In view of Saunders's demonstrable attention to introducing stylistic variation into his target chain, by what dispensation did Abe evade doing something similar in the source text? While no fully cogent answer to such a question can be ventured without considering language- and tradition-specific tolerance of repetition (cf. chapter 15), at least part of Abe's exemption from introducing stylistic variation can be understood in terms of the following general principle:

(**4.11**) All else being equal, a relatively Condensed form tends to bear rep-
     etition within a text more felicitously than a relatively Diffused form.

From (4.11) it should follow that *ootosanrin*, constituting one word, would bear repetition quite a bit more easily than Saunders's initial Diffusion into *three-wheeled pickup truck*. And it is in fact exactly the resistance of this phrase to repetition, in terms of (4.11), that explains the variety of Reductions so skillfully employed by Saunders throughout his target chain (3.13)—a series whose specific disposition is further guided by principle (3.14).[5]

4.3.3 Repackaging and De Novo Translation

Looking back at the discussion presented under the headings Diffusion (§4.1) and Condensation (§4.2), one may wonder why only two points were adduced under the latter while four appeared under the former. Although in part this difference reflects no more than the accidents of data sampling, I suspect it is also symptomatic of a genuine statistical imbalance between the two varieties of Repackaging. In particular, in looking back on translations from dense to loose organization—particularly in cases where the denseness bespeaks lexical unity, as in (4.3)—I have come to suspect that the relative looseness in the target organization is often symptomatic of what might be called OPEN-ENDEDNESS OF TRANSLATIONAL CHOICES. That is, when translators lack a prefabricated target element and hence must devise nonce trajectional plans while in the very act of translating, all else being equal they will tend to synthesize a response in the form of a combination of target elements, a procedure tending to produce verbosity.

NOTES

1. Under special circumstances one might also posit definitional Condensation; e.g. when a place would be known to the target audience by name only, while the source audience would also recognize it by description; cf. Lefevere's discussion of *Troy* (name) as opposed to its description (epithet) as *Dardanus' town* (1975:87f).

2. A naturalistic, unilinguistic analogue of (4.4at) may be seen in this excerpt from Thomas Pynchon's novel *Gravity's Rainbow*: Once he sat all day staring at a single white dodo's egg in a grass hummock. . . . He waited for scratching, a first [crack] reaching to net the chalk surface. (1974:127)

3. Other, discoursal units may vary similarly across languages (or literary traditions). Thus, Vinay and Darbelnet note the French penchant for dividing texts into more paragraphs than English (1972: 232)—a disposition for which French would rate higher in Diffusion.

4. These relations are recognized by Vinay and Darbelnet with their notions of 'dépouillement', 'étoffement', 'explicitation', and 'implication' (1972:9f).

5. It may now be seen that Saunders's Reductional strategy in (3.13) is congruent with the shortenings of definitional Diffusion illustrated in (4.4a–b), with the difference that while the latter shortenings were instantaneous, Saunders's procedure was cumulative, ranging from full-blown definition-Diffusional *three-wheeled pickup truck* at the first link (3.13a)—cf. the dictionary entry in (4.3d)— to laconic *truck* at (3.13j). A similar procedure with respect to Turkish *sünnet* (4.3e) is employed in M1986b:12, translating a joke from A:24f, where the first occurrence is rendered by *circumcised in accordance with Islamic law* and the second occurrence simply by *circumcised*.

Chapter *5*

REORDERING

5.0 PRELIMINARIES

Reordering (Rrd; AB → BA), whereby one or more target elements appear in a position different from that of the source text, is the only trajection lacking a converse and hence also a generic.

Very roughly speaking, the tighter the morphosyntactic bond between two source elements, the less likely it is that Reordering in the target text will become a critical conscious issue for the translator. But like all rough generalizations, this rule of thumb fails to cover all cases. Thus, while discrepancies of intraword morpheme order between source and target languages may pass unnoticed in most translational situations, there are cases where this order plays an important role within the source text that cannot be contravened without compensation in the target text. So, in the Turkish quatrain in (5.1), the *aaab* rhyme scheme depends crucially on the fact that each of the first three verses closes in a verb ending in a sequence of passive-voice plus past-tense allomorphs: *-il-di* ~ *-ül-dü*; e.g. *ver-il-di* an. 'give-PASSIVE-PAST' = 'was given', and likewise for *der-il-di* 'was gathered', *sür-ül-dü* 'was banished'. A pattern like this cannot be ignored when translating into a language whose morphosyntax does not follow suit in prescribing just such dovetailing verse closures. (The translation of this quatrain into English will be discussed in detail in chapter 14.)

At a level of syntactic bonding looser than the morphologic but still lacking great fluidity, the translator may have to proceed cautiously with respect to BINO-

(5.1) Dört kitaptan bize haber verildi
Kâmil olan akıl başa derildi
İblis lâin merdud olup sürüldü
Hakkın buyruğundan döneldenberi (Ahi Ali Baba, apud A:76)

MIAL GROUPS, such as *rightly or wrongly, from top to bottom, year in year out*, etc. If not hampered by the overriding possibility that the source-language order might be playing some special role, the translator must be ready to Reorder in case the target language has frozen (or at least jelled) the elements of its corresponding binomial into a different order. Thus, both German and Norwegian have binomials corresponding to English *here and there*, which, however, are fixed in the order 'there and here', a sequence under normal circumstances best reversed by Reordering for translation into English; for instance:

(5.2) **as**. angstvoll [hin und her] fliegend (G:519)
at. anxiously flying [here and there] (HS:706)
bs. [hist og her] en enslig, rød sopp (Mykle:32)
bt. [here and there] a solitary red mushroom (M1980b:97)

When it comes to higher-level syntactic elements, such as major sentential constituents (subject, verb group, complement, etc.), the question of order tends to be more open and hence more readily exploited by the source-text author for special effects. This might not require more than a mention were it not for the well-known fact that languages differ widely both in general syntactic flexibility and in their inventory of resources available for enhancing their syntactic flexibility such as it is. A variety of examples will be treated in later chapters (e.g. (6.9), (7.2), (12.15)). Three cases will be considered here (§5.1–§5.3).

5.1 REORDERING TO OPTIMIZE COMPREHENSION

It may be recalled from chapter 4 that two coreference chains were marked off in Thomas Mann's sesquipedalian sentence in (4.6) but that only one was briefly treated on that occasion. An excerpt containing the other chain is reproduced in (5.3). The initial translational problem posed by this piece of German syntactic clockwork is the overlong modifier of the noun *Hoffnung* 'hope' on lines (sg–sh), a modifier that *precedes* its head noun in the source text. (I have bracketed it off in curly braces { } for better visibility.)

(5.3) **sg**. {mit der bald sich nähernden, bald foppend
with the now   approaching now mockingly
sh. wieder ins Weite   schwindenden} [Hoffnung] darauf
again in the distance disappearing   hope   for-it
si. in einem nachgerade erbitterten [[Kampfe]]⟨b⟩ lag,
in an   ever more bitter   struggle   was engaged
sj. [[den]]⟨b⟩ durch   einen Gewaltstreich zu beenden
which   by means of bold action   to end

sk. er sich neuerdings geneigt zeigte (Mann:316)
he was showing himself ever more inclined

tg. [[wrestled]]⟨b⟩ with these [hopes] {of his, that now
seemed almost within his grasp,

th. now receded into the distance and mocked him there};

ti. the [[struggle]]⟨b⟩ grew daily more embittered,

tj. he even threatened to end [[it]]⟨b⟩ once for all

tk. by a single bold bid for liberty (Lowe-Porter:345)

Since English syntax does not allow a modifier of this complexity and structure to precede its head, Lowe-Porter naturally enough Reordered it to *follow* its
head noun in his target version, as can be seen in (5.3tg–th). Note, however,
that if this had been the sum total of Lowe-Porter's response, the larger excerpt
would have been rendered clumsy to the point of near incomprehensibility:

(5.4) **g**. *was engaged in an increasingly bitter [[struggle]]⟨b⟩
with these [hopes] {of his, that now seemed almost
within his grasp.

h. now receded into the distance and mocked him there}

i. [[which]]⟨b⟩ he was showing himself ever more

j. inclined to end by means of bold action

The trouble with the hypothetical version in (5.4) is that the modifier, now
Reordered to *follow* its head noun, sets up a major obstacle for comprehension by
overcrowding the space between the noun *struggle* (line (g)) and its relative pronoun *which* (line (i))—an obstacle which, crucially, is not present in the German
original, where the counterpart of *struggle, Kampfe* (on line (5.3si)), is separated
from its relative pronoun *den* (line (j)) by only one word. In summary, Lowe-
Porter's decision to Reorder, if implemented with no compensation, would have
touched off a dominolike reaction of infelicities elsewhere in the passage. In the
context of this quandary, his strategic response in (5.3t) is both simple and effective: he Amplifies the coreference chain of *Kampfe* into two—the verb *wrestled*
positioned before the hope-cum-modifier complex, and the noun *struggle* positioned after it—and so provides what might be called a SPAN to the subsequent
topic connected by *it* on line (j).

5.2   REORDERING RELATIVE TO NARRATIVE FLOW

While grammaticality and comprehensibility were at stake with the Reordering
of (5.3), what is involved in (5.5) is rather the manner in which the images of the
scenario are presented to the reader. Both Abe's Japanese original and Saunders's translation are artistically effective in conveying the vivid perceptions of a
motorist during the seconds immediately following his near collision with a boy
on skates, but syntactic differences between the two languages virtually reverse
the succession of images in Saunders's translation from their order in the original. Note in particular that the dynamic image of bloc (5.5sb–e) = (5.5te–b) is

portrayed CENTRIFUGALLY from the boy as center in Japanese, but CENTRIPE-
TALLY to the boy as center in English; and that the movement of bloc
(sh−j) = (tj−h) is ICONIC TO TIME in Japanese but COUNTERCLOCKWISE in English. What is noteworthy about (5.5) is that Saunders has purchased his different
but viable imagery at almost no trajectional cost. The differences between Japanese and English are such that the Reorderings in (5.5t) are virtually all predicted
by the path of least resistance.

(5.5) s.
  a. Sugu ni kaabu ni sasikakaru.
  b. Ti mo nagasazu, hone mo orazu,
  c. sinisokonatta syoonen o
  d. oogesa ni torikakomu
  e. onnatati no sikisai ga
  f. bakku-miraa no naka
  g. yoko ni tobi
  h. kawatte gazoo ga kieta ato no
  i. Buraun-kan no hyoomen no yoo na
  j. siroi sora ga arawareru. (Abe 1967:5)
  t.
  a. Suddenly the curb was there.
  e. The colors of the women
  d. clustered around
  c. the boy who had missed death
  b. with neither loss of blood nor broken bones
  g. flew to the side
  f. of my rear-view miror
  j. and clear sky appeared
  i. like the surface of a Brown tube
  h. after the picture has disappeared. (Saunders 1980:6)

5.3 REORDERING OF TARGET-ALIEN STYLISTIC PATTERNS (GREEK *HYSTERON-PROTERON*)

While the German/English nexus of (5.3) was essentially linguistic, the Jap-
anese/English nexus of (5.5) involved both the linguistic and the situational in a
largely cause-and-effect relation. The last example in this sequence, the Greek/
English nexus of (5.6), is almost purely STYLISTIC, involving not differences of
linguistic structure between the two languages but rather differences in poetic devices (FIGURAE). As mentioned by Monro in his commentary (ii: 423,382),
the actions described in the Greek passages are phrased in terms of the classical
figura called HYSTERON PROTERON (or PROTHYSTERON), whereby the most important event is stated first although chronologically it occurs second: thus, in
(5.6as) Achilles fears the seizure of Priam, though Achilles must see him before

he can seize him; and in (bs) opening the gates is the crux, though they cannot be opened unless their bolts are first pushed back.

As can be seen in (5.6t), Rouse omits prothysteron from his English translations altogether and Reorders pursuant to the natural chronology of events.[1]

(5.6) as. ei gar s'airēsei kai esopsetai ophthalmoisin (H ii:243[XXIV,206])
    an.'if he seizes you and sees you with his eyes'
  at. If he sets eyes on you—if he gets hold of you (R:286)
  bs. hoi d'anesan te pulas kai apōsan okhēas (H ii:188[XXI,537])
    an.'they pushed back the gates and ran back the bolts'
  bt. They ran back the bolts and pushed back the gates (R:254)

5.4 FEATURE REORDERING

We will end the discussion of Reordering with a few examples involving FEATURES (cf. §4.1.1). In his novel *Die Blechtrommel*, Günter Grass exploits the German case system and relatively liberal word order to the effect of (5.7s), which Ralph Manheim translates into English as (5.7t).

(5.7) s.   Ihn, Greff, mochte ich nicht. Er, Greff, mochte mich nicht. (Grass:239)
    an. him Greff liked   I   not he Greff liked   me not
  t.   I didn't like Greff. Greff didn't like me. (Manheim:280)

It can be seen that the source-text parallelism of subject, verb, and object takes the CHIASTIC form OVS SVO, superposed on the person parallelism in PERIODIC form (1 = first person, 3 = third person) 3V1 3V1, thus together $O_3V\ S_1\ S_3V\ O_1$.

With the use of feature representation, the source-target comparison may be displayed even more clearly as in (5.8), where the source chiasmus of case OSSO is traded off for chiasmus of person in the target 1331, and conversely for the periodic organization of the complementary features: 3131 in the source, SOSO in the target. Manheim's response may be called CAT'S-CRADLE REORDERING.

(5.8) s. Ihn   , Greff, mochte ich   nicht. Er   , Greff, mochte mich nicht.
    [+0]   [+S]   [+S]   [+0]
    [+3]   [+1]   [+3]   [+1]
  t. I   didn't like Greff. Greff didn't like me
    [+S]   [+0] [+S]   [+0]
    [+1]   [+3] [+3]   [+1]

Another case of feature Reordering is provided by the King James rendition of the phrase ʕerεv rav at Exodus 12,38 as *a mixed multitude*. Putting aside the Amplification of the English indefinite article, there is still a discrepancy unaccounted for: the Hebrew adjective *rav* does not mean 'mixed' but rather 'much, great', and conversely, the noun ʕerɛv does not mean 'multitude' but rather 'mixture, mixed company'—the upshot of which is that a literal English rendition of ʕerɛv rav is roughly 'large mixture (of people)'. But then everything falls analytically into place if we assume the trajection here involves *feature Reordering*, approximately as suggested by the following diagram:

(5.9) s (K:Exodus 12,38)   **t** (KJ)

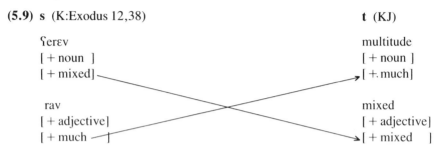

ʕerɛv
[+ noun]
[+ mixed]

rav
[+ adjective]
[+ much]

multitude
[+ noun]
[+.much]

mixed
[+ adjective]
[+ mixed   ]

NOTES

1. It is interesting that patterns that de facto constitute proteron hysteron sometimes emerge in spontaneous speech. Thus, in the following excerpt from a newspaper article, the effect (verbosity = ⟨b⟩) is asserted prior to the cause (drinking = ⟨a⟩), doubtless because the verbosity proves the crux of the point being made, the revelation of the sold secrets (= ⟨c⟩).

Mrs. Way, the neighbor who read tarot cards, said Mr. Walker sometimes called his former wife. 'He'd [be verbose]⟨b⟩ and [had a few drinks]⟨a⟩', Mrs. Way said Mrs. Walker had told her, 'and that's when he'd [get bragging that he was selling military secrets to the Soviets]⟨c⟩'. (Engelberg:B6).

Chapter 6

SOME DIMENSIONS OF TRAJECTIONAL ANALYSIS

6.0 PRELIMINARIES

If the theory of trajections as discussed and exemplified in the preceding chapters were to be taken as complete and sufficient unto itself, it would be easy to reduce the entire enterprise to absurdity. In fact, this could be done simply and dramatically by taking the first example of sentential Equation presented in this book (1.7) and reanalyzing it as an instance of all the (nongeneric) trajections *but* Equation:

(6.1) **a**. *Substitution*: *på*→ *at*, since the root sense of *på* is 'location as contact from above', i.e. a sense inviting Equation into English as *on*.

b. *Divergence*: *var* → *was*, since the past-tense paradigm of the English copula (*be*) has more forms than its Norwegian counterpart (*være*), in particular in containing the plural form *were*, while Norwegian *var* is unmarked for number.

c. *Convergence*: *det* → *it*, since Norwegian evidences a *common* (= masculine,feminine) ≠ *neuter* gender opposition for inanimate nouns, and *det* is specifically the neuter counterpart of *it*, while the appropriate common form would be *den*.

d. *Amplification*: *var* → *was* again (cf.(b)), since the past-tense paradigm of English *be* is informationally richer than that of *være*; in particular, *was* and *were* both convey number information, which the undifferentiated *var* lacks.

71

> **e**. *Reduction*: *de* → *the*, since *de* conveys more information than *the*, being specifically the *plural* definite article.
>
> **f**. *Diffusion*: voksnes → *grown-ups'*, inasmuch as the boundary between *grown* and *up* is morphosyntactically stronger than any boundary within *voksnes*, which patently comprises one word.
>
> **g**. *Condensation*: *foregikk* → *happened*, inasmuch as *fore* ('an.'before') is prefixal (or proclitic) to *gikk* (an.'went'), while the stem *happen* (of *happened*) is monomorphemic.
>
> **h**. *Reordering*: *voksnes* → *grown-ups'*, because the passive-participial suffix, which in this case happens to be *n* in both languages, is postpositive to the lexical stem *voks-* in Norwegian, while it interrupts the corresponding English lexeme *grow up*.

Fortunately, the cogency of such a challenge to the theory of trajections can in large part be neutralized by taking into account five factors in applying trajectional analysis. Of these five, three will be considered in this chapter, two hard-core factors (i–ii) and one soft-core factor (iii):

(i) Relativization of trajectional analysis to levels of composition (§6.1);

(ii) Recognition of certain formal relations holding between trajections (§6.2);

(iii) Recognition of trajections as applied-linguistic constructs (§6.3).

Two additional factors will be deferred until later chapters:

(iv) Supplementation of trajections by systemic analysis (§8.1);

(v) Relativization of trajectional analysis to strata of representation (§12.5).

6.1   LEVELS OF COMPOSITION: RECODING

As discussed in the Introduction (§0.2.4), all linguistic theories recognize the pervasively compositional nature of language, especially in its morphosyntactic organization. Consider, then, what it will mean for trajectional analysis if source and target texts are portrayed in terms of their compositional levels. Before any trajection can be posited, a decision will have to be made as to *which level or levels should be taken as analytically focal*. Thus, the trajection *de voksnes fest* → *the grown-ups' party* was first analyzed as Equation in (1.7), and just now in (6.1) it was (seemingly incoherently) reanalyzed as a medley of Reduction (e), Diffusion (f), and Reordering (h). The incoherence is only apparent, however since the strings in question may be analyzed into at least three distinct compositional levels, as in diagram (6.2), with corresponding differences for their trajections. Thus, although an analysis of *voksnes* → *grown-ups'* as Diffusion and Reordering is valid at the MORPHEMIC LEVEL (*voks* Diffuses to *grow up* and *n* Reorders between *grow* and *up*), yet these two trajections do not hold at the

WORD LEVEL, where the unit *voksnes* simply Equates to *grown-ups'*. Similarly, the discrepancy between *de → the* analyzed as Equation and its analysis as Reduction is resolvable between the word and phrase levels. The Reductional loss of information incurred by trajecting plural-marked *de* to number-neutral *the*, is cogent when the items are considered in isolation from their context on the word level. However, it is counteracted on the phrase level, where the English string *the grown-ups' party* is understood as plural, no less than the Norwegian group *de voksnes fest*. To be sure, the devices for marking plurality differ between the two languages, Norwegian investing this function in the specialized plural article *de* and English (orthographically) employing the plural-possessive suffix *-s'*. But these differences involve discrepancies at the morpheme and word levels. At the level of the phrase, both strings equivalently (and hence Equationally) convey 'the party held by and/or for a number of adults'.[1]

(6.2) C   *phrase* {de voksnes fest}   → {the grown-ups' party}
       O
       M
       P
       O
       S
       I   *word* {de}{voksnes}{fest}   → {the}{grown-ups'}{party}
       T
       I L
       O E
       N V
       A E
       L L *morpheme* {de}{voks}{n}{es}{fest}→{the}{grow}{n}{up}{s}{party}

If one asks how the appropriate compositional level for trajectional analysis should be determined, no fixed answer can be given. It will depend upon the specific situation addressed, and often enough the analyst will be best advised to experiment, by trying out several levels. An illustration of how level differences can be pertinent may be seen in the example from Manzoni/Colquhoun considered earlier in (2.6). If the trajection is analyzed on the word level, as in (6.3a), Colquhoun's likely mistranslation of the fifth term, *grida →*edicts*, is not thereby marked off. However, reanalysis on the *morpheme level* as in (6.3b), reveals the asymmetry of this term as being the only noun on the source side not ending in a plural suffix ({e} or {i}). This discrepancy in turn might very well constitute the decisive analytic clue that Colquhoun is missing something about patterning in the original text.

If the trajectional analysis of a given string may differ from one compositional level to another, the question naturally arises as to whether it might not be useful to study the trajections of strings on two or more levels *simultaneously*.

(**6.3**) **a.** {viottole}   → {paths}
       {rupi}   → {cliffs}
       {fughe}   → {escapes}
       {inseguimenti}   → {pursuits}
       √{grida}   → {edicts}
       {schioppettate}   → {musket-shots}
   b. {viottol}{e}   → {path}{s}
       {rup}{i}   → {cliff}{s}
       {fugh}{e}   → {escape}{s}
       {in}{segui}{ment}{i} → {pursuit}{s}
       √{grida}   → {edict}{s}
       {schiopp}{ett}{at}{e} → {musket}{shot}{s}

This is likely to be a promising area for general research, but only three points will be suggested here:

(i) Multiple trajectional-level analysis of a text may provide something of a SIMILARITY PROFILE for pairs of source and target languages. Thus, a cursory word- and phrase-level analysis of Genesis 1,1 between the Hebrew source and three target languages yields the comparison in diagram (6.4)—not a surprising result when one pits Hebrew's genetic-typological proximity to Arabic against its distance from English, and especially from Japanese.[2]

		Hebrew/Arabic	Hebrew/English	Hebrew/Japanese
(**6.4**)	W	2 Condensations	1 Amplification	4 Diffusions
	O			
	R	2 Reorderings	5 Diffusions	4 Reorderings
	D			
			1 Reordering	1 Amplification
				1 Divergence
	P	0	1 Reordering	1 Reordering
	H			
	R			
	A			
	S			
	E			
total		4	8	11

(ii) Certain types of level pattern will probably be found to correlate with specific types of translational nexus. Thus, a high score on Equation at more inclusive compositional levels (e.g. paragraph, discourse) would likely sympto-mize an overall successful, 'idiomatic' translation, while conversely, an exclu-sive preponderance of Equation at lower levels (perhaps notably the word level) would bid fair to be the hallmark of stodgy, overly literal translation (cf. Wilss(273); Greenstein (1983:24) ('concordant translation'); Chukovsky (47ff)).

(iii) Similarly, but from a local rather than a global vantage, it might be use-ful to grant special status to Equation at a given compositional level combined with any other trajection or trajections at the next-lower level. Such a bifocal tra-jection, to be called RECODING (Rec) and schematized $\{A\}_B \rightarrow \{A\}_E^3$, shows promise for capturing at least some of the essence of trajections like Old Irish *dha triochatt* → English *sixty*, considered in (4.7). As was pointed out, the diffi-culty with considering this trajection to be Substitution is that this tack by itself fails to capture the compositional equivalence of *2 × 30 = 6 × 10* which, how-ever transparently, subtends the trajection. But if the analysis is enriched from single-level Substitution-cum-Condensation ($A|B \rightarrow S_a^\frown S_b$) to dual-level Re-coding ($\{A|B\}_D \rightarrow \{S_a^\frown S_b\}_E$), the missing equivalence will at least be tallied by the device of higher-level Equation ($\{ \quad \}_D \rightarrow \{ \quad \}_E$).[4]

6.2 RELATIONS BETWEEN TRAJECTIONS

Relations between trajections are of two broad types, IMPLICATIONS (§6.2.1) and HOOK-UPS (§6.2.2).

6.2.1 Implications

Some readers may have been disturbed by an apparent discrepancy in the display of (6.1): if *det* → *it* (c) was analyzed as Convergence, because it was opposed to the potentially competing *den* → *it*, then why, in parallel fashion, shouldn't *de* → *the* (e) also be analyzed as Convergence, since it is opposed to potentially competing singular *det/den* → *the*? And indeed the same question might be stated the other way around: if (e) is analyzed as Reduction because '*de* conveys more information than *the*', why pari passu shouldn't (c) likewise be analyzed as Reduction, since presumably *det* also conveys more information than *it*?

If the trajections are modeled featurally, as in (6.5), the answer to these questions seems inescapable: the Convergence *det/den* → *it* implies Reductional loss of the feature distinction [±gender], while the Convergence *de/det/den* → *the* implies the even greater Reductional loss of [±gender] and [±plural].

Moreover, simple reversal of the arrows in (6.5) will show that trajection from Norwegian to English entails the converse relations: Divergence of *it* → *det/den* implies Amplificational gain of the feature distinction [±gender], and similarly for *the* → *de/det/den* vis-à-vis [±gender, ±plural].

(6.5) a. (cf. (6.1c))

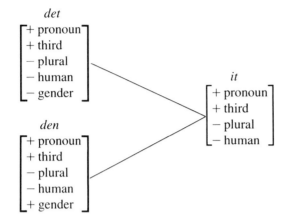

b. (cf. (6.1e))

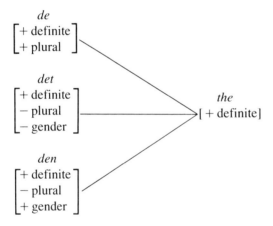

In fact, the implications demonstrated for (6.5) are actually special cases of an intertrajectional relation that might be stated as (6.6)(cf. also Jäger (136f)):

(6.6) Divergence implies Amplification, Convergence implies Reduction.

Principle (6.6), in turn, groups naturally with a similar relation:

(6.7) Substitution implies Recrescence.

The truth of (6.7) is simple to verify schematically. By definition, Substitution involves selection of a target-language element differing from its source counterpart in some plerematic aspect, e.g., semantically or syntactically. But then it follows that Substitution cannot take place without either gain (Amplification) or loss (Reduction) of some plerematic function. Indeed, in most instances there will be both gain and loss, in radical cases approaching the limit of total feature turnover.

In view of (6.6) and (6.7), the question looms as to whether Zigzagging (Divergence, Convergence) and Substitution should not be wholly restated in terms of Recrescence, and hence omitted from the inventory of trajections. If trajectional analysis were designed as a pure-theoretical mapping system rather than as an applied-linguistic heuristic tool kit (cf. §0.1.2), the inventory might indeed be so trimmed. But there are three reasons why Zigzagging and Substitution are advisedly maintained:

(i) Though Recrescence may affect Zigzagged or Substitutional elements when considered as pairs of context-free items, the effect is often negligible or altogether absent when the context is taken into account. A double example of this can be succinctly provided for Zigzagging with the mere title of one of Grimm's fairy tales, 'Die drei Männlein im Walde'/'The Three Little Men in the Wood' (G:60/HS:78). In isolation, the German plural article *die* Converges into English number-neutral *the* for the same reasons as Norwegian *de* considered earlier (6.5b); and conversely, the German noun *Männlein* Diverges into English *little men*, because nouns ending in the diminutive suffix *-lein* are not marked for number, and hence *Männlein* might alternatively traject into English *little man*. But in fact the Recrescence implied by *die* → *the* and *Männlein* → *little men* taken in isolation is completely neutralized when these elements are taken together as providing each other a reciprocal context: on the German side *die* disambiguates *Männlein* as plural, while in English *(little) men* disambiguates *the* as plural.[5]

Examples involving Substitution are common in coreference chains, where source and target texts frequently differ in their deployment of pronouns, names, and descriptions referring to the same entity. Numerous cases are to be found in Rouse's translation of the Iliad, where Greek pronouns or descriptions are frequently Substituted by proper names in the English version. Examples of both sorts of Substitution are given in the coreference chain snippet of (6.8), where both a definite description (*ho g'hērōs* 'the hero') and a personal pronoun (*ho* 'he') are Substituted in the target text by the proper name (*Teucros*) of the individual designated by the source description. Once again, however, the context ensures that these Substitutions incur no informational Recrescence, since the syntax and narrative conspire to make the reference unambiguous.

(**6.8**) s. [ho g'hērōs]⟨a⟩ paptēnas, epei ar tin' oïsteusas . . .
[ho]⟨a⟩ autis iōn païs hōs hupo mētera dusken,
eis Aianth'. (H i: 153[VIII,269–71])

t. [Teucros]⟨a⟩ would spy his man, and shoot . . .
[Teucros]⟨a⟩ dived back to Aias like a boy hiding behind his mother.
(R:97)

(ii) In a wide range of cases, the goal of the translator in using Zigzagging or Substitution will not be to increase or decrease information but merely to achieve (or replicate) an aesthetic or stylistic effect. In this regard, consider how one might proceed to translate either of the Spanish or English baseball texts considered in (2.7)–(2.8) into English or Spanish, respectively. What clearly might be helpful for such an enterprise would be a bilingual list of stylistic synonyms for various aspects of a ball game. But though the net effect of translating from such a list would certainly incur both Zigzagging and Substitution between the two languages, Recrescence in the informational sense would be weakly involved if at all. At most the texts might differ connotationally, losing or gaining something of a *gringo* or *jíbaro* aura to the ball game portrayed; but there would be no real Reduction or Amplification of cognitive meaning.

(iii) Similarly, a great deal of the traditional apparatus used by translators is de facto geared to a Zigzagging vantage on translation. Thus, entries in most bilingual dictionaries are set out in a one-to-many format that immediately invites a Divergent interpretation: a source-language item under which are characteristically listed several target-language counterparts. Reference grammars and other materials useful for the study of comparative morphology and syntax are also frequently organized in terms of paradigms that lend themselves to Zigzagging when used for translation and other cross-linguistic analyses or procedures. (Thus, in translating from Italian to French or English, one tends to develop a conceptual habit of mapping a four-member second person pronominal system (*tu, voi, Lei, Loro*) onto a two-member (*tu, vous*) or one-member system (*you*)—a procedure that is effectively Convergence, even as reversing the source and target languages would effectively constitute Divergence. To be sure, the tidiness of having such inventories at one's immediate disposal by no means always engenders automatic recipes for how the Zigzagging should be implemented in a given case; cf. (1.2), (1.3), and (2.10). But the inventories are psychologically real for all that and generally expedite a translator's work (cf. also Ray (1976:267)).

6.2.2 Hook-ups

The astute reader may have wondered why example (6.8) should not alternatively be treated as Convergence, specifically *ho g'hērōs/ho → Teucros*. A natural answer to this question will be suggested by an informal, common-sense review of the ingredients in (6.8). If we consider each of the elementary trajections in isolation from the other, it seems altogether clear that Substitution is involved in each case; it would be preposterous to consider that the noun *Teucros* might be the 'most straightforward counterpart available' (§1.1.2(a)) to the English language for either *ho g'hērōs/ho* 'the hero' or *ho* 'he'. On the other hand, however, when the links of the chain are taken together, it seems equally apparent that Convergence is involved, since 'two . . . distinct source text elements [*ho g'hērōs* and *ho*] . . . [are] mapped onto one and the same target element [*Teucros*]' (§1.1.2(b)).

The answer that follows from this review is simple and inescapable: (6.8) instantiates *both* Substitution *and* Convergence, specifically such that the Substitute (*Teucros*) is also the Convergens.

Nor is this phenomenon limited to Convergence and Substitution. A case involving three trajections was incidentally seen in (2.1), where the Divergence *ho* → *he/Patroclos* factors to the Equation *ho* → *he* and to the Substitution *ho* → *Patroclos*. And an even more intricate case may be seen in the first and last parallel lines of (6.9), which might be analyzed as involving three trajections:

(i) *Convergence*, since *was für ein Gewerbe er verstände* (sa) and *was er für ein Gewerbe verstände* (sc) of the source correspond to identical lines of the target: *what his trade was* = *what his trade was* (ta) = (tc);

(ii) *Reordering*, since source lines (sa) and (sc) differ only in the order of their elements, and hence Convergence to (ta) = (tc) necessarily entails Reordering; and

(iii) *Substitution*, since the closest idiomatic English to the German original would be *what trade he knew*.

(6.9) sa. was für ein Gewerbe er verstände und was er wüßte
        an. what for a   trade   he understood and what he knew
    sb. was für ein Gewerbe er verstünde und was er wüßte
        an. what for a   trade   he understood and what he knew
    sc. was er für ein Gewerbe verstände und was er wüßte
        an. what he for a   trade   understood and what he knew (G:117)
    ta. what his trade was, and what he knew
    tb. what was his trade, and what he knew
    tc. what his trade was, and what he knew (HS:154f)

The question as to how such HOOK-UPS might be represented schematically is easily answered: by placing the variables corresponding to one or more trajections, the LEAD-OFF(S), to the left of the arrow, and the variables corresponding to the FOLLOW-UP trajection or trajections to the right of the arrow. This is done in (6.10) for the three examples so far considered:

(6.10) a. B/C → S   (for (6.8))
    b. A → E/S   (for (2.1))
    c. AB/BA → E_aS_b (for (6.9))

For a variety of reasons, it will be useful to have available a notation for hook-ups alternative to that illustrated in (6.10), a notation trading off detail for convenience in highlighting the role of specific trajections. Letting X,Y, and Z stand for arbitrary trajections, X + Y = 'X is lead-off and Y is follow-up', (X,Y) = 'X and Y are both either lead-offs or follow-ups'. The examples in (6.10) may thus be represented as follows:

(6.11) a. Cnv + Sub   (for (6.10a))
    b. Div + (Equ,Sub)   for (6.10b))
    c. (Rrd,Cnv) + (Equ,Sub)
       or Rrd + Cnv + (Equ, Sub) (for (6.10c))

Hook-ups will be discussed again in §7.5.[6]

6.3 TRAJECTIONS AS APPLIED-LINGUISTIC CONSTRUCTS

Since the theory of trajections is intended as a conceptual and analytic instrument at the service of the practice and study of translation (§0.1.1–§0.1.2), all questions concerning the essence and dynamics of trajections should be framed with that instrumental function in mind. If, on the contrary, trajectional theory were intended as a domain of pure, theoretical linguistics, such extenuation would be inappropriate; rather, questions of essence and dynamics would then be fully answerable on the theory of trajections itself, for better or for worse.

There are at least two major correlates of this applied-linguistic essence relative to the stance of the analyst or translator on using trajections: (i) the legitimacy of a certain amount of what be called 'psychologism' in judging trajectional relations; (ii) the liberty to select, from the available alternatives, whichever specific trajection or combination of trajections seems useful or appropriate to the situation at hand.

To be sure, both of these points invite abuse and must be subject to reasonable constraints if trajectional analysis is to prove itself a useful technique rather than a whimsical game.

A constraint appropriate to point (i) might run along these lines:

(6.12) Psychological disposition to view a given nexus in terms of trajection X rather than genuine alternative Y may be legitimate, all else being equal, to the extent that the choice of X entails abstracting away from the nexus rather than altering the nexus.

An apt illustration of (6.12) is provided in association with example (6.5a): all else being equal, it is legitimate for a person to analyze *det/den* → *it* as Convergence rather than Reduction to the extent that the former implies abstracting away the loss of the feature [±gender]. Conversely, no amount of psychological disposition could justify analyzing *det/den* → *it* as, say, Reordering, which would require out-and-out alteration of the nexus rather than abstraction from it.

In essence, principle (6.12) is simply an attempt to limber up trajectional analysis without 'muscle-binding' the investigator to consider each and every detail of each and every translational situation, a sort of analytic freedom necessary in virtually every field.

Another prime application of principle (6.12) relates to Equation which, as intimated in §1.2, in a sense does not exist (cf. Jäger (122ff)). The sense in which it does not exist is really a special, translational case of a bit of linguistic wisdom accepted by virtually all language scholars. For A → E to hold unexceptionally would imply A = E with no qualifications. But that is impossible, since A and E are organic parts of different linguistic systems and, by virtue of that, contract at least some formally and substantively distinct relations. This in turn invests them with at least some distinct functions. Once again, however, principle (6.12) may legitimize the acceptance of A = E as a useful analytic function, given only the enabling condition that the elements be similar enough to allow their differences to be ignored for the purposes at hand.

Let us now return to the other correlate of the applied-linguistic nature of trajections, the liberty to select from available alternatives. The same general cautions apply: the applied-linguistic vantage cannot be construed as licensing any capriciously chosen trajection for any random nexus. If that were the case, trajectional analysis would be no more than a magic mirror show allowing people to shine back at themselves pseudo-scientific reflections of their own private biases and hunches. Indeed, it was with exactly this concern in mind that much of this chapter was elaborated: to help rein in the freedom of trajectional analysis to reasonably specifiable limits.

Anticipating the discussion of the systemic perspective in chapter 8, let us consider a nexus not straightforwardly amenable to the constraints so far developed. In (6.1) the trajection *på* → *at* was called Substitution, but by hook-up it is equally legitimate to claim Divergence to the extent that the specific choice of English preposition may vary from construction to construction, e.g. *tenke [på]* → *think [about]*, *minne [på]* → *remind [of]*, *sint [på]* → *angry [with]*, etc. But then, focusing on the target item *at*, cases like *[på] de voksnes fest* → *[at] the grown-ups' party*, *[ved] bordet* → *[at] the table*, *[hos] skredderen* → *[at] the tailor's*, etc. seem to warrant Convergence.

This analysis of one and the same trajection, *på* → *at*, as either of a pair of antithetical alternatives, Divergence or Convergence, would seem to push the analytic slack built into trajectional analysis to the danger point. This is so because the more slack thus built in, the closer the constructs approach the vanishing point of analytic usefulness; after all, a framework allowing any arbitrary pattern to be explained in terms of any arbitrary construct really succeeds in explaining nothing at all.

As will be seen at the outset of chapter 8, however, the actual situation is not as precarious as it might appear to be.

NOTES

1. Level analysis is brought to a high degree of rigor and precision by Harris (1954) and Hockett (1954). (Cf. also Catford's notion of 'level shifting' (1965:73)).

2. The target references are Jamiyaat (1963) for Arabic, KJ for English, and Kyookai (1954–55) for Japanese. (Incidentally, the morpheme level was excluded from the chart when the Arabic case system (cf. §0.5) was found to increase the morpheme-per-word ratio so as to obscure the translinguistic profile at the word and phrase levels. If the goal of (6.4) were more than illustrative, such an omission would require substantive justification.) As an afterthought, a sliding-scale nature of comparisons like (6.4) is suggested by later comparison of the first two paragraphs of the triad Sandel (1968)/Lindberger(1963) and M1983c, which showed the English translation (M1983c) to be notably more distant from the Norwegian original than the Swedish translation (Lindberger) of the same, which was virtually Equational. This result was obtained despite the fact that English and Norwegian are structurally closer than Arabic and Hebrew. On the other hand, the similarity of Swedish and Norwegian is so strong as to justify relation as dialects of the same language.)

3. The fact that the Equational part is schematized { }$_B$ → { }$_E$ rather than { }$_A$ → { }$_E$ (contra §1.1.2a) is immaterial, since the letters are used as variables devoid of intrinsic content (cf. §1.1.1).

4. Recoding bears some similarity to Vinay and Darbelnet's notions of 'chassé-croisé' (1972:6) and especially 'équivalence' (8f).

5. This point often holds when a text composed in a language with a case system (§0.5) pairs off in translation with a language lacking such a system. The example below is just one of a myriad from Jerome's translation of the Hebrew Bible into Latin. Of the two tokens of the original case-undifferentiated noun *yoom* 'day', the first Diverges into the target as accusative *diem* and the second as nominative *dies*. And yet, although the target words *diem* and *dies*, taken as individual items, are semantically distinct where the source word *yoom* is not, the overall Latin translation is no richer in meaning than the Hebrew original. This is so because the function of the cases in the target is in the source assumed by the *configurational* relation of the tokens of *yoom* to their context, i.e. their specific positions vis-à-vis other words and their levels of composition. (Cf. also Jäger's notion of 'absolutes Mehr' versus 'relatives Mehr' (136f)).

    s. wayyiqrɔɔ ʔɛ̌loohiim lɔɔʔoor [yoom] wəlaḥošɛx qɔɔrɔɔ lɔɔylɔɔ wayəhii-ʕɛrɛv wayəhii-voqɛr [yoom] ʔɛḥɔɔđ (Genesis 1,5)

    t. appellavitque lucem [diem] et tenebras noctem factumque est vespere et mane [dies] unus. (Jerome)

    'And God called the light [Day], and the darkness he called Night. And the evening and the morning were the first [Day]'.(KJ)

6. The concept of hook-ups bears comparison to Voegelin's 'multiple stage translation' (1954).

Chapter 7

SOME TRAJECTIONAL PARAMETERS

7.0 PRELIMINARIES

Throughout the preceding chapters, a large number of PARAMETERS OF APPLICATION for trajectional analysis were woven into the illustrations, for the most part with no comment as to their mutual relations or scope of application beyond the particular trajections being discussed. While several of these parameters were in fact largely specific to the trajections being illustrated, others have wider scope and interrelate in a variety of ways worthy of more general treatment. This chapter will supply that treatment and in the process introduce a few more parameters.

7.1 STRUCTURAL-STRATEGICAL PARAMETERS

Prototypically, STRUCTURAL refers to source-target differences imposed by exigencies of the languages involved, while STRATEGICAL refers to the trajectional response to those differences, whether operatively by the translator or analytically by the investigator (cf. §0.1.4)

An example is provided in (7.1), centering on Rabassa's translation of Márquez's Spanish string *procuró que se interesara*. The structural set-up is the fact that an overly literal rendition of this string as *she had tried that she should be interested* would run afoul of the source-target difference that the English verb *try*, unlike Spanish *procurar*, requires an infinitive or gerundal complement (*try to do, try doing*) rather than a clausal complement (**try that(someone)should do*). Rabassa's strategical response to this structural discrepancy was to Amplify by means of the string *to get her*, thus providing a SPAN (cf. §5.2, and §7.2.1 below), enabling satisfaction of the infinitival requirement for *try*. (This case will be given a more precise characterization in the discussion of bridge technique in chapter 12; cf. (12.6).)

(7.1) s. procuró que se interesara por los asuntos elementales de la casa
(Márquez:198)

t. she had tried [to get her] to be interested in basic domestic affairs
(Rabassa:221)

7.2 LINGUISTIC-STYLISTIC-SITUATIONAL PARAMETERS

Though when first introduced (§2.1), the terms linguistic, stylistic, and situational were used to classify cues available to the translator for guiding Divergence, they may actually be used in a considerable range of other circumstances. For example, two excerpts from Böll/X involving Substitution are given in (7.2), the first in response to a situational difference between (average) source and target audiences, the second responding primarily to a German/English linguistic difference (though one with unavoidable situational repercussions). In (7.2a) the lexical Substitution *Klinke* → *knob* reflects X's decision about how to deal with a practical difference between German and American doors: a run-of-the-mill German door is opened by pressing a *handle (Klinke)* rather than by turning a *knob*. The purely situational nature of this nexus is evident; no violence would have been done to English grammar or style had X decided to tell us the card was hung on the outer *handle*, any puzzlement on the part of American readers to such a choice notwithstanding.[1]

The case of (7.2b) is different. *Geduzt* is the past participle of the verb *duzen*, which means 'to address someone by the familiar second person pronoun *du* (as opposed to the formal *Sie*). As was seen in chapter 1 (§1.2, §1.3), standard Modern English simply has no counterpart to this device, and X accordingly responded to the corresponding source-target *linguistic* discrepancy by Substituting *called . . . by her first name*, a simple and natural expedient since Americans tend to call familiars by their first names.

(7.2) as. hängten den Zettel 'Bitte nicht stören'
draußen an die [Klinke] (B:18)

at. hung a 'Please Do Not Disturb' card on the
outer [knob] (X:23)

bs. Er hatte sie also doch [geduzt] (B:114)

bt. He had [called] her [by her first name] (X:124)

7.2.1 The Chiaroscuro Nature of Stylistic Patterns

Though the relations of the above three parameters (linguistic, stylistic, and situational) may suggest a trichotomy, it is best to take them as an ordered gradient, whereby stylistic factors shade off into either linguistic or situational factors or both. An example may be seen in (7.3), which basically turns on the difference between the German verb *gefallen* and the English verb *like*. As will be discussed in chapter 16, *gefallen* and *like* constitute a PARALLACTIC SET, such that the referents of the subject and object switch places between the two languages while the overall meaning of the two constructions remains more or less constant. This might strike some as a bizarre translinguistic situation, but in fact it is quite commonplace, and indeed English itself has a unilinguistic analogue, since the verb *please* is quite similar to *gefallen* in the pertinent respect. Within English, if *X pleases Y* then *Y likes X*; and in parallel fashion translinguistically (between German and English), if *X gefällt Y* then *Y likes X*.

(7.3) s. Er ließ sich das gefallen (G:210)
　　　 t. He liked the idea (HS:580)

If the situation were simply thus, we should expect (7.3t) *He liked the idea* to correspond most straightforwardly to the German equivalent of *The idea pleased him*; that is, something like *Der Vorschlag gefiel ihm* or, ignoring the fact that Hunt and Stern Substituted *the idea* for Grimm's original *das* 'that', *Das gefiel ihm*, an. 'that pleased him'. But in point of fact Grimm's original is *Er ließ sich das gefallen*, word-for-word 'He let himself that please', i.e., analytically 'He let that please him'.

At first blush one might think that Hunt and Stern's rendering as *He liked the idea* is a mistranslation and that a more accurate rendition might be along the lines of *He let the idea sink in and came to like it*.

In fact, however, Hunt and Stern's simple *He liked the idea* is far more accurate, because textual analysis reveals this to be one of the many cases in Grimm's fairy tales where the German verb *ließ*, an. 'let', is used not so much semantically as syntactically, in this case as a mechanism to bring the pronoun *er* 'he' to the front of the sentence.

The reason for the desirability of *er* being sentence-initial will be discussed in a moment, but first it will be useful to consider the general nature of syntactic helpmate mechanisms like *ließ*, a device of a type that in fact has already been illustrated under the name of SPAN (§5.2, 7.1). Suppose, on the one hand, that the most straightforward way to synthesize a message in some language is by the sequence of constituents XYZ; but on the other hand that the specific context, for whatever reason, would be best served by Z occurring in first position. Suppose, however, that the language disallows Z from occurring immediately before X, so that a simple permutation of XYZ to ZYX^2 is ruled out. What can be done? Under various circumstances in various languages, the performer may be fortunate enough to find some constituent W with two properties: (i) syntactic license to occur in the context *ZWXY*; and (ii) approximate synonymy of the resulting group *ZWXY* with *XYZ*. Such a constituent *W* is a span, in this case one mediating between *Z* and *XY*.

In the case of (7.3s), the effectiveness of *ließ* as a span follows from the approximate interchangeability, in many contexts, of the propositions *X likes Y* and *X lets himself/herself like Y*, since normally a person's liking something will bespeak a positive stance toward that something, and hence an attitude of permissiveness toward its occurrence, presence, or availability.

With this background, it will be easy to state why the focal source-sentence (7.3s), with *er* 'he' in initial position, is a better fit to its context than the simpler hypothetical alternative *Das gefiel ihm, an.* 'That pleased him', with *ihm* 'him' in final position. The reason will be seen to emerge from consideration of both PARALLELISM and INFORMATION FLOW.

The person in question, the referent of *er* in (7.3s), is the second of four brothers, each of whom meets a different stranger on the road who then persuades the brother to embark upon a certain career. The four brothers (1–4) are introduced into the story seriatim, and upon his introduction each first (i) meets the stranger, then (ii) receives the stranger's advice, and finally (iii) accepts that advice. Crucially, in each of (i) and (iii), the NP referring to the brother in question occurs in sentence-initial position, schematized as follows:

(7.4) *episode sentence and position of noun phrase*

1i	{NP	}
1iii	{NP	}
2i	{NP	}
2iii	{NP	}
3i	{NP	}
3iii	{NP	}
4i	{NP	}
4iii	{NP	}

Conversely, had (7.3s) been foregone for the simpler *Das gefiel ihm*, the symmetry of (7.4) would have been warped into this asymmetrical display (the checkmark marks the asymmetry):

(7.5)

1i	{NP		}
1iii	{NP		}
2i	{NP		}
√2iii	{	NP	}
3i	{NP		}
3iii	{NP		}
4i	{NP		}
4iii	{NP		}

With this in mind, we can see the merits of Hunt and Stern's translation (7.3t). Quite simply, since English *like* does not require the extra baggage of a span in order to position the Equational pronoun *he* sentence-initially, the translators wisely trajected the German span *ließ* out of the picture by Reduction.

In considering one last point about (7.3), we return to the original point this example was chosen to illustrate: the often chiaroscuro nature of stylistic patterns. To the extent that the symmetry modeled in (7.4) corresponds to the traditional notion of parallelism, the trajectional maintenance of *er* → *he* in sentence-initial position can indeed be considered as stylistic (cf. §8.1). But at the sime time, since the initial-positioned NPs of (7.4) reference the four brothers who are the joint TOPICS of the passage, from the vantage of DISCOURSE GRAMMAR their initial positioning is arguably a linguistic function (§0.2). Moreover, one might even argue for a situational function as well, since the distribution of the NPs is by and large correlated to the temporal order of events in the scenario involving the brothers. In other words, the linguistic structure is to that extent *iconic* to the situational message being conveyed (cf. the discussion of (5.5) and (5.6) in chapter 5).

7.3 COMPENSATORY-CLASSIFICATORY PARAMETERS

Though numerous instances of Amplification and Reduction lend themselves to subclassification as compensatory or classificatory (cf. most of the examples in chapter 3), it is not clear that these notions constitute a genuinely dichotomous class of wider application. However, this is not to rule out the applicability of either term, taken individually, to non-Recrescent trajections. This is particularly true of the compensatory factor; and indeed it seems likely that any trajection, with the possible exception of Equation, could in principle be used compensatorily. Thus, in line 6 of 'Ua Cearnaigh' (1981)/M1983e, I Substituted *don tír* 'for the land' by *for all of Ireland* to make it perfectly clear to American readers what land was meant; and in the next line I Substituted two place names unlikely to be familiar to American readers, *Airdí Chuain* and *Dún Mhaonmhaí*, by a pair both familiar from song and salient on most maps: *Belfast Lough* and *Bantry Bay*;[3] see (7.6):

(**7.6**) **s.** Saoirse [don tír]
    Ó [Airdí Chuain] go [Dún Mhaonmhaí] (Ua Cearnaigh 1981)
  t. Freedom [for all of Ireland]
    From [Belfast Lough] to [Bantry Bay] (M1983e)

7.4 PARADIGMATIC-SYNTAGMATIC PARAMETERS

This pair of terms, of varied and venerable application in linguistic theory (at least since De Saussure 1962[orig. 1915]), proves useful in trajectional analysis. Fundamentally, a PARADIGMATIC relation holds among the members of a class, while a SYNTAGMATIC relation obtains among the parts of a whole. An important manifestation of this distinction for trajectional analysis involves the question whether the pertinent translational elements actually co-occur within the text (syntagmatically) or rather constitute virtual resources for the text (paradigmatically), from which an actual selection must be made. This distinction may be illustrated for Divergence with two passages from the Bible. The example in (7.7) turns on the polysemy of the Hebrew noun -*lvav*, answering in English to either 'midst' or 'heart'. Hence, one can say that both the King James and Jewish Publication Society translations reflect PARADIGMATIC DIVERGENCE, since though both translators were faced with the same choice of resources (A → B/C = -*lvav* → *midst*/*heart*), each made a distinct selection from these resources.

(**7.7**)   s. Wattašliixeenii məṣuulɔɔ bi [lvav] yammiim (K:Jonah 2,4)
  ta. For thou hast cast me into the deep,
   in the [midst] of the seas (KJ)
  tb. For thou didst cast me into the depth,
   In the [heart] of the seas (Jewish Publication Society)

The situation in (7.7) may be contrasted with that in (7.8), which again turns on the polysemy of a Hebrew noun, *divree* ~ *dəvɔɔriim* as either 'words' or 'commandments'.[4] The King James translation in (7.8ta) obviously involves the choice of resources A → B/C = *divree* ~ *dəvɔɔriim* → *words*/*commandments*, but this time the Divergence is syntagmatic, since both choices (*words* and *commandments*) co-occur in the actual text. By way of contrast, the syntagmatic disposition of the Jewish Publication Society translation in (7.8tb) is not Divergent but rather constitutes SYNTAGMATIC MATCHING, in particular A → M = *divree* ~*dəvɔɔriim* → *words* taken twice.

(**7.8**)   s. wayyixroθ ʕal-halluuhooθ ʔeθ [divree] habbəriiθ
   ʕáśɛrɛθ had [dəvɔɔriim] (K:Exodus 34,28)
  ta. And he wrote upon the tables the [words] of the covenant, the ten [commandments] (KJ)
  tb. An he wrote upon the tables the [words] of the convenant, the ten [words] (Jewish Publication Society)

7.5 POSITIVE AND NEGATIVE HOOK-UPS

When the concept of trajectional hook-up was introduced in chapter 6, most of the discussion was devoted to symbology and description. In this section, the functional side of hook-ups will be considered briefly, and the notion of positive and negative hook-ups will be introduced.

As was seen in §6.2.2, a hook-up refers to a translational nexus comprising two or more trajections, such that the application of one (or more) of them is complemented by the application of the others(s). It is often the case that the function of the follow-up trajection(s) is COMPENSATORY (§7.3) with respect to some textual property jeopardized by the lead-off trajection(s). It is also commonplace for lead-off trajections to be STRUCTURAL and the follow-ups to be STRATEGICAL (§7.1).

The common properties of hook-ups introduced here may be conveniently illustrated with the example given in (2.10), where STRUCTURAL CONVERGENCE (*du/Sie → you*) hooked up with STRATEGICAL AMPLIFICATION (*X → X sonny*) as a compensatory corrective to the informational loss incurred by the Convergence. This hook-up was moreover POSITIVE, inasmuch as all of its trajections were SYNTAGMATIC (§7.4), in that they actually occurred within the text. The same was true of the three examples given in (6.10). A positive hook-up may be symbolized by a plus mark between the lead-off and follow-up; formulaically X + Y, e.g. Cnv + Amp in the case of (2.10). An example involving stylistic rather than situational compensation (§7.2, §7.3) can be provided on the basis of (3.3), the Abe(1962)/Saunders(1964) coreference chain of the Japanese noun *ootosanrin*. Since English does not have a unitary lexeme corresponding to *ootosanrin*, Saunders trajected the initial link by definitional Diffusion (§4.1.2) to *three-wheeled pickup truck*. But since English style would not bear maintenance of this long-winded Diffusional unit through the remaining links of the chain (cf. (4.11)), he next appealed to a medley of variational Reductions of the lead-off Diffusion. That is, he deployed a hook-up Dif + (Red,Red,Red, . . .).

A NEGATIVE HOOK-UP is one whose lead-off trajection is stated negatively with respect to a positive follow-up. Put differently, a negative hook-up is a potential trajection—the lead-off—avoided by means of another trajection—the follow-up. Phrased yet another way, a negative hook-up is one whose trajections are related paradigmatically (§7.4): the follow-up is chosen alternatively to the lead-off. An example was given in (2.11), where my refusal to Equate *ud[vey]* → *[way] out* provided the negative lead-off to the Substitutional follow-up *udvey* → *recourse*. As was discussed, I did this because I had already preempted the noun *way* as the translation of *mäd(en)*, both as the title of the story and, dependent on that, to translate an important recurrence chain throughout the story itself—a regularity I did not want to damage by misleading the reader with the unwarranted Convergence *-vey/mäd- → way*. Using the minus sign to modify the negative lead-off, this negative hook-up may be symbolized thusly: -Equ + Sub; or more fully, -(Equ,Cnv) + Sub.

7.6 TRANSLINGUISTIC-UNILINGUISTIC PARAMETERS

It is by no means unusual for linguistic and literary analysis to reveal trajection-like patterns within a single language, patterns for the most part representing options available to the performer for alternative encodings of one and the same message. An example was briefly discussed in §3.3.1, under the specific rubric of poetic Recrescence, but the phenomenon is much more widespread than intimated by that example and is by no means limited to poetic language.

For convenience, patterns of this sort will be referred to somewhat loosely as

UNILINGUISTIC TRAJECTIONS, a loose designation by virtue of the fact that trajectional theory has, as of this writing, been explicitly designed only for TRANSLINGUISTIC cases arising in the phenomenon of translation proper.

An instructive example of unilinguistic trajections was incidentally given in (6.9), three successive excerpts from Grimm's fairy tale 'The Devil with the Three Golden Hairs', concerning a youth who first meets a watchman, then a gatekeeper, and finally a ferryman, each of whom asks him the same question. As is obvious on even casual inspection, the three source-text excerpts are nearly but not quite identical—their differences being attributable to UNILINGUISTIC STYLISTIC VARIATION within the German text itself, the function doubtless being to reduce the monotony of otherwise unbroken repetition.[5]

As may be seen in the analytic translation, (6.9sa) is word for word 'what for [i.e. what kind of] a trade he understood and what he knew', and the first token of unilinguistic variation takes the form of substituting *verstände* 'understood' with the synonymous *verstünde* in (6.9sb), while the second token of variation is the reordering of *er* 'he' between (sb) and (sc). Note that there is also unilinguistic variation on the English side, though less than in the German original and differently distributed: reordering of *was* in (6.9tb).

When it comes to the translinguistic analysis of the German and English unilinguistic variation, i.e. to the trajections in the proper sense, we get a picture like that discussed in §6.2.2: translinguistic Convergence of the unilinguistic German reordering between lines (6.9sa) and (6.9sc) to (6.9ta) = (6.9tc), itself an instance of translinguistic Reordering; and an interplay of translinguistic Equation and Substitution making up the balance of the differences between source and target versions (cf. the schemata (6.10c) and (6.11c)).

NOTES

1. Cf. Wilss's example (288), from a German translation of Winston Churchill's autobiography, of *hat* → *Mütze* an. 'cap', with reference to the tophats once worn by boys at the British school Eton. At the same period (late nineteenth century), however, students in a German *Gymnasium* wore *Mützen* 'caps'.

2. Or copy to ZXYZ.

3. Most instances of what was called definitional Diffusion in §4.1.2 probably have a compensatory function, as do similar but rarer cases of Condensation, like Lefevere's example cited in note 1 of chapter 4.

4. The difference between the shapes *divree* and *dəvɔɔriim* is syntactic (the so-called construct versus absolute states) and has no lexicological import.

5. It will be convenient to distinguish unilinguistic analogues of trajections symbologically from genuine translinguistic cases by reserving capitalization for the latter: e.g. (translinguistic) Reordering versus (unilinguistic) reordering. The same differentiation will mark off occasional uses of quasi-trajectional cenematic patterns in chapters 13–14; e.g. equation, matching, diffusional substitution in §14.3.1.

PART TWO

Chapter *8*

SYSTEMIC AND FORMALISTIC TECHNIQUES

8.0 PRELIMINARIES

As was demonstrated in §6.3 with various expressions involving the Norwegian preposition *på*, one and the same nexus may be viewed as either Divergence or Convergence, depending on the analyst's perspective. But while it may be useful to shift one's analytic tools as occasion dictates, a technique that allows unprincipled freedom quickly degenerates from supple to flaccid. If, on the other hand, the analytic freedom can be demonstrated to be principled, one may confidently avail oneself of the technique and so profit by the increased analytic power that the freedom brings with it.

But how does one go about finding a principled basis for the analytic freedom inherent in trajections? An often fruitful rule of thumb is this: although analytic freedom bespeaks underdetermination of the technique in question (trajections in this case), the chances are reasonably good that the apparent 'slipperiness' in the data base (in this case, translational patterns) may give way to principled patterning from the point of view of some other technique. Thus, it is advisable to try out other techniques to supplement trajections if and as needed.

Part Two of this book will be devoted to discussion and illustration of two extremely general techniques with considerable power not only as supplements to trajectional analysis but also as translational analytic gear in their own right.

Like trajections, these two techniques—the SYSTEMIC and the FORMALIS-TIC—may more comprehensively be viewed as perspectives.

As will be seen, the systemic and formalistic perspectives are not disjoint but shade off into each other. This shading off is, moreover, rather in the manner of a cline whose systemic end tends to be general and conceptually free relative to the formalistic end, which is more structured and conceptually complex. In view of this, it will be wise to start Part Two systemically (this chapter) and conclude with two relatively formalistic chapters (11–12). But first it will be useful to provide brief characterizations of the two perspectives:

(i) Systemically, source and target texts and their relations are, where possible, viewed as orderly aggregates of orderly parts;

(ii) Formalistically, source and target texts and their relations are, where possible, viewed as structured phenomena ordered by principles amenable to scientific analysis—particularly analysis through the science of linguistics.[1]

8.1   The Systemic Perspective: Sets and Scatters

If there is one precept that leads directly to the systemic perspective, it is this:

(**8.1**) Never assume that a language datum is an isolate; always attempt to relate it to one or more other data so that the two (or more) comprise a patterned set.

A few supplements to this basic precept will be discussed later, but right now the case of Norwegian *på* will be picked up from chapter 6 and reviewed from the systemic vantage point. Harking back to §6.3, imagine first that one is faced with a translation of the phrase *[på] festen* into English as *[at] the party*,[2] and one wants to gain explicit understanding of how the nexus *på → at* fits into or derives from the Norwegian and English languages and their special relation as a translational pair. If the trajectional perspective is chosen, the results are more or less as was discussed. From the systemic perspective, the first desideratum is to know *what else* in Norwegian the deployment of *på* in the phrase *på festen* relates to. While it is doubtful that there is any unique first step in providing a full answer to this question, what might immediately come to mind is the fact that *på*, as a preposition, characteristically distributes in construction with various other NPs in addition to *festen*, e.g. *fjellet* 'the mountain'. A schema of the results might usefully be plotted as a SET, perhaps along the lines of (b) on the diagram in (8.2) (where the three vertical dots represent open-endedness). But then, the distribution of *på* in construction with *NP* also intersects with its government (systematic selection; cf. chapter 11) by various verbs (*VB*) and adjectives (*A*) like *tenke* 'think' and *sint* 'angry', which accordingly may also be plotted as a set (a). Finally, when this sort of setplotting has been carried out up to the point of usefulness for both source and target languages, the overall TRANSLATIONAL POTENTIAL may be represented by connective lines:

(8.2) (a) *VB,A på.*

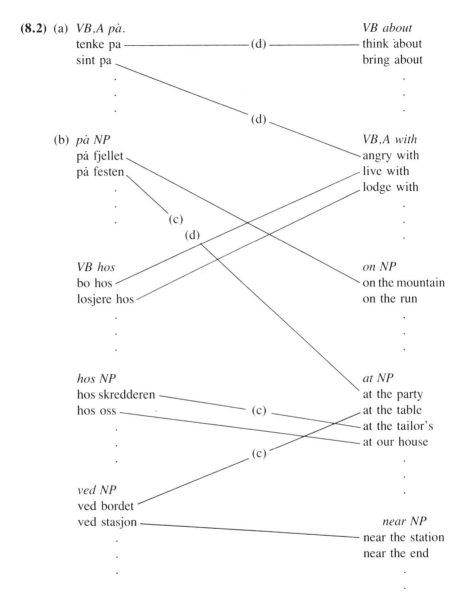

With this done, the case of trajectional 'slipperiness' may be picked up again and be shown rather to involve principled patterning from the systemic point of view. Note that the lines on diagram (8.2) tagged with (d) mark off the Divergent trajection discussed in §6.3, while those tagged with (c) mark off the Convergent alternative discussed in the same section. To summarize the most important points of this complementary interaction of the trajectional and systemic techniques, consider the crucial pivot line marked simultaneously with (d) and (c), *på festen* → *at the party*. Trajectionally, it is true that this nexus is indeterminate and may be viewed either as Divergence or Convergence, subject to convenience. However, the analytic freedom to choose is *not* unprincipled, the constraints of the choice being rather provided by the independent technique of systemic plotting. In short, trajectional analysis as Divergence will only be permissible when the systemic lines branch rightward (<); Convergence only when they branch leftward (>); and analyst's choice only where both branchings coincide (the middle bar—marked (d)(c)—or ⋛ in the diagram).

The discussion of (8.2) has ushered in the notion of set, a concept central to the systemic perspective. Because of the variety of useful applications of this notion in the analysis and practice of translation, it seems wise to provide a rather loose definition of this term:

(8.3) A set is any orderly multiple of linguistic forms, their orderliness determined formally and/or functionally.

By way of initial illustration, consider the provisionally unilinguistic examples in (8.4).

The first two cases instantiate ORTHOMETRIC sets (chapter 13), of types prevalent as euphonic figurae in various poetic traditions: the END-RHYMING set *attend* and *mend* in (a), characteristic of traditions such as the Medieval Arabic and Renaissance European; and the PARALLELISTIC sets *seakest* and *searchest, silver* and *treasures* in (b), important in the traditions represented by the Hebrew Bible and the Finnish Kalevala, among others (cf. also (10.5) in chapter 10).

Example (c), though formally similar to (b) and undeniably having similar poetic force, is essentially a SITUATIONALLY DETERMINED set, the orderliness of whose symmetrical parts is largely dictated by the extralinguistic nature of the referents.

With respect to the characterization in (8.3), the orderliness of a situationally determined set is primarily FUNCTIONAL, while that of an orthometric set is primarily FORMAL. However, this tendency can by no means be promoted to an absolute, since skilled writers frequently manage to enhance a functionally based set with formal similarity. (Thus, *wave offering* and *heave offering* in (c) have in common *VB offering*, in addition to which a syntactic symmetry pervades the entire passage.) What is more, good poets often fill out their formally symmetrical templates with functionally motivated elements. (Thus, the meanings contributed by rhyming *attend* and *mend* in (a) dovetail smoothly within the overarching message, as is typical with Shakespeare.)

Example (d) illustrates the fact that even colorless functor morphemes may crystallize into sets, here *neither* and *nor* and *both* and *and*.[3]

The remaining examples in (8.4) will be discussed in association with their calibrated translations or originals in (8.5).

When confronted with their translational counterparts, the examples of (8.4) bring out another dimension of sets, that of TRANSLINGUISTIC orderliness.

In (8.5ati) and (8.5atii) two Spanish translations of (8.4a) are presented, the

(8.4) **a**(s). The which if you with patient ears [attend],
What here shall miss, our toil shall strive to [mend].
(Shakespeare:882[Romeo and Juliet,prologue, 13–14])

b(t). If thous [seekest] her as [[silver]],
and [searchest] for her as for hid [[treasures]]
(KJ: Proverbs 2,4)

c(t). And thou shalt sacrifice the [breast] of the
[[wave offering]], and the [shoulder] of the
[[heave offering]], which is [[[waved]]], and
which is [[[heaved]]] up, of the ram of the
consecration (KJ: Exodus 29,27)

d(s). (*Benvolio*. My noble uncle, do you know the cause?)
Montague.I[neither]know it [nor] can learn of him.
(*B*. Have you importuned him by any means?)
M. [Both] by myself [and] many other friends.
(Shakespeare:884[Romeo and Juliet, I i 150–52)

e(t). Some have tasted of the [*Host of the Lamb*], only
a few of us of the [*Host of the Beast*] (X:218)

f(t). [His Lordship's] castle was the most beautiful of
castle's, and [her Ladyship] the best of all
possible baronesses. (Bair:4–5).

g(t). I can be found at the end of [place], on the border
between [place] and [nonplace]. So I can take you
from [place] to [beyond place] (P.Malone 1983:563).

first a metered translation by TRANSDUCTION (chapter 14) of Shakespeare's rhymed iambic pentameter into Spanish unrhymed hendecasyllabic meter, and the second prose translation. Both versions instantiate what will be called SET-TO-SCATTER translation, because the rhymed position-symmetrical set of the source, *attend* and *mend*, has become a nonset, or SCATTER, in both target texts: neither *atento* and *enmendar* (ati) nor *atención* and *enmendar* (atii) rhyme, and neither translation deploys its members in symmetrical positions.

The case of (8.4b), on the other hand, instantiates SET-TO-SET translation, with the interesting twist that the source-Hebrew CHIASTIC ORDER ([təvaqšɛnnɔɔ] . . . [[kɛsɛf]] . . . [[maṭmooniim]] [taḥpaśśɛnnɔɔ] (8.5bs) has been transduced to DIRECT ORDER in the English target ([seekest] . . . [[silver]] . . . [searchest] . . . [[treasures]]).

Case (8.5cs)-(8.4ct) also represents set-to-set translation, with two differences: (1) The linear arrangement of the sets and their members is Equational rather than Reordered (both *ababcc*). (2) While all three sets in both languages are functionally grounded, two are also formally grounded. Even as *wave offering* and *heave offering* have the morphosyntactic common denominator *VB offering*, so Hebrew *hattəfunnɔɔ* and *hattəruumɔɔ* have the common morphological base *hattəCuuCɔɔ*; and similarly *waved* and *heaved* shared *VB-ed*, while *huunaf* and *huurɔɔm* share *huuCVC*.[4] The remaining set lacks a formal base in either language: *breast* and *shoulder*, *ḥăzee* and *šooq*.

It is interesting that it is the Spanish prose version in (8.5dtii) that replicates Shakespeare's original with set-to-set translation in both cases (*neither* and *nor* → *ni* and *ni*, *both* and *and* → *así* and *como*). Conversely, the metered version in (8.5dti) defaults into set-to-scatter at least in verse 152 (*both* and *and* → *así*). In the case of verse 150, on the other hand, the two-to-three trajection *neither* and *nor* → *no* and *y* and *no* is arguably set-to-set, to the extent that one sort of symmetry is traded off for another.

Example (8.4e-8.5se) exemplifies a phenomenon of some frequency in literary language: the deployment of a functional set as a vehicle for a THEMATIC OR SYMBOLIC REFRAIN. In this case the German to English set-to-set correspondence *Sakrament des Büffels* = *Host of the Beast* functions as a totem of Nazism and Nazi sympathizers, while *Sakrament des Lammes* = *Host of the Lamb* totemizes the powerless, silently suffering German opponents of Nazism, a dialectic that pervades Böll's novel. In such THEMATIC SETS, authors frequently underscore the functional basis with some formal symmetry, a lead that the translator will normally be well advised to follow. Both Böll and X have done so here, with *Sakrament des N*-s and *Host of the N* respectively.

Finally, (8.4f) and (8.4g) are similar in instantiating Substitutional implementations of set-to-set mapping, where the translator either presses into special service (f) or coins (g) target-language counterparts to source elements which,

(**8.5**) **ati**. Si lo escucháis con el oído [atento]
procuraremos [enmendar] las faltas. (Manent:14)

    atii. Si la escucháis con [atención] benévola, procuraremos
[enmendar] con nuestro celo las faltas que hubiere (Marín:15)

    bs. ʔim-[təvaqšennɔɔ] xak [[kɛsɛf]]
wəxam[[maṭmooniim]] [taḥpaśśɛnnɔɔ] (K:Proverbs 2,4)

    cs. wəqiddaštɔɔ ʔeθ [ḥăzee] [[hattəfuunɔɔ]] wəʔeθ [šooq]
[[hattəruumɔɔ]] ʔăšɛr [[huunaf]]] waʔăšɛr [[[huurɔɔm]]]
meeʔeel hammilluuʔiim (K:Exodus 29,27)

    dti. **M**. Yo [no] la sé [y] por él [no] puedo hallarla.
M. [Así] lo hicimos ya con los amigos (Manent:21)

    dtii. **M**. [Ni] la sé, [ni] logro conseguir que la descubra.
M. [Así] yo [como] otros muchos amigos (Marín:21)

    es. die einen haben vom [Sakrament des Lammes] gegessen,
wenige nur, Alter, vom [Sakrament des Büffels] (B:204)

    fs. le château de [Monseigneur le baron] était le plus
beau des châteaux, et [Madame] la meilleure des
baronnes possibles (Voltaire:4–5)

    gs. vaani nimca be[sof hamakom], ʕal hagevul šebeyn [makom]
ve[eyn makom]. ʕal ken ani yaxol laset etxem el ašer
[1emaʕala min hamakom] (Yaari:199)

for one reason or the other, resist Equation. Thus, in (f), Bair renders Voltaire's source set *Monseigneur le baron* and *Madame (la baronne)* by *his lordship* and *her ladyship*, despite the nonequivalence of these titles in British peerage and French *noblesse titrée* (this case will be discussed immediately below); and in (g), P. Malone coins the nonce-noun *nonplace* and stretches English syntax for all four *place*-tokens, to capture a somewhat analogous neologistic deployment of Yaari's source-Hebrew *makom* 'place'. P. Malone thereby deploys what may be called a NEO-SET in the target text.

8.2 CHARTS AND DIAGRAMS: SET-TO-SET SUBSTITUTION; SET-TO-SCATTER EQUATION

Let us pick up example (8.4f-8.5fs) again to see exactly how Bair has managed to translate set-to-set while at the same time incurring Substitution, and to speculate on his motives for doing so. A suggestive answer to the latter point emerges from considering how he might have gone about Equating *Monseigneur le baron* and *Madame (la baronne)* into his English text. Quite simply, he could *not* have used Equation, because English has few if any conventionalized appellations of the form *honorific (the) title*: and a target pair like *Monsignor (the) baron* and *Madam(e) (the) baroness* would be cumbersome at best and might even incur downright false friendship (§1.4.2(iv)).

It would seem, in fact, that Bair was faced with only three plausible alternatives: carry-over Matching (§1.4.1) (to *Monseigneur le baron* and *Madame la baronne*); Reduction (to *the baron* and *the baroness*); or Substitution. Inasmuch as he has manifestly chosen to Substitute, the systemic perspective may prove helpful in seeing exactly how he has proceeded. Since the SEMANTIC FIELD of the core source expressions, *baron* and *baronne*, is that of French titled nobility (*nobless titrée*),[5] it may help to start with a list or diagram showing the focal terms in their connections to closely related terms. This is done in (8.6), where it can be seen that the pair of titles *baron* and *baronne* occupy the fifth rank in the system of traditional French *noblesse*, just below *vicomte-vicomtesse* and just above *chevalier-chevalière*.

When the cross section of the French system in (8.6) is aligned with its closest British counterpart in (8.7), we will have gained a sufficiently clear and simple picture of the potential relations to characterize Bair's set-to-set translation precisely. Since the English appellations *Lordship* and *Ladyship* are restricted in reference to members of the peerage, Bair has effectively Substituted a GENERIC for a HYPONYM (SPECIFIC), as in (8.8). (Cf. also chapter 9.)[6]

As may have been suggested by the preceding example, systemic analysis is greatly enhanced by lists, charts, and diagrams—whether ready-made or synthesized by the analyst.[7] In this regard, a frequent nexus for translation involves source-target discrepancies in METROLOGICAL SYSTEMS, i.e. culture- and/or language-specific methods of assigning and computing measurements, dates, kinship roles, and the like. A commonplace occasion is the necessity of bridging

(8.6)

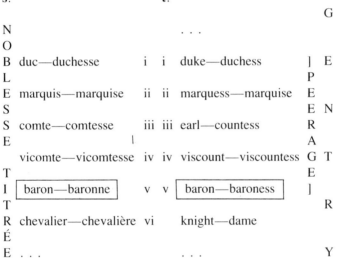

```
N                         rank
O
B   duc—duchesse          i
L
E   marquis—marquise      ii
S
S   comte—comtesse        iii
E
    vicomte—vicomtesse    iv
T
I   ┌ baron—baronne ┐     v
T   └──────────────┘
R   chevalier—chevalière  vi
É
E
```

(8.7) s.   t.

```
                                             G
N                          . . .
O
B   duc—duchesse      i   i   duke—duchess      ]  E
L                                               P
E   marquis—marquise  ii  ii  marquess—marquise E
S                                               E  N
S   comte—comtesse    iii iii earl—countess     R
E                  ∖                             A
    vicomte—vicomtesse iv iv viscount—viscountess G  T
T                                               E
I  ┌ baron—baronne ┐  v   v  ┌ baron—baroness ┐ ]
T  └──────────────┘          └───────────────┘  R
R   chevalier—chevalière vi     knight—dame
É
E  . . .                    . . .               Y
```

differences between the metrical system and the traditional British system of linear measurement, a confrontation that can be rendered quite perfunctory and
harmless by using a simple slide-rule converter (datalizer), available at any sta-
tionery store. It may very well have been with the aid of such a device, for example, that Saunders converted Abe's original metrical specifications of rope-
ladder length into terms of feet in (8.9a)—and it was indeed thus that I
transposed Mykle's metrical figures for another rope ladder into terms of yards in
(8.9b).

The set-relevant properties of such translations can be brought out with a
simply devised chart like that in (8.10), where lines contain equivalent measure-

(8.8)

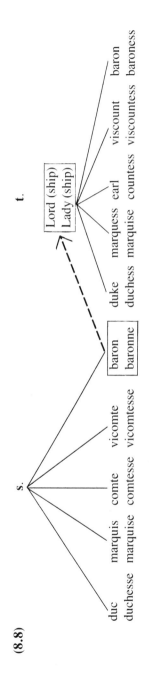

(8.9) as. Saiwai, [sanzis-senti] de tomatte kureta (Abe 1962:155)
　　　　　　an.'thirty centimeters'
　at. Fortunately, the stretching stopped after [about a foot] (Saunders 1964:171)
　bs. han skulle ha [fem meter] tau til leketøy for en liten landkrabbe (Mykle:29) an.'five meters'
　bt. all he wanted was [six yards] of rope for a little landlubber's toy (M1980b:95)

ments (thus, 1 centimeter = ¹/₁₀₀ meter = .39 inches = .03 feet = .01 yard), whole numbers or fractions represent terms of pragmatic salience which might be called FOCI (e.g. 1 centimeter = ¹/₁₀₀ meter, 1 inch = ¹/₁₂ foot), and decimal notation marks nonfocal measurements, to be called PERIPHERALS (e.g. 2.54 centimeters, .39 inches).

(8.10) Metrical System　　　　　British System

centimeters	meters	inches	feet	yards
1	1/100	.39	.03	.01
2.54	.025	1	1/12	1/36
(as) 30		→ (at').9		
30.48	.3	12 →	(at) 1	1/3
91.4	.91	36	3	1
100	1	39.37	3.28	1.09

If we now systematically characterize foci as sets and peripherals as scatters, we can account for the translational strategies of (8.9) in terms of the hypothesized principles of (8.11). By way of illustration, Saunders's case of (8.9a) is plotted in (8.10), where it may be seen that his actual trajectory ((as) *30* (centimeters) → (at) *1* (foot)) constitutes set-to-set Substitution, as opposed to what might have been set-to-scatter Equation ((as) *30* (centimeters) → (at') *.9* (feet)).

(8.11) a. In many text types not requiring quantificational precision, metrological information is optimally encoded focally rather than peripherally.
　b. In translation, principle (a) is often implemented by rounding off a potential target peripheral to a focus; that is, by trajecting through set-to-set Substitution rather than set-to-scatter Equation.

It may be noted that principle (8.11b) would never be applicable if the metrical and British systems were in phase such that the foci of one aligned with the foci of the other. It is, however, commonplace for metrological systems to be OUT OF PHASE, and the resulting asymmetries can exercise a translator's resourcefulness in any number of ways. another case in point involves the traditional Hebrew calendar, whose months are systematically out of step with the Gregorian calendar, so that the beginning of a Gregorian month falls near the middle of a Hebrew month and vice versa; cf. (8.12).

I had to confront the consequences of this skewed interface in translating a

(8.12) Hebrew | Gregorian

Hebrew	Gregorian
	(1) January
Šəvȧṭ	
	(2) February
ʔĂđȧr	
	(3) March
Nisȧn	
	(4) April
ʔIyyȧr	
	(5) May
Siwȧn	
	(6) June
Tammuz	
	(7) July
ʔȦv	
	(8) August
ʔElul	
	(9) September
Tišri	
	(10) October
Ḥɛšwȧn	
	(11) November
Kislew	
	(12) December
Ṭeveθ	

poem by the medieval Jewish-Spanish (Sephardic) poet Samuel ha-Nagid, the first stanza of which is given in (8.13). As a comparison with (8.12) will reveal, the three Hebrew months referred to in the source comprise a bloc out of phase with either of the corresponding Gregorian triplets: *July, August, September* (7,8,9) or *August, September, October* (8,9.10). Now the specific problem for translation was that neither set-to-set Match straightforwardly conveyed the crucial source-text message of the drop from the heat of summer to the chills of autumn, at least for English-language readers with average Northern Hemisphere temperate-zone expectations in matters climatic: target series (7,8,9) is not chilly enough at the end (*September*); and series (8,9,10) may even be too extreme in this regard (*October*), while conversely its warm extreme (*August*) conveys too little of what, to my sensibilities, should be the summer half.

As may be seen in (8.13t), I attempted to deal with this problem by foregoing set-to-set translation of either sort, settling instead for a set-to-scatter pastiche which I hoped would be redeemed by conveying more or less the right feel for the seasonal change from hot to cold.[8]

(8.13) s. Meθ [ʔàv] umeθ [ʔelul] umeθ ḥummàm
　　　　　gam nɛʔɛ̌saf [tišri] umeθ ʕimmàm
　　　　Bảʔu yəme haqqor, wəhattiroš
　　　　　ʔảḍàm wəqolo bakkəli ḍàmam (Samuel
　　　　　ha-Nagid, apud Schirmann i:167)
　　　t. [August's] gone, the heat of [summer's] dead
　　　　　Even [early autumn's] blown away;
　　　　Chill's upon the air, the wine is red
　　　　　Ready now to yield us its bouquet (M1983f:372)

8.3 JAPANESE SELF-REFERENT PRONOUNS; FRENCH *DIZAINES* VERSUS ENGLISH *DOZENS*; SCATTER-TO-SET TRANSLATION

As was shown in the preliminary examples in (8.4d), sets may be built of functors no less than of contentives. Interesting cases of set-to-set Substitution involving functors may often be found where languages differ in deployment strategies for various rhetorical or narrative functions. Thus, in some cases where in English narrative third-person pronouns may be used by a protagonist in thoughts and reflections both self-referentially and other-referentially, in Japanese narrative, self-reference may be conveyed by a first-person pronoun and other-reference by a second-person pronoun. An example from Abe(1962)/Saunders(1964) is given in (8.14a), with its set-to-set Substitutional disposition sketched in (8.14b) via the dotted arrows.

It sometimes happens that the choice between set-to-set Substitution and set-to-scatter Equation places the translator between the horns of a dilemma. Thus, the Romance languages differ from English in having a quasi-productive word-formation rule for constructing collective nouns on the basis of the cardinal numerals, especially those signifying the decades. See the examples in (8.15), and contrast the parsimony of the English equivalents. Note also the formal heterogeneity of the English items, while the Romance nouns are with few exceptions (e.g. Italian *centinaio*) built up by uniform suffixes (*-ena, -ina, -aine*).

Not surprisingly, Romance-language speakers freely avail themselves of these lexical riches, and the lower-level decade nouns in particular—especially *decena, diecina, dizaine*—have become stylistic favorites for synthesizing rough estimates of groups numbering less than two digits or so. Since English has no all-purpose noun numerically corresponding to *decena, diecina,* or *dizaine,* one strategy in translating a text containing such nouns is set-to-set Substitution to *dozen,* the systemically closest English counterpart. But a moment's reflection will suggest that Substitution of '10' by '12' may often incur mistranslation by dint of overestimating the sum of referents so rounded off. See the French example in (8.16), where this problem does in fact emerge: 'several dozens of six-hundred-odd' would certainly overstate the count intended by 'several "tens" of six-hundred-odd' (*plusieurs dizaines des quelque six cent*).

(8.14) as. Sara ni buraku no siuti no koto o kangae ni irereba,
[ore] ga uketa higai wa, tootei keisan situkusenai hodo ni
naru . . . [[Omae]]o; koko ni hikitomete oku mono no,
zyootai o, hihubyoo no kasabuta o hagu yoo na konki
de, tutukimawasu koto ni sita (Abe 1962:173f)

at. When he thought about what the villagers had done,
he realized that it would be almost impossible to
calculate the harm´[he] had suffered . . . He had
decided he would try to get at the reason that kept
[[her]] in the hole with the same patience one has
in picking at a scab left from some skin disease (Saunders 1964:191)

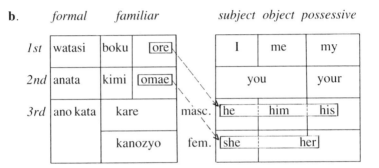

b.

	formal	familiar		subject	object	possessive
1st	watasi	boku	ore	I	me	my
2nd	anata	kimi	omae	you		your
3rd	ano kata	kare		masc. he	him	his
		kanozyo		fem. she		her

	Spanish	*Italian*	*French*	*English*
(8.15) '10'	decena	diecina	dizaine	—
'12'	docena	dozzina	douzaine	dozen
'20'	veintena	ventina	vingtaine	score
'30'	treintena	trentina	trentaine	—
'40'	cuarentena	quarantina	quarantaine	—
etc.	etc.	etc.	etc.	—
'100'	centena	centinaio	centaine	(a)hundred

(8.16) s. Washington, aidé par la forte pression d'organizations
comme Amnesty International, a déjà réussi à persuader
les Duvalier de relâcher plusieurs [dizaines]
des quelque six cent prisonniers politiques
qu'ils détiennent (op.cit. in (3.3a):9)

t. Washington, with the strong backing of organizations
like Amnesty International, has already persuaded
the Duvalier regime to release several *[dozens]
of the six-hundred-odd political prisoners
being held (JM)

Thus far, examples and discussion have been provided of a range of cases involving both set-to-set and set-to-scatter translation, but no instances have been seen of SCATTER-TO-SET translation. While a priori, it might be thought that this would be a rare, quirky phenomenon in any event, experience has taught me that this is not the case, and reflection upon the matter has suggested a plausible reason why scatter-to-set translation is not so rare after all. If the source language happens to have a functional set which is a formal scatter, and if, moreover, the target language at the time of translation simply lacks any adequately corresponding terms, the translator may very well cope by *coining terms via definitional Diffusion* (§4.1.2)—a procedure a priori likely to produce a formal set for the simple reason that the extralinguistic similarities of the referents will, all else being equal, be encoded by linguistically similar forms. An example is given in (8.17), where the ancient Hebrew sacrificial concepts *minḥaθ* (base form *minḥɔɔ*) and *nisk-* (base *nesɛx*) were Diffused by the King James translators into the formal set *meat offering* and *drink offering*. The formal symmetry of the resulting set (*N offering*) directly reflects its semantic composition.

(8.17) s. wəʔeθ hakkɛvɛś haššeenii taʕáśɛɛ been hɔɔʕarbɔɔyim
kə[minḥaθ] habbooqɛr ux[nisk]ɔɔh taʕáśɛɛ-lɔɔh
ləreaḥ nihoaḥ ʔiššɛɛ lYHWH (K:Exodus 29,41)

t. And the other lamb shalt thou offer at even, and
shalt do thereto according to the [meat offering]
of the morning, and according to the [drink offering]
thereof, for a sweet savor, an offering made by fire
unto the LORD (KJ)

8.4 FORMAL AND FUNCTIONAL SETS

Though the freedom of pitting groups of forms as sets against other groups as scatters provides the analyst with a handy way of highlighting a variety of translational differences, the reader may have noted that the classification *set ≠ scatter* does not truly constitute an all-or-none, discrete opposition. To illustrate this with the last example, in (8.17s) the group *minḥaθ* and *nisk-* was said to constitute a functional set but a formal scatter, a cross-classification that would be contradictory if the attributes of set and scatter were intended to be mutually exclusive.

Nevertheless, while the set-scatter concept would be rendered needlessly restrictive by redefining it as truly binary, under certain circumstances it might be analytically useful to firm up and clarify the concept by subsidiary techniques. One such technique is that of FEATURES (§4.1.1), and though feature analysis can be brought to any desired degree of precision and detail, the illustration to be adduced here will be limited to just the two specifications that have been most prominent in the exposition thus far: those of form (featurally [+f]), and function in its typical manifestation as meaning (featurally [+m]). Examples will be provided from the vocabulary of Spanish and English legal language, per Robb (1955).

Consider first what kind of nexus might be implied by set-to-set translation in both meaning and form, featurally $[+m, +f] \rightarrow [+m, +f]$: that is, a group of items mutually related by both meaning and form $([+m, +f])$ is trajected into the target text in terms of a group of items similarly related. The English pair *complainant* and *defendant* is such a group, $[+m]$ by virtue of having as referents the set of opposing litigants in a court case, and $[+f]$ by dint of the common structure *VB-ant*. As it turns out, Spanish legal language has an analogous set, *demandante* and *demandado*, with the common denominator *demanda-SUFFIX* (see 8.18a).

It also happens that both English and Spanish have synonyms to this set (thus $[+m]$) lacking the formal cohesion (thus $[-f]$), *plaintiff* and *defendant* and *actor* and *reo*. Hence, we have (8.18b), and by interchanging set members, (8.18c).

If source and target each have $[-m]$ groups, the items in question are not related in meaning, though in form they may (8.18d) or may not be (8.18e). Cases like (8.18e) simply instantiate scatter-to-scatter translation and as such have little theoretical interest per se. On the other hand, cases like (8.18d), and especially mixed cases like (8.18f), are not uncommon and can be troublesome. Case (d) depends upon the quirk that in both languages the items *right = derecho* are polysemous in the same way, meaning either 'opposite of left' (*right side*) or

(8.18) a. $[+m, +f]$ $[+m, +f]$
    complain-ant   ← — →   demanda-nte
    defend-ant   ← — →   demanda-do
 b. $[+m, -f]$ $[+m, -f]$
    plaintiff   ← — →   actor
    defendant   ← — →   reo
 c. $[+m, -f]$ ← — → $[+m, +f]$
    plaintiff   ← — →   demanda-nte
    defendant   ← — →   demanda-do
 d. $[-m, +f]$ $[-m, +f]$
    right side   ← — →   lado derecho
    copyright   ← — →   derecho de autor
 e. $[-m, -f[$ $[-m, -f]$
    defendant   ← — →   reo
    copyright   ← — →   derecho de autor
 f. $[-m, -f]$ $[-m, +f]$
    administrative law   ← — →   derecho administrativo
    antecedent right   ← — →   derecho antecedente
 g. $[+m, +f]$ $[-m, +f]$
    administrative law   ← — —   derecho administrativo
    *antecedent law   ← — —   derecho antecedente.

'lawful due' (*copyright*), while (f) depends upon a further Spanish-specific polysemy of *derecho*, which can mean either 'lawful due' (*derecho antecedente*) or 'legislation' (*derecho administrativo*). The formal agreement in cases like this can sometimes beguile the translator into mistranslations on the assumption that identity of form should imply identity of meaning, an occasion for error magnified when, as here, the [− m, + f] nexus occurs syntagmatically, in one and the same text. When such mistranslation actually does occur, as in the Spanish-to-English case of (g), the phenomenon of FALSE FRIENDSHIP is incurred (§1.4.2(iv)): form *without* meaning in the source ([− m, + f]) has erroneously induced form *with* meaning in the target ([+ m, + f]). Like (g), most cases of [− m] → [+ m] or [+ m] → [− m] will symptomize mistranslation of one type or another.

The examples in (8.18) were, for convenience and precision, taken from legal language, but though 'legalese' has an extremely high premium on functional sets ([+ m]), the occurrence of formal sets ([+ f]) is for the most part incidental, being situationally determined (cf. (8.4c)-(8.5c)). A text-type with a high premium of formal sets, on the other hand, is literary language, where form often carries either aesthetic or symbolic weight.[9] Cf. §15.1.1, §15.2.1.

NOTES

1. The systemic and formalistic perspectives were first discussed in M1981b:36ff.

2. Replacing *på de voksnes fest* → *at the grown-ups' party*, which seemed too cumbersome and special for general illustration.

3. Functor sets may sometimes become hallmarks of some orthometric traditions; cf. the case of *koliko* and *toliko* (an. 'as much' and 'that much') cited by Kerewsky-Halpern as 'common in many Serbian oral genres' (1983:314). (The case of Hebrew *wə-* ~ *u-* given in (2.9) may possibly be another case in point, vis-à-vis Biblical narrative.)

4. The representations *hattəCuuCɔɔ* and *huuCVC* are informal abbreviations for interlocking complexes of characteristically Semitic 'internal-flective' morphology (M1985c). The difference between *a* and *ɔɔ* in *huunaf* and *huurɔɔm* derives from a phonological rule (cf. chapter 13).

5. To be sure, the characters in question are supposed to be Germans, but Voltaire's terms of address and reference appear to be purely Gallic for all that.

6. For the titular systems of (8.7)–(8.8), see the article 'Nobility' in Britannica (1911:esp.729a).

7. To cite just two cases in point: Fuller (1984) is in large part an annotated list of French and Spanish vocabulary likely to pose difficulties for the translator; and Ray reports that in translating Bengali poetry she plots language levels (e.g. formal, familiar) on a graph as she works her way through the source text (1976:267).

8. In a similar vein, it is interesting to note that Márquez (154), writing in and about a region in South America (Colombia) just below the equator, counts *diciembre* 'December' as a month in New World, Southern-Hemispheric *verano* 'summer', rather than Old World, Northern-Hemispheric *invierno* 'winter'—a practice followed (Equated) by his translator Rabassa (173).

9. To be sure, what constitutes formal similarity is subject to considerable language-specific variation. Thus, in Classical Arabic, where morphological repetition is prized as a literary embellishment,
what passes for repetition depends largely on the peculiarly Semitic internal-flective morphology (cf.
note 4), with the consequence that, for example *taṣawwuf, taʾalluf, taṭarruf,* and *tanaqqin* all pass
muster as identically structured, despite the apparent deviance of the last form cited (Frank:76f).
(Moreover, the appreciation of and conditions for such repetition are likely to date from Common Semitic, to judge by millenia-earlier cases like that of Akkadian *adād, ānab, āšuš, amṭi(na)* cited in
Cooper (512).)

Chapter 9

TAXONOMIES

9.0 PRELIMINARIES

In (8.8), TREE DIAGRAMS were tacitly used to represent the structure of Bair's Substitutional translation of *(Monseigneur) le baron* and *(Madame) la baronne* by *(His) Lordship* and *(Her)* Ladyship. Tree diagrams lend themselves to perspicuous modeling of numerous linguistic relations among which (as in this case), that of a GENERIC (or CLASS) to its HYPONYMS (or MEMBERS) occupies an important place in the work of linguists, anthropologists, and language-philosophers.[1]

A network of generic-hyponymic relations is called a TAXONOMY, and the fundamental principle for tree-representing taxonomic relations is simple to state. A generic is symbolized by a NODE placed above its hyponyms and connected to them by lines called BRANCHES, a configuration called DOMINATION. Thus, in (8.8t) the generic appellations *Lordship* and *Ladyship* may be said to dominate their family of hyponymic titles *duke-duchess, marquess-marquise*, etc.

Before turning to more cases involving translation, it will be useful to adduce three additional properties of taxonomies:

(i) A taxonomic node, or TAXON, may or may not be labeled. A possible example for colloquial English will be seen later in (9.9t), where the subgroup of sentient beings labeled in scientific English as *amphibian* has no widely accepted standard name, despite folk recognition that frogs, toads, etc. 'go together'.

(ii) Though the taxonomies of (8.8) each contain two levels of taxa, taxonomies with three or more levels are not uncommon, in which case intermediate taxa simultaneously function as hyponyms to dominating taxa and as generics to dominated (subordinate) taxa. For example, the diagram in (8.7t) can be converted into the three-level taxonomy of (9.1), where *peer* is simultaneously a hyponym of *(member of the) gentry* (peerage being a kind of gentry) and generic to *duke, marquess,* etc. (since dukes, marquesses, etc. are kinds of peers).

(iii) Finally, taxonomies are TRANSITIVE, in that the class-membership relation of adjacent-level taxa is passed on from node to node to taxa at greater vertical distance. Thus, in (9.1), if a *peer* is a member of the *gentry* and a *duke* is a kind of *peer*, then by transitivity a *duke* is also a member of the *gentry*.

(9.1)

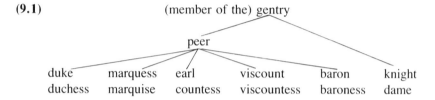

(member of the) gentry

peer

duke   marquess   earl   viscount   baron   knight
duchess marquise countess viscountess baroness dame

9.1 TAXONOMIC CONFLATION

Coming now to the relevance of the foregoing discussion to translation, the most interesting cases are those in which a term of the source language is a component in a taxonomy which, in one fashion or another, is out of line with the closest corresponding taxonomy in the target language. And while there is a considerable variety of such cases, among the most important — and potentially troublesome — are those involving what will be called a CONFLATED TAXONOMY, that is, a taxonomy containing one and the same term on two or more taxic levels. Thus, in the schema of (9.2) the conflated term is T, which simultaneously functions as a generic to the set of hyponyms X,Y,Z,T and as a member of that set. It will sometimes be convenient to symbolize a conflated term in a generic role with a subscripted 'g' (hence T_g), and in parallel fashion a subscripted 'h' will be used for a hyponymic role (T_h).

(9.2)

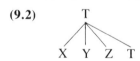

T

X Y Z T

As may be deduced from the preceding characterization of taxonomic conflation, a conflative term is semantically always a POLYSEME, that is, a term having two or more related meanings. This follows from the fact that a pair of generic-hyponymic terms are by definition both semantically distinct and semantically related. Some unilinguistic examples from English are given in (9.3), instantiating a kind of conflation whereby a term unambiguously female in reference (*she, spokeswoman*) is paradigmatically coupled with a complementary term referentially ambiguous, out of context, as either specifically male or sexually generic (*he, spokesman*). Taxonomies of this sort, involving what might be called SEX-BASED CONFLATION, are extremely widespread in the world's languages, and have in recent years rightly (if not always clearmindedly) become the object of criticism for the danger of miscommunication that may easily be incurred when the context fails to provide sufficient cues as to whether specifically male or generically male-female reference is intended.

(**9.3**) **a.**   he$_g$ **b.**   spokesman$_g$

    she   he$_h$ spokeswoman   spokesman$_h$

In translation, the dangers of conflation-induced ambiguity may easily be perpetuated when source and target languages happen to evince similar taxonomic disposition—though an alert translator may take measures to obviate the ambiguity in the target text. Thus, the Semitic languages are like English (and most other Indo-European languages) in employing sex-conflated pronouns with the structure of (9.3a), a similarity that apparently lulled the King James translators into perpetuating the Hebrew ambiguity of the Biblical passage in (9.4a) into the English version. (The intended sense is that the death of either servant or maid be punished (*umee*ϑ⟨a,b⟩) = *he*⟨a,b⟩ *die*), not just that of the servant (**umee*ϑ⟨a⟩ = *he⟨a⟩*die*).) On the other hand, translator ʿAlī was perspicacious enough to neutralize a similar ambiguity in another Semitic language, Arabic, in the Qoranic passage in (9.4b). The trajection ʿAlī used in this case is one of the most widespread and effective in disambiguating conflation: Diffusion of the source generic (in this case *lahu* an. 'he') into syntagmatic co-occurrence of the target hyponyms (*he, she*); cf. (9.5). (See also the discussion of the second type-case in M1986e.)

(**9.4**) **as.** wǝxii-yakkɛɛ ʔiiš ʔɛθ-ʕadoo⟨a⟩ ʔoo ʔɛθ-ʔămɔɔθoo⟨b⟩
        bašševɛṭ umeeθ⟨a,b⟩ taḥaθ yɔɔḏoo nɔɔqoom yinnɔɔqeem
        (K:Exodus 21,20)

   at. And if a man smite his servant⟨a⟩, or his maid⟨b⟩, with
        a rod, and he⟨a,b⟩ die under his hand; he shall
        surely be punished (KJ)

   bs. Waʔin kaana raǰulun⟨a⟩ yuuraθu kalaalatan ʔawi 'mraʔatun⟨b⟩
        wa[lahu]⟨a,b⟩ ʔaxun ʔaw ʔuxtun falikullin waaḥidin
        's-sudusu (Qur'ān:192)[IV,12])

   bt. And if a man⟨a⟩ or a woman⟨b⟩, having no children
        leaves property to be inherited and [he (or she)]⟨a,b⟩
        has a brother or sister, then for each of them is the
        sixth ('Alī:192)

As has been illustrated several times in earlier chapters (e.g. (3.13), (6.8)), it is a stylistic commonplace for coreference chains to be diversified by varying

(9.5)

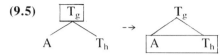

the NP designating the referent from link to link. A frequent resource for such variation is provided by taxonomies, whereby different links of a chain may be filled with generic-hyponymically related elements at different taxic levels. Thus, in the German example of (9.6s), a wolf is first referred to by the specific noun *Wolf* and subsequently by the generic noun *Tier*, a chain apparently Equated by Hunt and Stern in their English translation as *wolf* and *beast*, respectively (9.6t). Snippets of the relevant taxonomies are given in (9.7) where, at least for colloquial German and English of the period (nineteenth century), the lexemes *Tier* and *beast* function as generic terms for undomesticated sentient beings like wolves, lions, bears, and so forth.

(9.6) s. Als der [Wolf]⟨a⟩ seinen Hunger gestillt hatte,
trollte er sich fort, legte sich draußen auf der
grünen Wiese unter einem Baum und fing an zu
schlaffen . . . 'Jetzt geht und sucht Wackersteine,
dem gottlosen [Tier]⟨a⟩ den Bauch füllen, solange es
noch im Schlafe liegt' (G:33f)

t. When the [wolf]⟨a⟩ had satisfied his appetite he
took himself off, laid himself down under a tree
in the green meadow outside, and began to sleep . . . 'Now
go and look for some big stones, and we will fill
the wicked [beast's]⟨a⟩ stomach with them while
he is still asleep'. (HS:40–42)

(9.7) s.

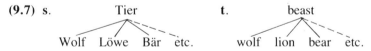

With (9.6) and (9.7) in mind, we may turn our attention to (9.8) and ponder the felicity of following suit with the trajection *Tier(e)* → *beast(s)*. For many or most readers, the lexeme *beast* will just not seem appropriate in these cases — and in fact, as will be seen, is not the word that Hunt and Stern actually chose here. The question is, since *Tier* → *beast* works in (9.6), why shouldn't it go over equally well in (9.8)?

If we compare the first-link hyponyms in (9.8) with the hyponyms in (9.7), an important difference emerges: the referents of the latter are mammals, while the referents of the former are not. And indeed, it turns out that English and German make further differentiations of wild sentient beings, so that as a first step toward a solution of the translational problem confronting us, the trees of (9.7) should be incorporated into overarching taxonomies along the lines of (9.9). On the English side, this portrayal captures the problem with (9.8): at least in this

(9.8) **as**. Der Ameisenkönig war mit seinen tausend und tausend
[Ameisen]⟨a⟩ in der Nacht angekommen, und die
darkbaren [Tiere]⟨a⟩ die Hirse mit grosser Emsigkeit
gelesen (G:78)

at. The ant-king had come in the night with thousands and
thousands of [ants]⟨a⟩, and the grateful *[beasts]⟨a⟩
had by great industry picked up all the millet-seed (HS:101)

bs. Die Mutter hörte, daß das Kind mit jemand sprach, und
als sie sah, daß es mit seinem Löffelchen nach einer
[Unke]⟨b⟩ schlug, so lief sie . . . heraus und tötete das
gute [Tier]⟨b⟩ (G:361)

bt. The mother . . . heard the child talking to someone, and
when she saw that she was striking a [paddock]⟨b⟩ with
her spoon, ran out . . . and killed the good little
*[beast]⟨b⟩ (HS:481)

style of English, *beast* does not smoothly function as a generic for *ant* or *pad-
dock* (= *toad*) and hence may not felicitously serve in a coreference chain with
either term.[2]

(9.9) **s**.

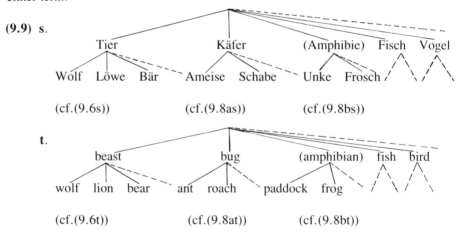

There remains one central portion of the problem to be addressed: the felicity of the German originals, (9.8as-bs). If *beast* is ill-suited to (9.8at-bt) because
of (9.9t), why, in parallel fashion, shouldn't *Tier* in (9.8as-bs) be counterin-
dicated by (9.9s)? The answer is quite simple when it is recognized that the German taxonomy of (9.9s), unlike its English counterpart (9.9t), is CONFLATIVE,
whereby the lexeme *Tier*, in addition to its NARROW-SENSE function as a generic
over wild mammals, also functions in the WIDE-SENSE as a supergeneric over all
wild sentient beings; see the filled-out trees in (9.10s). The final piece in the picture is Hunt and Stern's actual translation of *Tier(e)* in (9.8at-bt) as *creature(s)*,
which implies the nonconflative taxonomy of (9.10t).[3]

(9.10) s.

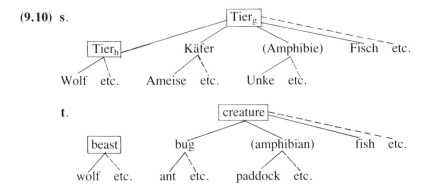

9.2 MATCHING AND DIFFUSIONAL DECONFLATION

Since an optimal translational response to taxonomic conflation in a source text will very often result in effective deconflation in the target text, whether for structural or strategical reasons (e.g. (9.8) and (9.4b), respectively), it is useful for translators to gain a rough-and-ready overview of at least some of the most common guises that deconflation may assume. One handy perspective is to classify deconflations trajectionally in terms of what might be called Matching and Diffusional techniques and to cross-classify this breakdown in terms of whether the conflative source element is sensically generic or hyponymic. In the case of source generics, both subtypes of trajectional deconflation have incidentally been presented up to this point: Matching (Substitution) of German *Tier*$_g$ by *creature* in (9.10), and Diffusion of Arabic *lahu* into *he (or she)* in (9.4).

A case of Diffusional deconflation of a conflative source hyponym may be seen in (9.11). Unlike the English noun *attempt*, Spanish *atentado* is conflative in having both a generic sense 'attempt in general' and a special, hyponymic sense 'attempt against a person's life'. Since it is the hyponymic sense intended in (9.11s), Rabassa appropriately renders the sense explicit in his English version (9.11t) by Diffusional addition of the modifying phrase *on his life*. One can appreciate both the sensical difference between the Spanish and English lexemes and the unobtrusive success of Rabassa's ploy by reading (9.11t), with *on his life* omitted. (The relevant taxonomic differences are plotted in (9.12).)

(9.11) s. Escapó a catorce [atentados], a setenta y tres
          emboscadas y a un pelotón de fusilamiento. (Márquez:93)
      t. He survived fourteen [attempts on his life],
          seventy-three ambushes, and a firing squad. (Rabassa:104)

An example of Matching deconflation of a source hyponym may be seen in (9.13a), with reference to the taxonomies of (9.13b): while Irish is like the Romance languages in having one lexeme with the wide sense of 'woman (in general)' and the narrow sense of 'wife' (cf. French *femme*, Italian *moglie*, Spanish *mujer*, Portuguese *mulher*), standard modern English unambiguously invests the two senses in the two distinct lexemes *woman* and *wife*, respectively.

(9.12) s.

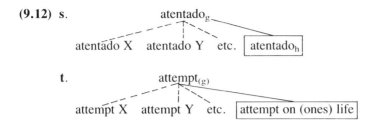

(9.13) as. 'Tá mo [bhean]—marbh' (Ní Shúilleabháin 1976:12)
   at. 'My [wife] is—dead' (M1980c:21)

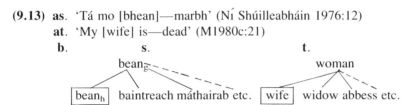

However, while many cases of Matching deconflation are just as simple and straightforward as (9.13a) appears to be, this case actually forms part of a nexus that demonstrates that deconflation cannot always be carried out with impunity to the function of the source text. Taken in isolation, the translation *bean* → *wife* in (9.13a) is fine.[4] The difficulty emerges when the excerpt is restored to its context, a dialogue in which the speaker, Tom, is talking with Liz, a woman with whom he is living extralegally in England, where they have run off together, deserting their respective spouses back in Ireland. The occasion of Tom's uttering (9.13as) is his guilty grief at his discovery that his legal wife has just died in Ireland. Liz, in turn, resenting and fearing Tom's sudden emotion toward the wife he had abandoned, reacts as in (9.14s):

(9.14) s. 'Mise do [bhean]', a mheas a sí a rá,
           ach ná dúirt (Ní Shúilleabháin 1976:12)
       t. 'I'm your [wife]', she thought to say,
           but didn't speak (M1980c:21)

The problem is not with (9.13as), (9.13at), or (9.14s), but with (9.14t). In the Irish dialogue, the fact that *bean* is a unitary lexical item despite its generic-hyponymic polysemy (cf. (.13bs)) allows Tom's utterance of *mo bhean* in (9.13as) to act as a stimulus to Liz's response *do bhean* in (9.14s), despite the fact that Liz need *not* be interpreted as specifically asserting 'I am your *wife*'— in fact, she could not be literally so interpreted, since patently it is the dead woman in Ireland who is Tom's wife. Indeed, there is nothing in the structure or function of the Irish text to warrant any interpretation narrower than the generic 'I am your *woman*', the switch from Tom's clearly intended 'wife' in (3.13as) notwithstanding. The LEXICAL integrity of the Irish noun *bean* is sufficient to render the connection between Tom's and Liz's utterances organic and so constitute an important type of RECURRENCE CHAIN (§3.2.2).

On the English side of the nexus, however, all is not so well. My translation of both tokens of *bhean* as *wife* necessarily induces a homogenization of sense from (9.13at) to (9.14t), which in turn forces a METAPHORICAL interpretation of Liz's thought as 'I'm your wife', a metaphor with no counterpart in the original 'Mise do bhean'. But under the circumstances, I felt I could do no better. English simply has no one lexical item whose semantic functions interact with its taxonomic structure as do those of *bean* (9.13), as the source text required. In this case, I decided that on balance it would be better to sacrifice a bit of the meaning (the sense switch between *mo bhean*$_h$ and *do bhean*$_g$) and retain the stimulus-response cohesiveness of the recurrence chain (*my wife*$_h$ . . . *your wife*$_h$), than to break the chain for the sake of retaining the sense switch (*my wife*$_h$ . . . *your woman*$_g$). (Cf. the similar case of *meall* 'deceive, lure' treated in M1979b.)

9.3 NONCE CONFLATION

Let us turn to the important notion of NONCE CONFLATION. A superficial examination of Tolstoy's original Russian phrase *ubijstva i careubijstva* in (9.15s) reveals a formal hint of something at first disguised in Edmonds's translation *murder and regicide*. The syntagmatic connection of three nouns in the conjunctive phrase *grabeža, ubijstva i careubijstva* leads us to expect that the referents jointly add up to some cohesive semantic whole, an expectation required equally, of course, of the translation *plunder, murder, and regicide*. But the second of the source nouns, *ubijstva*, an. 'murder', is morphologically included in the third noun, *care-ubijstva*, an. 'king-murder', a formal relation that languages often exploit in encoding the relations of a generic (included) to a hyponym (including). In fact, this seems patently true of this very case in Russian itself, since nouns denoting various kinds (hyponyms) of murder (*ubijstvo*[5] are in fact built up just like *care-ubijstva: otce-ubijstvo* 'parricide' (an. 'father-murder'), *brato-ubijstvo* 'fratricide' (an. 'brother-murder'), and so on.

But if these considerations rightly lead us to conclude that *careubijstva* 'regicide' (an. 'king-murder') is a kind of *ubijstva* 'murder', what kind of interpretation are we invited to give the phrase *grabeža, ubijstva i careubijstva* = *plunder, murder, and regicide?* Clearly this grouping is meant to convey a sample of heinous crimes, of which equally clearly either of the pairs *grabeža, ubijstva* (*plunder, murder*) or *grabeža, careubijstva* (*plunder, regicide*) succeeds in imparting two exemplars apiece. But what is meant to be imparted by the pair *ubijstva, careubijstva* (*murder, regicide*)? If this pair were to be understood in the same way as the other pairs, we would clearly not be presented with two independent exemplars of heinous crime, because by normal taxonomic definition *careubijstva* is a hyponym of *ubijstva*, so that open assertion of the latter automatically includes reference to the former; cf. (9.16).

(9.15) s. —Da, idei grabeža, [ubijstva i carcubijstva]—
        opjat' perebil ironičeskij golos (Tolstoy i:22)
   t. 'Yes, the idea of plunder, [murder, and regicide,]'
      an ironical voice interjected again (Edmonds i: 21)

(9.16)

The odd interpretation of (9.15) bespoken by (9.16) must certainly give way to a commonsense interpretation fully supported by the context: that Tolstoy did intend his three nouns to convey three exemplars of heinous crime, something like 'plunder, regicide, and *other* murders' or 'plunder, and murder of kings and commoners alike'. To do this, he availed himself of a device widespread in many languages, probably all languages, whereby a generic term (here *ubijstva*) is pressed into service as a NONCE HYPONYM, to be understood as semantically complementary to whatever other conventional hyponym or hyponyms (here *careubijstva*) are syntagmatically associated with it in the context. Thus the NONCE-CONFLATIVE TAXONOMY of (9.17s), whose nonce (neologistic) character consists in the special, context-bound usage of $ubijstvo_h$ to mean 'any or all instances of $ubijstvo_g$ except those of *careubijstvo*'. Note also that Edmonds's translation puts exactly the same interpretation on nonce-conflative $murder_h$, despite the morphological opacity of the English noun *murder* as compared to the noun *regicide*; (9.17t). Hence, despite the adlibitum character of the entire nexus, the trajection $ubijstva_h \rightarrow murder_h$ is at basis Equational.[6]

(9.17) s.

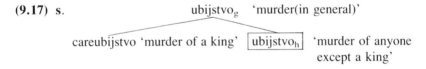

t.

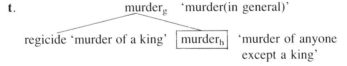

Through all the preceding discussion of conflation, the central role of SYNTAGMATIC OPPOSITION will have been noted. As has just been seen, it is a necessary condition for nonce conflation that the nonce-conflative hyponym ($ubijstvo_h$ = $murder_h$ of (9.17)) be co-occurrently paired with at least one conventionalized hyponym (*careubijstvo* = *regicide* of (9.17)); and in the case of ordinary conflation, the operation of Defusional deconflation was seen to be fundamentally syntagmatic: e.g., in (9.4b) Arabic $lahu_g$ (an. 'he') was disambiguated on the target side by pitting the conflative he_h against its opposing hyponym *she* in the group *he (or she)*.[7] In light of this importance, the suspicion arises that syntagmatic opposition might always induce the taxonomic relation of cohyponyms between elements of an otherwise appropriate type. For the great majority of cases, this might in fact be so. But I have run across superficially similar situations, especially in poetic language, where syntagmatic opposition appears to induce relations other than that of cohyponyms. A likely case in point from the Biblical psalms appears in (9.18a), a nexus that I had originally taken to be conflative along the lines of (9.18b). However, the philological-exegetical analysis of D.D. Brown et al. throws the matter into an entirely different light. According to them (1978:750), kɔɔliil (base form of -xɔɔliil) is employed as a 'descriptive synonym' of ʕoolɔɔ, and so presumably constitutes a sort of poetic highlighting mechanism devoid of (cognitive) semantic import. If so, the binomial phrase ʕoolɔɔ wəxɔɔliil would be semantically equivalent to either of its monomial components taken alone, and the King James version would be misleading at best.[8]

(9.18) **as.** ʔɔɔz taḥpoṣ zivḥee-ṣɛdɛq [ʕoolɔɔ wəxɔɔliil]
(K:Psalms 51,21)

at. Then shalt thou be pleased with the sacrifices of righteousness, with [burnt offering and whole burnt offering] (KJ: Psalms 51,19)

bs. ʕoolɔɔ_g — ʕoolɔɔ_h — kɔɔliil

bt. burnt offering_g — burnt offering_h — whole burnt offering

NOTES

1. Some of the work in this general area that I have found most relevant is that of Cecil Brown, Stanley Witkowski, and their associates (see the Bibliography for samples), though I hasten to add that these scholars should not be held responsible for this chapter, which was developed independently (drawing heavily on the more comprehensive but somewhat dated M1979b).

2. The parentheses around *Amphibie* and *amphibian* mark the questionable status of these terms colloquially (cf. §9(i)).

3. Independent evidence for *Tier* in the narrow sense (*Tier*ₕ of (9.10s)) may be seen in the Biblical enumeration of creatures in Genesis 1,30: *und allen[Thieren]⟨a⟩ der Erde, und allem [Geflügel]⟨b⟩ des Himmels, und allem, [das sich reget auf Erden]⟨c⟩* . . . (Alioli) = *and to every [beast]⟨a⟩ of the earth, and to every [fowl]⟨b⟩ of the air, and to every [thing that creepeth upon the earth]⟨c⟩* . . . (KJ). Here, *Thieren* (dative plural of *Tier* in the old spelling) is clearly referentially distinct from both fowl and creeping things.

4. The spelling *bhean* reflects a phonological modification induced by the proclitic *mo*.

5. Within the source text, the forms end in *-a*, which marks the genitive case. The forms in nominative-accusative *-o* constitute normal Russian citation forms for nouns.

6. Nonce conflation appears to be an extremely commonplace phenomenon, and since becoming analytically aware of it I have accrued a large and varied collection of examples. (Some are analyzed in M1979a, including a syntactic rather than a lexical case.) Note just one recent unilinguistic example, from a short story:

'They [squirrels] come right down out of the trees and climb in your pockets and help themselves to [nuts], [peanuts] or whatever you might have' (Schuler:13).

Clearly, *nuts* here denotes 'nuts other than peanuts'.

7. The incipient appearance of nonce-conflative items PARADIGMATICALLY, with no accompanying (and opposing) conventionalized hyponyms, may signal the emergence of true conflative polysemy; see Brown (1984b) for discussion and examples.

8. Similar to taxonomies are PARTONOMIES, semantic arrays where higher taxa stand to lower taxa in the relation of PART TO WHOLE. As was treated in M1979a:§6, partonomies share many translation-relevant properties with taxonomies, including conflation: for instance, Russian *ruka* may Diverge into English *arm* qua name-of-the-whole (e.g. Tolstoy i:549/Edmonds i:660), but into *hand* qua name-of-the-part (e.g. Tolstoy i:304/Edmonds i:359). The concept of partonomy stems from C. Brown et al. (1976); see also Witkowski and Brown (1985).

Chapter *10*

ZEROES

10.0 PRELIMINARIES

The concept of ZERO (NULL), first introduced by Roman Jakobson, has served theoretical linguistics long and well in an impressive variety of areas, and it is hence not surprising that it should prove useful in applied linguistics also. A number of translational cases will be discussed here.

Looked at informally, most uses of zero in linguistics involve its role as a SLOT FOR OR TRACE OF SOME ELEMENT. This might be illustrated by fitting out the schemata for Amplification and Reduction (§1.1) with zeroes, the conventional linguistic symbol for which is '∅'. Thus, Reductional AB → A becomes AB → A∅, where the ∅, as it were, designates a trace of the lost B; and Amplificational A → AB becomes A∅ → AB, where the ∅ may be said to mark a slot for the B to be gained—a pair of usages that were incidentally illustrated with example (1.4). It will be convenient to refer generically to both slot and trace zeroes as PLACEHOLDERS.[1]

10.1 ZEROES IN RECURRENCE AND COREFERENCE CHAINS; BIBLICAL HEBREW PARALLELISM

Recrescental zeroes may be used in combination with coreference and recurrence chains to mark off certain links as placeholders. Among other things, such a procedure with a coreference chain can supply a rough measure of the referential information implicit in a text. Two examples are given in provisional form in (10.1) and (10.2), which repeat (parts of) (1.3a) and (2.1), respectively. In (10.1s), the German coreference chain $Sie\langle a\rangle$, an. 'you$\langle a\rangle$ . . . you$\langle a\rangle$', is trajected by Reduction onto $\emptyset\langle a\rangle$ . . . $you\langle a\rangle$ in (10.1t). The trajection of the first link, $Sie\langle a\rangle \rightarrow \emptyset\langle a\rangle$, represents both a similarity and a difference between the German and English imperative constructions: while under normal discourse conditions an imperative verb in both languages is understood as second person, only in German is this information *explicitly* conveyd by the pronoun Sie *(hören Sie*, an. 'listen you'), English rather conveying the same information *implicitly (listen)*. The explicit-implicit difference is represented by the Reduction $Sie \rightarrow \emptyset$, while the similarity in reference is captured by the indexical Equation $\langle a\rangle \rightarrow \langle a\rangle$; conjointly, $Sie\langle a\rangle \rightarrow \emptyset\langle a\rangle$.

(10.1) (= (1.3a))

    s. Nun hören Sie$\langle a\rangle$ einmal zu, Neuer, sind Sie$\langle a\rangle$
       katholisch? (B:201)

    t. listen $\phi\langle a\rangle$, new one, tell me, are you$\langle a\rangle$ a Catholic? (X:216)

An example in the opposite direction, involving Amplificational gain of a pronoun in the English target, is given in (10.2), a portion of the Homeric Greek example treated in (2.1). In this case the trajection $nukse\ \emptyset\langle b\rangle \rightarrow stabbed\ him\ \langle b\rangle$ reflects the difference that the Greek source dispenses with an object pronoun (*nukse*, an. 'stabbed') which English requires (**Patroclos came quite close and stabbed* would be poor), while the identity of reference is captured by the identity of indices in $\emptyset\langle b\rangle \rightarrow him\langle b\rangle$.

(10.2) (= (2.1))

    s. ho de$\langle a\rangle$ Thespora$\langle b\rangle$, Ēnopos huion, deuteron
       hormētheis . . . ho d'$\langle a\rangle$ egkheï nukse $\phi\langle b\rangle$parastas
       (H ii:81[XVI,401–404]

    t. Next he$\langle a\rangle$ drove at Thespor$\langle b\rangle$ . . . Patroclos$\langle a\rangle$ came
       quite close and stabbed him$\langle b\rangle$ (R:194f)

As mentioned above, examples (10.1) and (10.2) were said to be given 'in provisional form'. The reservation concerned a tacit liberty taken with the zeroes, which must now be corrected and discussed. For preliminary convenience, the target $\emptyset\langle a\rangle$ in (10.1t) was positioned correlatively to its source correspondent $Sie\langle a\rangle$ in (10.1s), which is to say, immediately following the verb *listen*, just as Sie immediately follows its verb *hören*. Similarly, the source $\emptyset\langle b\rangle$ in (10.2s) was positioned correlatively to the target $him\langle b\rangle$, in (10.2t), postpositively to the verb (*nukse* = *stabbed*) in both cases. However, to get maximum benefit from the use of zero in translational analysis, it is advisable to position zeroes in accordance with the rules and patterns specific to the language in focus, rather than on the analogy of the paired translational language. This precept is straightforwardly demonstrable for case (10.2s), where $\emptyset\langle b\rangle$ should precede *nukse*, since in Homeric Greek object pronouns, when they are used, normally distribute prepositively to the verbs that take them as arguments: e.g. *phrazōmesth ' hōs ken [[min]][aressamenoi pepithōmen]* (H i: 165[IX,112]), an. 'let-us-consider how [[him]] [appeasing we-might-persuade]' = *Let us consider how we can [appease][[him]]* (R:104).

Similar reasoning leads us to change (10.1t) from *Listen ∅⟨a⟩* to *⟨∅⟩a listen*, since in cases when the pronoun *you* is overtly used with an imperative verb, to punctuate the urgency of the command or the like, the normal order is *you VB*; e.g., *You listen to your mother, Sal!*, not **Listen you to your mother, Sal!*[2]

These corrections are given in (10.3), pursuant to the rule of thumb summarized in (10.4):

(**10.3**) **a**. ɸ⟨a⟩ listen, new one, tell me, are you⟨a⟩ a
 Catholic? (replaces (10.1t))
 b. ho de⟨a⟩ Thespora⟨b⟩ Ēnopos huion, deuteron
 hormētheis . . . ho d'⟨a⟩ egkheï ɸ⟨b⟩ nukse parastas
 (replaces (10.2s))

(**10.4**) **a**. Where possible, zeroes should be distributed in
 accordance with the rules and patterns of the
 language in question.
 b. *Zeroes as links in coreference chains.* As a special
 but important case, zeroes should
 be positioned in the same slots that would be occupied
 by coreferent overt forms, had the latter been used.

There are areas where accurate positioning of zeroes assumes special importance, areas that generally speaking have in common requirements of textual symmetry which, under certain circumstances, can be achieved by either overt forms or zeroes. A fine illustration can be provided from Edward Greenstein's pioneering work reanalyzing Biblical parallelism from the vantage point of modern syntactic theory (1974, 1982, 1983).[3] In Biblical parallelism, an example of which was seen in (8.4b = 8.5b), the two hemistichs of a verse are syntactically either identical or symmetrically related (notably by chiasmus), and morphologically filled out by semantically related forms distributed in a one-to-one fashion. Thus, the partially chiastic example of (8.5b) might be schematized *CONJ VB PP ‖ CONJ' PP' VB'*, where *CONJ* = the conjunction *ʔim-*'if' in the first hemistich and *CONJ'* = the conjunction *wə-* 'and' in the second hemistich; the same holds for the paired verbs *VB* = *təvaqšɛnnɔɔ* 'thou-seekest-her' and *VB'* = *tahpaśśɛnnɔɔ* 'thou-searchest-for-her', and the prepositional phrases *PP'* = *xakkɛsɛf* 'as-silver' and *PP'* = *xammaṭmooniim* 'as-hid-treasures'. (As was seen, the King James translation of this verse (3.4b) by and large maintains the parallelistic effect of the Hebrew original, though modified by Diffusion and Reordering.)

Simply stated, part of Greenstein's discovery is that numerous cases of what had traditionally been analyzed as DEFECTIVE PARALLELISM can be reanalyzed as full (or nearly full) parallelism if zeroes are posited in one or more slots of the second hemistich. This may be nicely illustrated with the three consecutive verses from Psalm 33 given in (10.5) (cf. Greenstein 1982 46f). Thus, if in (sa) the conjunction *kii*, 'for' leading off the first hemistich, is answered by a zero leading off the second hemistich, the verse ascends from defective-parallelistic *CONJ PRN VB VB* ‖ *PRN' VB' VB'* to fully parallel *CONJ PRN VB VB* ‖ *CONJ' PRN' VB' VB'*. Similarly, in (sb), if lead-off *YHWH* '(the ineffable name of) God' is answered by a zero in the second hemistich, defective *NP VB NP* ‖ *VP' NP'* becomes full *NP VB NP* ‖ *NP' VP' NP'*. Example (sc) involves a correspondence at the end of the hemistichs, the verb *taʕămoḏ* 'standeth' and ∅, whence fully parallelistic *NP PP VB* ‖ *NP' PP' VB'*.

It may be noted that while all the zeroes in (10.5s) are placed in accordance with general clause (a) of rule of thumb (10.4)—in each case, respectively, a conjunction, noun phrase, or verb could legitimately occupy the slot of the zero—only in case (10.5sb) does a relation of COREFERENCE obtain between an overt NP (*YHWH*⟨b⟩) and the zero (∅⟨b⟩). In (sa) and (sc), on the other hand, the indices do not stand for coreference but rather for IDENTITY OF SENSE, or SYNONYMY. This can be most clearly appreciated in (sc), where the instance of 'standing' predicated by the verb *taʕămoḏ* of God's counsel in the first hemistich (cf. (tc)) is not the same instance as that predicated of His heart in the second hemistich. Rather, the MEANING of 'stand' is taken to be identical in both cases, even though predicated of distinct referents.

(10.5) **sa**. kii⟨a⟩ huu ʔɔɔmar wayyɛɛhii ‖
    ф⟨a⟩ huu-ṣiwwɔɔ wayyaʕămoḏ (K:Psalms 33, 9)

    sb. YHWH⟨b⟩ heefiir ʕăṣaθ-gooyiim ‖
    ф⟨b⟩ heenii maḥšăvooθ ʕammiim (33, 10)

    sc. ʕăṣaθ YHWH ləʕoolɔɔm taʕămoḏ⟨c⟩ ‖
    maḥšăvooθ libboo ləḏoor wɔɔḏoor ф⟨c⟩ (33,11)

    ta. For⟨a⟩ he spake, and it was done;
    ф⟨a⟩ he commanded, and it stood fast (KJ)

    tb. The LORD⟨b⟩ bringeth the counsel of the heathen to naught:
    he⟨b⟩ maketh the devices of the people of none effect (KJ)

    tc. The counsel of the LORD standeth⟨c⟩ for ever,
    the thoughts of his heart ф⟨c⟩ to all generations (KJ)

The upshot of this difference between (10.5sb) on the one hand and (10.5sa-sc) on the other is the addition of a second special-case clause (10.6) to the rule of thumb of (10.4):

(10.6) (= (10.4c))
    Zeroes as links in recurrence chains. Zeroes should be
    positioned in the same slots as would be occupied by
    synonymous overt forms, had the latter been used.

It may now easily be seen why a principled distribution of zeroes is so vital for the analysis of parallelism along the lines suggested by Greenstein's innovative work. To illustrate the point with (10.5s), if any of the three zeroes had been distributed without regard to the structural contours of Hebrew, the parallelistic effect would be impaired or even destroyed. Thus, for $\emptyset = NP'$ in (sb), only *NP VB NP* $\| \emptyset VB' NP'$ manifests parallelism. Any other positioning would break the pattern: e.g. *NP VB NP $\| VB' \emptyset NP'$, *NP VB BP $\| VB' NP' \emptyset$.

Let us turn briefly to the King James versions of these verses, in (10.5t). As is characteristic of the King James translators, they have by and large replicated the parallelism of the original—and to that extent have responded Equationally, though to the tune of a good deal of structural Diffusion generally symptomatic of English's looser morphological organization (e.g. in the extrusion as independent words of numerous functors like *he, it, the, and, of, to*, which in Hebrew are signaled by modification of a noun or verb). Note finally the response of the translators to the source-text zeroes. In the two cases where English syntax would allow it, ((a) and (c)), these have been Equated into the target. In the remaining case, (b), pronominal Amplification was used ($\emptyset\langle b\rangle \rightarrow he\langle b\rangle$). (I suspect that this Equational-Amplificational response is accurately representative of the general King James strategy in trajecting parallelistic zeroes, but validation of this suspicion must await study of a much larger sample of verses.)

(10.7) s. On$\langle a1\rangle$? $\phi\langle a2\rangle$ P'janica! $\phi\langle a3\rangle$ Učitelem byl—
vygnali $\phi\langle a4\rangle$. $\phi\langle a5\rangle$ Propilsja, $\phi\langle a6\rangle$ pišet v gazety,
$\phi\langle a7\rangle$ sočinjaet prošenija. $\phi\langle a8\rangle$ Očen' podlyj
čelovek! (Gorky:316)

t. He$\langle a1\rangle$? He$\langle a2\rangle$'s a drunkard! He$\langle a3\rangle$ was a schoolteacher,
and $\phi\langle a4\rangle$ got turned away. He$\langle a5\rangle$ has drunk all he had,
and now he$\langle a6\rangle$ writes for the newspapers, and $\phi\langle a7\rangle$
invents petitions. He$\langle a8\rangle$'s a real bad 'un!
(Montefiore and Jakowleff:70)

10.2 ZEROES IN THE STUDY OF STYLE AND TEXTUAL AMBIGUITY

Zeroes will be seen below to play a vital role in combination with other techniques at several junctures, but we may conclude this chapter with brief illustrations of two case types to which postulation of zeroes seems particularly well geared: (i) the analysis of textual conciseness or terseness (laconism, telegraphism, clipped style, etc.); (ii) the analysis of textual ambiguity.

(i) There is a style of colloquial Russian well known for its conciseness of expression, a conciseness enhanced (though not predetermined) by various morphosyntactic properties alien to various important target languages (perhaps notably English and French) and hence not easily replicable in translation. An example from a short story by Gorky is given in (10.7), where a simple word-count ratio (Russian 15/English 34) probably vindicates the strong impression of the bilingual reader that the English translation by Montefiore and Jakowleff fails to reconstruct the quintessential terseness of the original. But though several facets of Russian conspire to this overall telegraphic effect, construction of a conference chain for the character being denigrated here is quite revealing of much of the terseness: except for the lead-off $On\langle a1 \rangle$ 'he', all seven remaining links are zeroes. The English translation, on the other hand, succeeds in replicating only two of these zeroes ($\langle a4 \rangle$, $\langle a5 \rangle$), all the others being Amplified to he — a strategy which, compounded by considerable Diffusion elsewhere in the passage, virtually destroys the stylistic impact of the original.

(ii) Many languages allow omission of pronominal subjects of verbs under a wide range of circumstances, and though the potential loss of information thereby incurred is often counteracted linguistically (e.g. by compensatory markings on the verb) or situationally (contextually), the danger of ambiguity is sometimes real indeed. Thus, Spanish freely omits subject pronouns under most circumstances, and though informational loss is in large part offset by differential suffixes on the verb, there is no such morphological protection against the loss of gender differences when the pronouns $él$ 'he' and $ella$ 'she' are suppressed.

A situation of this type, even an intricate one, can become a facile object of analysis through the use of coreference chains with zero links. For instance, the passage in (10.8s) is unusual, particularly for the writing of Gabriel Márquez, in containing two reference switches, $\emptyset\langle b2 \rangle$ and $\emptyset\langle c1 \rangle$, providing no structural cues at all, and at best retroactive contextual cues, as to the intended reference. Thus, $\emptyset\langle b2 \rangle$, *Nunca llevó amistad íntima con nadie* could, even in the immediate con-

(10.8) s. $\phi\langle a1 \rangle$ Pasaba la mayor parte del día encerrado en el
despacho, y en las pocas ocasiones en que $\phi\langle a2 \rangle$
salía a la calle $\phi\langle a3 \rangle$ regresaba antes de
las seis, para acompañarla$\langle b1 \rangle$ a rezar el rosario.
$\phi\langle b2 \rangle$ Nunca llevó amistad íntima con nadie. . . .
Sonaron dos aldabonazos perentorios en el portón, y
$\phi\langle b3 \rangle$ le abrió a un militar apuesto$\phi\langle c1 \rangle$, de ademanes
ceremoniosos, que tenía una cicatriz en la mejilla
y una medalla de oro en el pecho. $\phi\langle c2 \rangle$ Se encerró
con su padre en el despacho. (Márquez:176)

t. He$\langle a1 \rangle$ spent most of his time locked up in his study
and the few times that he$\langle a2 \rangle$ went out he$\langle a3 \rangle$ would
return to recite the rosary with her$\langle b1 \rangle$. She$\langle b2 \rangle$
had intimate friendships with no one. . . . Two
peremptory raps of the knocker sounded at the door
and she$\langle b3 \rangle$ opened it to a well-groomed military
officer$\langle c1 \rangle$ with ceremonious manners who had a scar
on his cheek and a gold medal on his chest. He$\langle c2 \rangle$
closeted himself with her father in the study. (Rabassa:196)

text, be misunderstood as *$He\langle a4 \rangle$had intimate friendship with no one* rather than *She$\langle b2 \rangle$ had intimate friendship with no one*, as intended by Márquez and correctly rendered by Rabassa. In a case of this sort, the use of zeroes in the source text makes it possible to assess the structure and felicity of the translation modeled as a series of Divergent Amplifications of the paradigmatic form $\emptyset \rightarrow$ *she/he*, differentially implemented syntagmatically as $\emptyset \rightarrow$ *she* (e.g. at $\langle b2 \rangle$) versus $\emptyset \rightarrow$ *he* (e.g. at the second trouble spot, $\langle c1 \rangle$).

Notes

1. The term 'trace' is not being used in the technical sense of so-called government and binding (GB) theory (e.g. Chomsky 1982), though various of the examples to be treated below would in fact pass as GB traces.

2. Notwithstanding the more or less set expression *Listen, you!*, where the pronoun is best taken as an appositional vocative per se independent from the imperative construction; cf. the nonimperative *Hey, you!* or *You listen, Sal!*, a syntagm that brings out both the vocative nature of the postverbal slot and its opposition to the genuine preverbal subject.

3. For detailed discussion of Biblical parallelism, see also O'Connor (1980).

Chapter *11*

ABSTRACT
SYNTACTIC
REPRESENTATIONS

11.0 PRELIMINARIES: THE NOTION
OF "GOVERNMENT".

An important notion of long heritage within the grammatical tradition of the Occident is that of GOVERNMENT, according to which certain aspects of a sentence's form and function are determined, or GOVERNED, by some specific element within the same sentence. While both the variety of governing elements and the range of forms and functions determined by them are rather large and, as will be seen later, have been growing even larger under explication by modern linguistic theory, the phenomenon of government is perhaps best (and most infamously) known to students of Classical Greek and Latin from two areas that can prove quite vexing to the beginner: the government of various noun cases by verbs or prepositions, and government by a main-clause verb of the form and function of a subordinate clause.[1]

11.1 THE LATIN ACCUSATIVE-WITH-INFINITIVE
CONSTRUCTION

While a few examples have incidentally been provided of case government (e.g. (1.9), (2.1)), the focus here will be on the more complex issue of government by main-clause verbs of subordinate clauses. A well-known example from Latin is the so-called ACCUSATIVE WITH INFINITIVE construction, wherein the verb of a subordinate clause appears as an infinitive, and its subject assumes the accusative case. What makes this construction an instance of government is the fact that its use is restricted to sentences whose main clauses contain specific verbs. Moreover, the inventory of governing verbs is by no means constant across Latin authors. Thus, Furneaux's discussion of Tacitus's use of the construction starts off with these words — '*The accus. with infin.* — is used by Tacitus with *adnecto*, IV 28,2; *illacrymo* II 71,4; *incuso* III 38,4' (Furneaux:15) — the sense of which is that, among Tacitus's conditions for using the accusative with infinitive construction, is the appearance in the main clause of one of the verbs (in some conjugational form) *adnecto* 'connect', *illacrymo* 'lament', or *incuso* 'criticize'.

It will be instructive to track down these examples to their sources, in (11.1s), where the intercalated analytic translations should provide some feel and structural understanding of how the accusative with infinitive construction works.

In each case the verbs are set off in brackets, that of the main clause preceding the infinitival one of the subordinate clause (e.g. respectively, [adnectebatque] and [ministravisse] in (sa)), while (a key portion of) the infinitive's accusative subject is italicized (e.g. *Caecilium Cornutum* in (sa)).

Consideration of Grant's English versions in (11.1t) immediately suggests that the idiosyncracies of a source-language's government patterns cannot be expected to traject uniformly (let alone Equationally) into a target language, which will have its own governmental peculiarities. Thus, in (tb) and (tc) Grant clearly Diverges Tacitus's accusative with infinitive, pursuant to the governmental characteristics of the English main-clause verbs *lament* and *criticize*: in the one case into a finite-verb construction introduced by the complementizer *that* (*that . . . has fallen*), and in the other case into a gerundial construction introduced by the preposition *for* (*for not avenging*). Grant's response is more oblique in (ta), where he has, by Reduction, omitted trajecting *adnectebatque* altogether, leaving its force to be deduced from the context, and then upgrading the source subordinate clause to main-clause status.

Nor by any means need the diversity in government always be on the target side, a point that is demonstrated by the complex excerpt in (11.2). In this case, the main-clause verb *censuit* 'proposed' governs a series of four subordinate clauses split over two distinct constructions: the accusative with gerundive construction for the first two subordinate verbs ([eradendum], [publicandam], glossed in the analytic translation, 'deletable', 'confiscatable'); and for the last two, a subjunctive verb construction ([concederatur], [mutaret] = 'should-be-allowed', 'should-change'), introduced by the complementizer [ut] ('that').

Variation in government constructions along the lines illustrated in (11.1) and (11.2) will be found to be the rule rather than the exception, whatever the languages involved, and the question of how best to model it for translational purposes deserves care and precision. This will be the focus of the next section.

(11.1) sa. [adnectebatque] *Caecilium Cornutum* praetorium
[ministravisse] pecuniam (Tacitus: 181[IV 28,2])
an.'[and-he-connected] *Caecilius Cornutus*
praetor [to-have-provided] funds'

  sb. etiam quos invidia erga viventem movebat,
[inlacrimabunt] quondam florentem et tot bellorum
superstitem muliebri fraude [cecidisse] (Tacitus: 121[II 71,4]
an.'even those-whom envy toward the-living-man moved,
[will-lament] once flourishing and so-many wars
survivor by-womanly treachery [to-have-fallen]'

  sb. neque minus *Rhoemetalcen* . . . [incusans] popularium
iniurias inultas [sinere] (Tacitus: 147[III 38,4])
an.'nor less *Rhoemetalces* . . . [criticizing] people's
wrongs unavenged [to-permit]

  ta. funds [had been provided] by an ex-praetor,
Marcus Caecilius Cornutus (Grant:171)

  tb. even those who envied me in my life, [will lament]
[that] the once flourishing survivor of many campaigns
[has fallen] to a woman's treachery (Grant:112)

  tc. and Rhoemetalces was as forcibly [criticized] . . .
[for not avenging] his people's wrong (Grant:138)

(11.2) s. consul . . . *nomen* Pisonis [eradendum] fastis [censuit],
partem bonorum [publicandam], *pars* [ut] C. Pisoni
filio [concederetur] *is*que praenomen [mutaret]
(Tacitus: 137[III 17, 8])
an.'consul . . . *name* of-Piso [deletable] from-the-calendar
[proposed], *half* of-property [confiscatable], *half*
[that] to-Cnaeus Piso son [should- be-allowed] and-*he*
first-name [should-change]'

  t. the consul's proposal was that Piso's name could be
deleted from the calendar; that half his property
should be confiscated and the other half allowed to
his son Cnaeus, who should change his first name (Grant:127)

11.2 SOME GUIDELINES FOR SYNTHESIZING ABSTRACT SYNTACTIC REPRESENTATIONS (ASRs)

Since, as has been illustrated in (11.1) and (11.2), government patterns evince variation both unilinguistically and translinguistically, it would be useful for analytic purposes to start with some relatively neutral representation of relevant clause structures, so that the differential workings of government can be modeled as differential formal and functional impact on the neutral representations. An effective way of doing this is through an adaptation of the theoretical linguist's notion of DEEP or UNDERLYING STRUCTURE, which, in what follows, will be called ABSTRACT SYNTACTIC REPRESENTATION (ASR)—a portrayal of morphosyntactic relations designed to maximize both semantic transparency and, as a partial by-product of that, uniformity of structural modeling. Several *guidelines* will be introduced as helpmates to build up ASRs, the first of which has the function of neutralizing differences between subordinate and main clauses (henceforth to be called EMBEDDED and MATRIX clauses, respectively):[2]

(11.3) To the extent useful or possible, embedded clauses may be represented as if they were synonymous matrix clauses.

Using paired curly braces to mark off clause boundaries, guideline (11.3) is quite simple to implement in the case of English *that*-clauses: omit the complementizer *that*. This procedure leads to rerepresenting the first part of (11.2t) as *{the consul's proposal was {Piso's name could be deleted from the calendar} }*—a notation that may alternatively be either simplified by omitting the matrix braces (*the consul's proposal {Piso's name could be deleted from the calendar}*), or enriched by tagging both clauses ($_0$ *{the consol's proposal was* $_1$ *{Piso's name would be deleted from the calendar}*$_1$*}*$_0$, where conventionally '0' tags the most inclusive matrix clause—the so-called ROOT CLAUSE—and successively embedded clauses are tagged '1', '2', . . . 'n', pursuant to depth), or a combination of both (*the consul's proposal was* $_1$ *{Piso's name could be deleted from the calendar}*$_1$), all subject to expository convenience.

Abstract representation of most other embedded clause types in English will normally entail other factors, as may be seen in the question that immediately arises if we follow the lead of (11.2t) and attempt to rerepresent (11.1tc) using only (11.3). If we isolate *{for not avenging his people's wrong}* as the surface (concrete) string corresponding to the embedded clause, and proceed on the analogy of *that*-removal to remove the *for* and *-ing*, which mark a gerundial clause of this type as being embedded, we end up with the structurally and conceptually incomplete *{not avenge his people's wrong}*. The factor that most saliently marks this string as unclause-like is its apparent lack of a sujbect NP. A guideline to rectify this can, in the present context, be viewed as ancillary to (11.3), though it is actually an independent principle:

(11.4) Elements semantically present but morphosyntactically absent may be structurally represented.

In regard to the implementation of (11.4), we already have one device that may be used in coreference and recurrence chains—that of COINDEXED ZEROES (cf. (10.4), (10.6)), a technique that leads to an abstract representation of (11.tc) along these lines: *and Rhoemetalces⟨a⟩ was as forcibly criticized {Ø⟨a⟩ does not avenge his people's wrong}*. Alternatively, a semantically implicit but formally missing element may be given by generalizing the form of some non-null link in its own chain and so modeling a coreference chain as a RECURRENCE CHAIN. Thus: *and Rhoemetalces⟨a⟩ was as forcibly criticized {Rhoemetalces⟨a⟩* does not avenge his people's wrong}.

Though in this case coindexing happens to provide one means of implementing (11.4), tagging elements for coreference is actually a desideratum of abstract representation in its own right. Thus, we have a third guideline:

(11.5) Coreference relations may be indicated.

In fact, the independence of (11.5) from (11.4) can also be illustrated with (11.1tc), since the pronoun *his* of *his people's wrong* refers to Rhoemetalces, despite its concrete morphosyntactic presence. Thus: *{Rhoemetalces⟨a⟩ does not avenge his⟨a⟩ people's wrong}*, or using the recurrence technique: *{Rhoemetalces ⟨a⟩ does not avenge Rhoemetalces'⟨a⟩ people's wrong}*.

The reader may have noted that in applying guideline (11.3) to (11.1tc), the negative gerund *not avenging* was tacitly replaced by the finite group *does not avenge*, a decision that might be questioned. Why might not the replacing string have been DID *not avenge,* since the matrix verb is in the past tense? Indeed, reasonable arguments could be made in favor of either choice, but to insist too strongly on either would be to overlook an important fact about most types of embedding. By their very nature, embedded clauses tend to be formally and semantically parasitic on the matrix clauses within which they are set, so that often the attempt to rerepresent them as if they were fully independent matrices (root clauses) in their own right will simply fail. To deal with this, the following guideline is useful:

(11.6) Properties of an element determined syntagmatically by other elements may be omitted from an ASR.

In the specific case of (11.1tc), the gerund *avenging* is susceptible to (11.6) because of at least two omissible properties: *tense,* as determined by the matrix verb *was . . . criticized*; and *subject-person,* as determined by the abstract *Rhoemetalces⟨a⟩* or *∅⟨a⟩* (itself determined by the matrix subject in terms of (11.4) and (11.5)). While it is often possible to avail oneself of feature notation (§4.1.1) to provide formally explicit models of abstract elements deprived of properties by (11.6), it will in many situations be sufficient to use informal abbreviations. In the case of verbs like *avenging* in (11.1tc), capitalization of the bare stem will be employed. Hence, *AVENGE* = 'any specific form of the verb *(to) avenge* determined syntagmatically'. Thus: *{Rhoemetalces⟨a⟩ not AVENGE Rhoemetalces'⟨a⟩ people's wrong}*.

One last guideline for synthesizing ASRs will be presented in this section, an important but rather involved principle whose formulation is best staved off until we can examine some data motivating it. Let us start with the unilinguistic case in (11.7), comparing the nineteenth-century British dialect syntax in (a) with its constructed contemporary American counterpart in (b). The first problem with these strings is that application of the guidelines introduced thus far fails to provide a uniform abstract representation of the embedded clauses, despite their presumed synonymy and identical government by the matrix verb *asks*. Guideline (11.3) is inapplicable to (11.7a), since {*does he know the name of Rouncewell thereabouts*} already has the form of the synonymous root question; nor can it remove the *whether* in (11.7b) without losing the interrogative meaning of the clause, since {*he knows the name of Rouncewell thereabouts*} is formally identical to a root declarative, not to a root question. Guideline (11.4) is patently inapplicable, and though (11.5) and (11.6) might irrelevantly apply to neutralize subject agreement in *does* to *DO* and *knows* to *KNOW*, and coindex *he* with *workman*, the essential problem would be unchanged:

(11.7) a. the trooper . . . asks a workman {does he know the name of Rouncewell thereabouts} (Dickens 1980[orig.1853]:847)

     b. The trooper . . . asks a workman {whether he knows the name of Rouncewell thereabouts} (constructed)

The general problem with cases like (11.7) is that of dissimilar formal means encoding similar meanings. In particular here, whilte the interrogative nature of the embedded clause is signaled MORPHEMICALLY in (11.7b), by the complementiser *whether*, the same interrogative value in (11.7a) is encoded TAGMEMICALLY, by manipulating the word order of the subject and verb (with the help of the auxiliary-verb *does*; cf. the discussion of (11.13) in §11.3).

Moreover, the type of morphemic-tagmemic discrepancy instantiated unilinguistically in (11.7) is quite widespread translinguistically, notably but not exclusively in interrogative clauses. Thus, the Irish original of the tagmemically signaled English interrogative root clause in (11.8at) evidences morphemic organization, via the lead-off element *ná-*, a root-clause negative analogue of *whether* (an. 'Whether-not-was beautiful the color of-hair that was on-her'; (cf. declarative *níor dheas* . . . an. 'Not-was-beautiful . . . ' with the same word order, meaning 'She didn't have beautiful hair'). On the other hand, the Russian original of the morphemically signaled English embedded interrogative in (11.8bt) shows mixed morphemic-tagmemic structure: different order from non-interrogative *on ne sdelal*, an.' he not did (anything reprehensible)', plus intercalation of the interrogative morpheme *li*: *ne sdelal li on*, an. 'not did whether he'.

(11.8) as. nár dheas an dath gruaige a bhí uirthi? (Ní Shúilleabháin 1977:5)

     at. Didn't she have beautiful hair? (M1983b:83)

     bs. I P'er, so straxom vspominaja, {ne sdelal li on
čego-nibud' predosuditel'nogo}, krasneja, ogljanulsja
vokrug sebja (Tolstoy i: 204)

     bt. And Pierre, frantically trying to think {whether
he had been guilty of anything reprehensible},
crimsoned and looked about him (Edmonds i: 237)

From among the variety of pure-linguistic solutions that have been proposed over the years for the problem of morphemic-tagmemic discrepancy, I have synthesized guideline (11.9), which I believe is, on balance, probably the most useful for translational purposes:

(11.9) a. The elements of a clause may be represented in the most neutral order possible. For many languages, such an order will be that of a positive indicative declarative active sentence with no special informational emphasis; but language-specific differences will often dictate other properties.

   b. Tagmemes may be rerepresented as abstract morphemes.

Returning now to (11.7), guideline (11.9) dispatches the problem in the following way. For (11.7a), procedure (11.9a) dictates a change to {*he knows the name of Rouncewell thereabouts*}, the most neutral analogue of the embedded clause {*does he know the name of Rouncewell thereabouts*}. However, since this neutralization has, in the process, lost the interrogative tagmeme signaled by the special order {*does he know . . .*}, procedure (11.9b) dictates that this marking be reinstated in the form of an abstract morpheme synonymous with the neutralized tagmeme. Following one convention we may use the symbol 'Q' for the abstract interrogative morpheme and position it in the same slot where overt complementizers occur in English, i.e. clause-initially: {*Q he knows the name of Rouncewell thereabouts*}.

Going back to (11.7b), we note first that (11.9) is not applicable: the elements of {*whether he knows . . .*} are already in neutral order, and there are no tagmemes to replace. However, we also note that this clause differs from the just-abstracted {*Q he knows . . .*} only by having the concrete complementizer *whether* in lieu of the abstract *Q*. Moreover, *whether* is itself an interrogative morpheme. Therefore, it is legitimate and desirable to replace *Q* by *whether* in the abstract version of (11.7a), so that the embedded clauses of both it and (11.7b) now appear as {*whether he knows the name of Rouncewell thereabouts*}. Having done this, our goal of providing both clauses with a uniform abstract representation is achieved, and we can put on the finishing touches by applying (11.5) and (11.6): {*whether the workman⟨a⟩ KNOW the name of Rouncewell thereabouts*}.

11.3 DERIVATIONS, RULES, AND STRATA OF REPRESENTATION

The guidelines and examples in the preceding section have been presented rather haphazardly and fragmentedly. In this section, much of that looseness will be consolidated and filled out, through the important notions of DERIVATION, RULE, and STRATUM OF REPRESENTATION.

Before starting, it should be made clear that abstract representation is by no means limited to governed embedded clauses, a clarification that may have been intimated by the appearance of a nongoverned, root clause (11.8a) in the midst of the discussion in the last section. Governmental examples were chosen simply because they lend themselves to illustrating several important syntactic-semantic points in one and the same string.

Henceforth, governmental and nongovernmental examples will be used indiscriminately, and we may begin by returning to example (11.1tc) to develop an abstract representation of its ungoverned matrix clause to synthesize with that of its governed embedded clause developed in §11.2 as {*Rhoemetalces*⟨a⟩ *not AVENGE Rhoemetalces'*⟨a⟩ *people's wrong*}. Proceeding to the matrix onset of the sentence, *Rhoemetalces was as forcibly criticized* . . . , it will be sufficient for the present purposes to coindex (11.5) the subject with that of the embedded clause to give *Rhoemetalces*⟨a⟩ and abstract away number agreement from *was*

(=   BE   ) to give BE.
  [+past, +singular]   [+past]

Putting this result aside for a moment, let us turn to the important notion of DERIVATION, a pure-linguistic concept that may be characterized as a complex linguistic representation consisting of two or more STRATA related by a set of RULES which apply successively and unidirectionally from stratum to stratum.

As a first step toward developing analogues of derivations for translational purposes, we might explore working up the guidelines introduced in §11.2, an a priori promising idea, since the notions of abstract and surface (concrete) representations easily lend themselves to duty as strata, and guidelines (11.3,4,5,6,9) are essentially rulelike concepts. Moreover, the function of the guidelines in building up abstract from surface representations bears some resemblance to the successive stratum-to-stratum operation of a derivation. In fact, a derivation-like construct along these lines is easily synthesized, as in (11.10), using the example of (11.1tc), where the surface representation is taken as the input stratum (top line), the ASR as the output stratum (bottom line), and the guidelines function as rules successively mapping the former onto the latter.

11.10)

surface Rhoemetalces was as forcibly criticized {for not avenging his people's wrong}
guideline a (qua rule 1)
guideline b (qua rule 2)
guideline c (qua rule 3)
guideline d (qua rule 4)
ASR   Rhoemetalces⟨a⟩   BE   as forcibly criticized {Rhoemetalces⟨a⟩
                          [+past]
          not AVENGE Rhoemetalces'⟨a⟩ people's wrong}

However, a guideline-based derivation like that sketched in (11.10) will not work out, because, unlike rules, guidelines of the type developed in §11.2 are not intentionally formulated to complement one another with a rigorous division of formal labor in a derivation. Rather, the guidelines were purposely devised to maximize their usefulness to the analyst as informal helpmates, a goal not best served by hermetic, nonoverlapping formulation. This difference may be appreciated by comparing the three guidelines (11.3), (11.4), and (11.5) with respect to their potential for service as *guideline (a)* in (11.10). Guideline (11.3) is simply too global and indeterminate to serve as a structural rule; it fails to prescribe any specific formal operation on the embedded clause {*for not avenging his people's wrong*} that might change it to a 'synonymous matrix clause[s]'. Moreover, both (11.4) and (11.5) *do* contain formal operations of the type that a genuine rule-analogue of (11.3) would require, since both the presence of a subject (11.4) and its identification (11.5) are among the hallmarks of most matrix clauses. However, the situation is not improved by trying out (11.4) and (11.5) in the role of rule(1) in (11.10): (11.4) cannot indicate that 'Rhoemetalces' is a 'semantically present' subject of *avenging* without coindexing by (11.5), but there is nothing for (11.5) to coindex until a construct (zero or other) is provided by (11.4).

To be sure, these limitations could in many instances be overcome simply by making guidelines more rulelike, in which case (11.10) would be no more than a straw man. However, there are two good reasons for refraining from such a program:

(i) As already intimated, it would be counterproductive to make guidelines excessively rulelike: the gain in rigor would be offset by a loss in helpfulness;

(ii) Derivations in most contemporary linguistic theories differ from that schematized in (11.10) by mapping in the *opposite direction*, from underlying (abstract) to surface (concrete). Hence, it will be most useful for our purposes to build derivational analogues counterdirectional to (11.10), and in the process develop rule like constructs independent of the guidelines.

It is actually not a complex matter to implement this advice. Once a satisfactory ASR has been worked out, all that need be done is to map this representation backwards step by step onto the surface representation from which, with the help of the guidelines, it originated. To be sure, as in all applied-linguistic enterprises, the closer the results to those of solid pure-linguistic findings, the sharper and deeper they are likely to be. Nevertheless, good results can often be obtained simply by exercising caution that each derivational step be implemented by a rule-analogue carefully devised to ensure that it (a) brings closer to the surface stratum a specific aspect (or group of related aspects) of structure; and (b) interacts coherently and complementarily with any other rule-analogues similarly devised.

From this point on we will, for the most part, use rule-analogues similar in function to, but lacking the detail and rigor of, pure-linguistic counterparts studied in the contemporary literature. We will sometimes borrow the conventional names of such rules, in the interests of facilitating access to readers interested in exploring the pure-linguistic literature on their own.[3]

With this in mind, (11.10) may be abandoned in favor of something like (11.11).

The four rule-analogues (henceforth, barring ambiguity, to be called simply 'rules') used in (11.11) bear some discussion:

Equi ('Equi-NP-deletion') is a rule that deletes (replaces by zero) one or more links in a coreference chain under identity with a specific trigger-link, the so-called ANTECEDENT. Equi is an extremely widespread rule among the world's languages, though details of its application and form vary considerably from language to language. Functionally, Equi is akin to pronominalization (see below), and it is not unusual for source and target languages to differ precisely in the fact that where one uses Equi, the other pronominalizes.

Pron ('Pronominalization') replaces a link in a corereference chain by a personal pronoun under identity with the antecedent. Characteristically, a pronoun will assimilate to itself features both of the antecedent and of the syntactic frame in which the pronoun occurs, the details again varying from language to language. Thus, *his*⟨*a*⟩ picks up its feature [+masculine] from the antecedent *Rhoemetalces*⟨*a*⟩ (≠ *her,*its), and [+genitive] from the frame 's people's wrong (≠ *he, *him).

Agr ('Agreement') copies certain features from an NP onto a verb in construction with that NP, details again differing from language to language. Agr in English, unlike its robust cousins in more conservative Indo-European languages, is quite residual, in regular cases limited to marking a present-tense verb as having a third-person singular subject. The copular verb *be* is unique in also marking a limited amount of past-tense agreement, as here: *was* ≠ *were*.

Ger ('Gerund Formation'), a rule triggered by specific matrix verbs (here *criticize*), always marks a bare verb stem with the suffix *-ing* and under some conditions (as here) also with the preposition *for*.

Note that (11.11) also illustrates the common property of derivations that their rules are at least partially determined as to the order of their application. In particular here, if Agr applied before Pron, we would get the incorrect result of *avenges* being in agreement with *Rhoemetalces*, a result which then would inappropriately block Ger, abutting finally on incorrect **Rhoemetalces was as forcibly criticized not avenges his people's wrong*.

Since it is normal for the rules of a language to evidence a fixed order across all derivations, it will be useful to consider each rule as belonging to a specific INTERMEDIATE STRATUM, to be tagged with a lower-case letter in alphabetic order. Thus, in (11.11) Equi and Pron are assigned to an intermediate stratum tagged (b), Agr to the next (c), and Ger to the third (d). This order is then maintained in (11.12), deriving example (11.2t), in that Agr maintains its order as a stratum-(c) rule, and ThatIn is relegated to stratum (d) for its similarity in function to Ger as one of a family of processes marking embedded clauses.[4]

ThatIn ('*That* insertion') has been taken by some to be the default case of embedded-clause marking, applying whenever it is not preempted by some other rule. Whether or not this is indeed the case, ThatIn may be taken here de facto to be governed by the nominalized matrix verb *proposal*.

We will conclude this section by providing derivations for two final exam-

(11.11) (cf. (11.1tc))

ASR   Rhoemetalces⟨a⟩   BE   as forcibly criticized{R⟨a⟩not AVENGE R's⟨a⟩ people's wrong}
                                 [+past]

b. *Equi,Pron*   ∅⟨a⟩   his⟨a⟩
c. *Agr*   was
d. *Ger*   for   avenging
surface   Rhoemetalces⟨a⟩ was as forcibly criticized{for ∅⟨a⟩not avenging his⟨a⟩ people's wrong}

(11.12) (cf. (11.2tc))

ASR   The consul's proposal   BE   {Piso's name could be deleted from the calendar}
                                        [+past]

c. *Agr*   was
d. *ThatIn*   that
surface   The consul's proposal was{that Piso's name could be deleted from the calendar}

(11.13) (cf. (11.7a))

ASR   The trooper ASK a workman⟨a⟩{whether the workman⟨a⟩KNOW the name of R. thereabouts}

b. *Pron*   he⟨a⟩

c. *Agr*   asks   knows

d. *Qform*   does he   know

surface   The trooper asks a workman⟨a⟩{does he⟨a⟩ know the name of Rouncewell thereabouts}

(11.14) (cf. (11.8at))

ASR   whether she not had beautiful hair

d. *Negform*   didn't she have

surface   Didn't she have beautiful hair?

ples from §11.2, given here as (11.13) and (11.14). Note in particular the two new rules introduced on stratur (d): *Qform* ('Question formation') and *Negform* ('Negative formation') are presented as a compacted version of what theoreticians have taken to be the conjunction of several rules designed to capture the peculiar tagmemics and morphemics of the English negative and interrogative constructions. Both involve the auxiliary-verb *do*, which deprives the main verb of agreement (*does he know* ≠ *do he knows) as well as other marks such as tense and negation (*didn't she have* ≠ **do she hadn't*); and Qform additionally involves sacrifice of the abstract morpheme *whether* for tagmemic displacement of the subject to a position behind the first verb word, whether it be the auxiliary verb *do*, as here (*does he know* versus noninterrogative *he does know*), or some other auxiliary (*will he know* versus *he will know*, etc).

At this point the reader may be disconcerted that the discussion of the last two sections has been solely unilinguistic. This narrowness of focus was intentional; we are now equipped to return to translinguistic issues in the next chapter.

NOTES

1. Once again, as with the term 'trace' (see note 1 of chapter 10), the term 'government' will be used throughout in the informal (and traditional-grammatical) sense rather than in the technical (and neologistic) sense lent it in GB theory (Chomsky 1982). There will, however, be a good amount of incidental overlap between both senses of the term in the examples adduced (cf. again note 1 of chapter 10).

2. The hedge-verb 'may' in the formulation of (11.3) and other guidelines below is used intentionally, given the noncoercive, practical nature of these guidelines as applied-linguistic helpmates as opposed to pure-linguistic axioms or theorems (cf. §0.1 and §11.3).

3. Because of disconcertingly rapid changes in linguistic theory, it is often quite different to extract a unitary picture from the contemporary literature without long-term familiarity with that literature. However, I can fortunately cite a single reference work that will provide a theoretical basis for most of the syntactic rule-analogues to be developed below: Stockwell, et al. (1973). (Though this book is in several regards outmoded theoretically, it is more useful to our purposes than much contemporary theoretical research which, despite its promise, has not yet been tried out for translational application.)

4. The sequencing starts with (b) rather than (a) in order to leave space for earlier-ordered rules in later derivations, e.g. *Rais* in (12.5). (Also in this vein, similar rules are tagged with identical stratum-letters across languages; e.g. French Equi and Pron with (b) in (12.1). This homogenization is solely expository in nature, however, and could not in fact be maintained if a larger sample of rules were adduced.)

Chapter *12*

BRIDGE TECHNIQUE

12.0 PRELIMINARIES

In large part, the work of the preceding chapter was preparatory to the business of this chapter, the rapprochement of source and target derivations of a translational nexus via a procedure to be called BRIDGE TECHNIQUE.

12.1 BASIC PROPERTIES OF THE TECHNIQUE

By way of preliminary illustration, let us consider a sentence from Balzac/Waring:[1] *Je tâcherais de m'y conformer* (s269)/*I would try to accommodate myself to them* (t226). To start with the target version, the guidelines of §11.2 easily supply an abstract representation—*I⟨ a⟩ would try {I⟨a⟩ ACCOMMODATE I⟨a⟩ to them}*—where the coindexed (11.5) first-link pronoun *I⟨a⟩* is generalized to fill in the implicit subject of the embedded verb (11.4) as well as to replace the syntagmatically determined object form *myself* (11.6). Abstraction of the French original proceeds similarly but not identically:

JE⟨a⟩   TÂCH-   {JE⟨a⟩   *CONFORM-*   JE⟨a⟩   y   }—where   TÂCH-
[+ conditional]   [+ conditional]

abstracts away (11.6) the first-person singular suffix *-erais*, a step unnecessary for the suffixless English counterpart *would try*; surface *m'y* (an.'me to-them') moves from the front to the rear of the verb per French syntax at large (cf. the

145

constructed *de conformer Arabelle aux goûts de Félix*, 'to accommodate Arabelle to Felix's tastes').

The device of bridge technique now comes to the fore when these ASRs are brought together with their respective derivations in (12.1). The metaphor behind the name 'bridge technique' is suggested by the structure and function of a bascule lift bridge, whose left and right PYLONS (towers), which may be lifted and lowered in coordination, correspond to the source and target derivations respectively, and whose vertically shiftable TRUSS (roadway) corresponds to the horizontal stratum on which the translational nexus is focused, in this case the stratum of ASR (note the arrow in example 12.1).

Coming now to the specific attributes of bridge technique, note that the work of describing the relations between a source and target string has by virtue of the bridge structure been preapportioned into two distinct modes: once TRANSLIN-GUISTICALLY—on the truss—and twice UNLINGUISTICALLY—once in each pylon in terms of the differences between source and target derivations. Thus, in (12.1), while English and French share the rules of Equi, Pron, (cf.(11.11)), and *Inf* ('Infinitivization'),[2] only French requires Agr (cf. (11.11)) to mark subject agreement on *tâcherais*, an.'agree-would-I', and English has no analogue of the rule *Clis* ('Clisis'), prevalent in the Romance languages, whereby pronouns in construction with a verb are grouped in a fixed order and positioned to that verb as either prepositive PROCLITICS (as here) or postpositive ENCLITICS.

Turning now to the translinguistic portrayal of the nexus on the truss of (12.1), and examining this nexus trajectionally, we may complete our inventory of source-target relations by analyzing three instances of Equation in the coreference chain $JE\langle a \rangle. . . JE\langle a \rangle. . . . JE\langle a \rangle \rightarrowtail I\langle a \rangle. . . I\langle a \rangle$ one again in the abstract verb *CONFORM-* $\rightarrow$ *ACCOMMODATE, and two cases of Diffusion:*

$$\hat{TACH}\text{-} \rightarrow \text{would try, and } y \rightarrow \text{to them.}$$
$$[+conditional]$$

While this examination of (12.1) has provided a succinct introduction to most of the basic properties of bridge technique, it might also provoke a legitimate question as to appropriateness: Though it may be wondrous and worthy in the realm of pure linguistics to analyze sentences in terms of derivations with underlying representations and rules, does such elaboration really throw any new light on a translational nexus as apparently simple and straightforward as this unassuming little excerpt from Balzac/Waring?

A question such as this touches on the important issue of ways and means to guard against OVEREXTENDING applied-linguistic distillates of pure-linguistic concepts. As a care in point, bridge technique can and should be modified to fit the requirements of a given analytic situation, and while there are no hard and fast procedures for determining in advance just what such requirements may turn out to be, the nature of bridge technique lends itself to framing and implementing various rules of thumb. One of the clearest of these is the frequent omissibility of rules common to source and target derivations, especially when such rules occur on corresponding strata and otherwise figure analogously in both derivations.

(12.1)

s.

JE⟨a⟩ TÂCH- {JE⟨a⟩CONFORM-JE⟨a⟩ y}
[+conditional]

b. *Equi,Pron*

c. *Agr* tâcherais m'⟨a⟩

d. *Inf* 0⟨a⟩

e. *Clis* de conformer

de m'y conformer

Je tâcherais de m'y conformer (Balzac: 269)

→

t.

I⟨a⟩would try{I⟨a⟩ACCOMMODATE I⟨a⟩to them}

b. *Equi,Pron*

0⟨a⟩myself⟨a⟩ **d.** *Inf*

to accommodate

I would try to accommodate myself to them (Waring:226)

Furthermore, if the overall disposition of the derivations allows it, the omission of such rules can be achieved by 'lowering the truss' an appropriate number of strata. Thus, since in (12.1) French and English share both rules (Equi and Pron) of level (b), the abstract level may be modified by assuming application of these rules and so be 'lowered' one notch to the space vacated by the stratum so omitted; see (12.2) on p. 149.

In some cases, the omitted stratum will have to 'jump over' an intervening stratum to meld into the abstract stratum. This is demonstrated in (12.3), a modified version of (12.2) in which the ASRs have absorbed stratum (d) by virtue of the fact that the two languages share the rule of Inf; see p. 149.

It will be noted in (12.3) that trust-lowering has effectively lost all the target rules, with the consequence that the English ASR is identical to its surface representation. If this were the case on *both* target *and* source sides, the truss would be coterminous with the surface stratum, which in turn is tantamount to saying that the null case of the technique would have been reached. Such a result in turn would allow a simple, summary evaluation: since source and target derivations would have been identical (homologous) by virtue of identical (homologous) rules, there would probably be no point in applying bridge technique in the first place. Moreover, such cases often betray themselves to the analyst in advance, in that source and target strings may approach Equation. For instance, in the nexus Norwegian *Men kanskje vi kunne lage en taustige* (Mykle:28) → English *But maybe we could make a rope-ladder* (M1980b:95), source and target agree word for word. Bridge technique in a case like this would merely corroborate the source-target homology perceived in the surface strings themselves, and so, barring some special analytic goal, could most likely be dispensed with.

Observe finally that while shared rules may provide a particularly salient occasion for modifying bridge technique, such a condition is neither necessary nor sufficient. This point will be tacitly operative throughout the discussion of more complex cases in §12.2ff but might be schematically illustrated here on the basis of (12.1) and (12.3).

On the one hand, the source-specific rule of Agr in (12.1) might be melded into the abstract level, giving *JE⟨a⟩ tâcherais* {*JE⟨a⟩ CONFORM- JEκa⟩ y*}, subject to analytic convenience. Note, however, that there is often a trade-off price to pay for such liberties. In this case, while unmodified TÂCH- trajects to
$$[+\text{conditional}]$$
would try by Diffusion, modified *tâcherais* incurs the extra trajectional expense of Reduction (because *would try* lacks any counterpart to the subject part of the suffix *-erais* an.'I-would'). Generally speaking, the more an ASR is modified in the direction of its surface derivative, the more trajectionally complex it becomes.

As for the non-necessity of omitting shared rules from bridge technique, just observe that a priori the ASRs in (12.1) may prove analytically superior in any number of foreseeable or unforeseeable ways to their modified counterparts in (12.2) and (12.3). For one thing, the functional homology of source and target strings is simply more visible to the analyst in (12.1), where it is minimally de-

(12.2)

s.

Je⟨a⟩   TÂCH-   {∅⟨a⟩ CONFORM- m'⟨a⟩y}   →   **t.**
        [+conditional]   I⟨a⟩would try{∅⟨a⟩ACCOMMODATE myself⟨a⟩to them}
        tâcherais

c. *Agr*   de conformer
d. *Inf*   de m'y conformer   to accommodate   **d.** *Inf*
e. *Clis*   (surface strata as in (12.1))

(12.3)

s.

Je⟨a⟩   TÂCH   {∅⟨a⟩ de conformer m'⟨a⟩y}   →   **t.**
        [+conditional]   I⟨a⟩ would try {∅⟨a⟩ to accommodate myself⟨a⟩ to them}
        tâcherais

c. *Agr*   de m'y conformer
e. *Clis*   (surface strata as in (12.2))

tracted from by language-specific morphological reflexes introduced into the modified ASRs of (12.2) and (12.3). As will be apparent in the next section, such visibility can be a very important asset heuristically.

12.2 SPANNING: FRENCH *TÂCHER* AND SPANISH *PROCURAR* VERSUS ENGLISH *TRY*

Bridge technique comes into its own when syntactic relations are complex or subtle, particularly when the complexity or subtlety falls out differently from source to target. The problem may be localized in the source text, in the target text, or distributed over both. In any event, the focus of the technique may vary with the purpose at hand; for example, complexity in the source may pose a challenge for the operative mode while conversely a complex target text may exercise the analytic mode (cf. §0.1.4).

Let us begin by looking at an excerpt from Balzac bearing a deceptive similarity to the string given in (12.1): *Mais je tâcherai qu'il soit fidèle à ses premières affections* (Balzac:244), an.'But I will try that he should be faithful to his first affections'. The problem is simply that the analytic translation is hopeless in English, despite the fact that this sentence is structurally no more complex than (12.1), both involving distinctly simple embedded clauses governed by a form of the matrix verb *tâcher* 'try'. As will be seen, Waring has succeeded in translating this sentence into quite acceptable and straightforward English, and it would be absurd to imagine that he used bridge technique in the process. Thus, the major focus of this example will be on the analytic rather than (reconstructively) on the operative mode.

We first want to know exactly what it is about this ostensibly simple French sentence that resists an Equational response into English. We will then want to examine Waring's actual translation and see precisely what facet of the English language he has pressed into service in the process. Consider the partial bridge laid out in (12.4), where on the French side, in addition to Agr (cf. (12.1)), we need only call upon *QueIn* ('*Que*-insertion'), the French analogue of ThatIn (cf. (11.12)), and *Subj* ('Subjunctivation'), which invests the embedded verb with subjunctive mood under government by *tâcher*.

On the target side, however, the English ASR is doomed from the start. Despite the rough synonymy of English *try* with French *tâcher*, the two verbs have crucially different GOVERNMENT PROPERTIES: while *try* requires that the embedded subject be coreferent with the matrix verb (thus e.g. $I\langle a\rangle \ldots I\langle a\rangle$ in (12.1)), *tâcher* does not. Thus, in standard English we cannot say things like *$I\langle a\rangle$ *will try {that he$\langle b\rangle$ should be faithful . . . }* as a way of conveying an intended effort whose goal is someone else's action or state. In French, however, it is perfectly possible to convey such meanings in that way, and hence the unimpeachableness of Balzac's sentence in (12.4).

Waring's actual response to this problem, fitted out by bridge technique as the actual target pylon to (12.4), appears in (12.5) on p. 151.

(12.4)

s.
Mais je⟨a⟩ tâcherai {il⟨b⟩ ÊTRE fidèle à ses premières affections}

$\rightarrow$

t.
But I⟨a⟩ will try {he⟨b⟩ BE faithful to his first affections}

c. *Agr*
d. *Queln,Subj*

ÊTRE
[+3rd, + singular]
qu'il soit

Mais je tâcherai qu'il soit fidèle à ses premières affections (Balzac:244)

(12.5) t.
$_0${but I⟨a⟩ will try $_1${I⟨a⟩ MAKE $_2${HE⟨b⟩ BE faithful to his first affections}$_2$}$_1$}$_0$
MAKE HE⟨b⟩ $_2${0 BE
0⟨a⟩ MAKE him⟨b⟩$_2${0 0
to make

a. *Rais*
b. *Equi,Pron,CopDel*
d. *Inf*

but I will try to make him faithful to his first affections (Waring:204)

151

Even as the ASR in (12.4) made clear the crucial difference between French and English, so the ASR in (12.5) affords us a clear view into Waring's solution. Since matrix *try* requires its subject to be coreferential with that of the immediately embedded clause, Waring has skillfully interpolated a *span clause* (§7.2.1) between that of $I\langle a \rangle$ *try* $(_0\{ \quad \}_0)$ and $HE\langle b \rangle$ *BE* $(_2\{ \quad \}_2)$, that of $I\langle a \rangle$ *MAKE* $(_1\{ \quad \}_1)$, which not only has the required coreference but moreover does no violence to the required semantic relation between the 'trying' and the 'being faithful'.

With this understanding of the ASR in (12.5), the derivation itself consists exclusively of mainstream English syntactic rules, of which only two are new here:

> *Rais* ('Raising'), a widespread rule type among languages, in this case 'raises' an embedded subject $(HE\langle b \rangle)$ up into the matrix clause, where it is subsequently treated by Pron (cf. (11.11)) as if it were the object of the matrix verb (*make him⟨b⟩*). (Raising will receive more discussion below, (12.13)–(12.14).)

> *CopDel* ('Copula deletion') under various circumstances makes for the optional omission of an embedded form of *be*. (If the option of CopDel were not chosen here, the string would emerge as . . . *make him (to) be faithful*; cf. example (12.6), where CopDel is in fact not used, hence . . . *get her to be interested* . . . rather than . . . *get her interested* . . . .)

It may be recalled that a similar Spanish case from Márquez/Rabassa was briefly treated in (7.1), with the matrix verb *procurar*. If we fit out that example here with indices and brackets (12.6), its parallelism to the French case of *tâcher* in (12.5) will be apparent, as will the fundamental difference between them: while Waring chose as a span the verb *make*, Rabassa chose the largely synonymous *get*. These two items are the most common CAUSATIVE verbs in English and as such are natural candidates as spans to mediate between a matrix of 'trying' and an embedded clause to be understood as the semantic object of that 'trying'. In most real-world situations, if a person X 'tries' to bring about a given situation Y through the agency of another person Z, it will probably be accurate to infer that by dint of that X is 'trying' to 'cause' Z to bring about Y.[3]

(12.6) (= (7.1))
s. $\emptyset\langle a \rangle$ procuró {que $\emptyset\langle b \rangle$ se interesara por los asuntos elementales de la casa}
t. she$\langle a \rangle$ had tried {$\emptyset\langle a \rangle$ to get her$\langle b \rangle$ {$\emptyset\langle b \rangle$ to be interested in basic domestic affairs}}

12.3 REFASHIONING: ANTISPANNING, LEXICALIZATION

Though from the trajectional point of view, Waring's and Rabassa's use of the spans *make* and *get* constitutes Amplification (and perhaps also Diffusion, to the extent that these verbs might constitute lexical extrusions of features implicit in the matrix *try*), it will be useful to have a generic term for any 'corrective' response by a translator to a source-target obstacle revealed by bridge technique. In such a case, the translator will be said to employ REFASHIONING.[4]

It is interesting that even as refashioning may take the Amplification form of clause-building spanning, as has just been seen, there are also situations where refashioning goes in the opposite direction, via Reductional 'antispanning' deletion of clause structure. A Spanish-to-English case from Cervantes/Ormsby will be presented below, involving RELATIVIZATION, but it will be wise to work up to that by first reviewing a simpler case of relativization from the same source/target pair; see (12.7) on p. 154.

Starting for convenience on the target side of (12.7), it should be readily apparent that the ASR can be developed from the surface representation by the guidelines of §11.2: since the implicit object of the surface relative clause {*I never heard*} refers back to the antecedent *a word*, (11.4) and (11.5) dictate an ASR like *a word$\langle a \rangle${I never heard the word$\langle a \rangle$}* for the entire group, which in turn satisfies (11.3). (Guideline (11.9) doesn't apply, and while (11.6) could, it isn't needed.)

Analogous reasoning justifies the source ASR, an. 'it is a word$\langle a \rangle$ {I have not heard the word$\langle a \rangle$ in all the days of my life}', a string whose trajection into the English ASR deviates from Equation in a few minor tokens of Substitution and Reduction irrelevant to this discussion. This source ASR relates to its surface representation by three rules:

(i) *RelPr* ('Relative pronominalization'), whereby the antecedent-coreferent NP *el vocábulo$\langle a \rangle$* an. 'the word$\langle a \rangle$' (the so-called ANAPHOR) is replaced by the relative pronoun *que* (an. 'which');

(ii) *RelCo* ('Relative Copy'), whereby the relative pronoun is moved to the front of the relative clause, leaving behind a personal-pronominal COPY agreeing with the antecedent in appropriate features, in this case *lo* (an. 'it'); and

(iii) The Spanish analogue of *Clis* (cf. (12.1)), whereby *lo* is moved to preverbal position.

Turning now to the target derivation, note that the two languages share only RelPr (stratum (b)). Though many nonstandard varieties of English do have an analogue of *RelCo*,[5] standard literary English instead employs *RelCh* ('Relative Chop'), whereby movement of the relative pronoun to the front of its clause is not compensated by a pronominal copy. Rather, the relative pronoun is simply 'chopped' out of its original slot, leaving no segmental trace behind; a copy pronominalized (e.g. **a word {which I never heard it}* would go over poorly in standard literary English.

Finally, the optional rule of *RelDel* ('Relative Deletion') may apply to drop the relative pronoun introduced by RelPr.

With example (12.7) in mind, let us turn to the partial bridge in (12.8), a double-embedded case where one relative clause ($_2${   }$_2$) is nested in another ($_1${   }$_1$). Despite its syntactic complexity, the message conveyed is rather straightforward (cf. the analytic translation at the base of the source pylon), and the Spanish derivation, despite appearances to the contrary, involves no more than commonplace rules. To begin with, RelPr applies twice in clause $_2${   }$_2$,

(12.7)

s.

es [vocábulo$\langle a\rangle$] {no he oído [el vocábulo $\langle a\rangle$]
en todos los días de mi vida}

b. *RelPr* {no he oído que$\langle a\rangle$
c. *RelCo* {que$\langle a\rangle$ no he oído lo$\langle a\rangle$

e. *Clis* {que$\langle a\rangle$ no lo$\langle a\rangle$ he oído

Es vocábulo que no lo he oído en todos los
días de mi vida (Cervantes:511)
an. 'It is a word which I have never heard it
in all the days of my life'

$\rightarrow$

t.

it is [a word$\langle a\rangle$] {I never heard[the
word$\langle a\rangle$] in all my life}

b. *RelPr* {I never heard which$\langle a\rangle$
c. *RelCh* {which$\langle a\rangle$I never heard $0\langle a\rangle$
d. *RelDel* {0 I never heard

It is a word I never heard
in all my life (Ormsby: 302)

(12.8)

s.

O valeroso [Roque$\langle a\rangle$] $_1${ no hay [límites$\langle b\rangle$]
en la tierra $_2$[llos límites$\langle b\rangle$] encierren
[la fama$\langle c\rangle$] [de Roque$\langle a\rangle$]}$_2$}$_1$

b. *RelPr*

O valeroso [Roque$\langle a\rangle$] $_1${no hay [límites$\langle b\rangle$]
en la tierra $_2${que$\langle b\rangle$ encierren
cuya$\langle a\rangle$ [fama$\langle c\rangle$] }$_2$}$_1$

c. *RelCo* }
e. *Clis* }

O valeroso [Roque$\langle a\rangle$] $_1${cuya$\langle a\rangle$ [fama$\langle c\rangle$]
no hay [límites$\langle b\rangle$] en la tierra $_2${que$\langle b\rangle$
la$\langle c\rangle$ encierren }$_2$}$_1$ (Cervantes:646)
an. 'O valiant [Roque$\langle a\rangle$] $_1${whose$\langle a\rangle$ [fame$\langle c\rangle$]
there are no [limits$\langle b\rangle$] on earth $_2${which$\langle b\rangle$
might bound it$\langle c\rangle$ }$_2$}$_1$'

$\rightarrow$

t.

O valiant [Roque$\langle a\rangle$] $_1${there are
no [limits$\langle b\rangle$] in earth $_2${[the
limits$\langle b\rangle$]might bound[Roque's$\langle a\rangle$][fame$\langle c\rangle$]}$_2$}$_1$

O valiant [Roque$\langle a\rangle$] $_1${there are
no [limits$\langle b\rangle$] on earth {which$\langle b\rangle$ **b.** *RelPr*
might bound whose$\langle a\rangle$ [fame]$\langle c\rangle$}$_2$}$_1$

replacing *los límites*⟨b⟩ ('the limits') with *que*⟨b⟩ ('which'), and *de Roque* ⟨ a⟩ ('of Roque, Roque's') with *cuya*⟨a⟩('whose')—which also switches position with its sister NP: *cuya fama* ≠ **(la) fama cuya*. Next, the application of RelCo is unexceptional but requires comment on three points not demonstrable in the simple example (12.7):

(i) When, as in this case, there are two or more relative clauses that might ambiguously be construed as the domain for frontward movement of the relative pronoun, the choice is determined by the resulting proximity to the antecedent; thus, *cuya*⟨a⟩ moves to the front of $_1${ }$_1$, closest to Roque, while *que*⟨b⟩ is appropriately already at the front of $_2${ }$_2$, nearest to *límites*⟨b⟩;

(ii) When the fronted relative pronoun is a genitive (possessive) like *cuya* ⟨a⟩ ('whose'), its movement 'pied-pipes' its sister NP along with it; thus, the entire string *cuya*⟨a⟩ *fama*⟨c⟩ ends up being clause-initial;

(iii) The copying part of the rule does not apply with *que*⟨b⟩, which is already appropriately clause-initial (cf. point (i)) and reacts to the sister of the relative pronoun in *cuya*⟨a⟩ *fame*⟨c⟩ giving *la*⟨c⟩ rather than **lo*⟨a⟩. Finally, this *la*⟨c⟩ is repositioned by Clis, giving *la*⟨c⟩ *encierren* from *encierren la*⟨c⟩.

We will quickly come to the problematic part of this nexus when we attempt to derive a target string from the English ASR. RelPr goes through smoothly, as indicated. But when it comes next to RelCh, there is trouble. The resulting string is not only unacceptable English, it is well-nigh incomprehensible: **O valiant [Roque]⟨a⟩ $_1${[whose]⟨a⟩[fame]⟨c⟩ there are no [limits]⟨b⟩ on earth $_2${[which]⟨b⟩ might bound}$_2$}$_1$.*

The problem here is that application of RelCh has run afoul of a universal syntactic constraint against the removal of morphological elements from a clause (S') contained within an NP, as suggested by either of the arrows in (12.9a). A violation would be instantiated by the English case in question, as may be seen in (12.9b). On the other hand, it is avoided by the Spanish source since copying, unlike chopping, does not entail the REMOVAL of morphology but rather its REPLACEMENT (by the pronoun, (12.9c)). The constraint is also obviated by cases of simple chopping relativization like (12.7t), since the target of the removal does not go beyond the NP (12.9d).[6]

(12.9) a. ↑ NP{   S'{   ∅   }S'   }NP   ↑

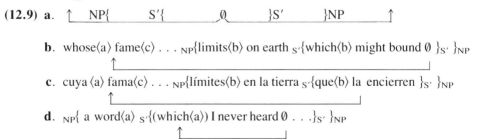

b. whose⟨a⟩ fame⟨c⟩ . . . $_{NP}${limits⟨b⟩ on earth $_{S'}${which⟨b⟩ might bound ∅ }$_{S'}$ }$_{NP}$

c. cuya ⟨a⟩ fama⟨c⟩ . . . $_{NP}${límites⟨b⟩ en la tierra $_{S'}${que⟨b⟩ la encierren }$_{S'}$ }$_{NP}$

d. $_{NP}${ a word⟨a⟩ $_{S'}${(which⟨a⟩) I never heard ∅ . . .}$_{S'}$ }$_{NP}$

b. *RelPr*

Refashioning

c. *RelCh*

(12.10) (completes (12.8t))

O valiant [Roque⟨a⟩] $_1${there are no [limits⟨b⟩] on earth $_2${which⟨b⟩ might bound whose⟨a⟩ [fame⟨c⟩]}}$_2$}$_1$

O valiant [Rouque⟨a⟩] {no [limits⟨b⟩] on earth might bound whose⟨a⟩ [fame⟨c⟩]}

O valiant [Roque⟨a⟩] {whose⟨a⟩ [fame⟨c⟩] no [limits⟨b⟩] on earth might bound ∅}

(*Other adjustments:* Passivization, loss of *might*)

O valiant Roque, whose fame is bounded by no limits on earth! (Ormsby:438)

(12.11) as. [una camisa de cuello postizo⟨a⟩] $_1${que⟨a⟩ no sabía $_2${de quién había heredado ∅⟨a⟩}$_2$}$_1$ (Márquez::303)

an.([a shirt with an artificial collar⟨a⟩] $_1${that⟨a⟩ he did not know $_2${from whom he had inherited ∅⟨a⟩}$_2$}$_1$

Reordering →

at. [a shirt with an artificial collar⟨a⟩] $_2${that⟨a⟩ he had inherited ∅⟨a⟩ $_1${from he did not know whom}$_2$}$_1$ (Rabassa:335)

bs. Después se llevaron [los tres sacos de oro⟨a⟩] $_1${que⟨a⟩ sólo ellos y su víctima sabían $_2${donde ∅⟨a⟩ estaban escondidos}$_2$}$_1$ (Márquez:312f)

an. 'Then they took out [the three sacks of gold⟨a⟩] $_1${which⟨a⟩ only they and their victim knew $_2${where ∅⟨a⟩ were hidden }$_2$}'

Reordering and Condensation →

bt. Then they took out [the three sacks of gold⟨a⟩] from [the hidding place⟨b⟩] {which⟨b⟩ was known only to them and their victim} (Rabassa:346)

cs. Te⟨a⟩ lo⟨b⟩ ∅⟨c⟩ dejamos bien. ∅⟨a⟩ procura {que ∅⟨c⟩ lo⟨b⟩ encontremos mejor} (Márquez:93) an. 'We⟨c⟩ leave it⟨b⟩ to you⟨a⟩ in good shape, ∅⟨a⟩ try {that we⟨c⟩ should find it⟨b⟩ in better shape}'

Substitution and Diffusion →

ct. We⟨c⟩ leave it⟨b⟩ to you⟨a⟩ in good shape; ∅⟨a⟩ try $_1${∅⟨a⟩ to have it⟨b⟩ in better shape $_2${when we⟨c⟩ return}$_2$}$_1$ (Rabassa:104)

It is now time to redeem the promise, given in concluding the discussion of Amplificational span-refashioning in (12.5) and (12.6), that (12.8) would usher in a case of Reductional 'antispan'-refashioning. We can understand how Ormsby did, in fact, use such refashioning to break the impasse posed by (12.8t) by counterposing two structures: that of (12.9b), which represents the brunt of the impasse per the schema of (12.9a), and that of (12.9d), a string that obviates the constraint of (12.9a). Comparison of these structures suggests that if the double-embedded relative clause in (12.8t) can somehow be simplified to a single embedding, without thereby incurring (major) semantic change, the problem will ipso facto be solved—simply because, as has been seen in (12.9d), single embedding cannot entail the configuration prerequisite to violation.

Turning back now to (12.8t), we can see that the offensive structure lends itself to a solution along these lines, because the semantic content of the matrix part of the middle clause $_1\{$ $\}_1$ is minimal. A biclausal statement *There are no X {which might Y}* is nearly equivalent to the uniclausal statement *No Y might Y*, the former differing only by explicitly asserting the nonexistence of the *X*, while in the latter case the nonexistence is inferential.

It is exactly this refashioning strategy that Ormsby has exploited, as may be seen in (12.10). Note that such REDUCTIONAL ANTISPANNING has something important in common with AMPLIFICATIONAL SPANNING of the sort illustrated in (12.5) and (12.6). In either case, the span or antispan must, in the context, be more or less semantically neutral, so that the overall target message is minimally affected by its respective addition or subtraction.

The proceeding examples are not meant to suggest that refashioning need always proceed by Amplification or Reduction. On the contrary, quite a variety of refashioning techniques may be called on by the skillful translator, even when responding to nearly identical structures. A few abbreviated examples to this effect from Márquez/Rabassa are given in (12.11), where paired source and target structures are bracketed and indexed to facilitate visibility of the refashioning trajections given at the arrow. In (as) and (bs), Spanish evinces not RelCo, as in (12.7), but RelCh (cf. (12.7) for English) from clause $_2\{$ $\}_2$, in a way resisted by literary English (cf. the clumsiness of the analytic translations). In (at) Rabassa has skillfully dodged the problem, in part by Reordering clauses $_1\{$ $\}_1$ and $_2\{$ $\}_2$, so that the relative pronoun *that* is fronted without ever leaving its own clause. Case (bt) also relies on Reordering but crucially also involves LEXICALIZATION of the clause $_2\{donde\ \emptyset\langle a\rangle\ estaban\ escondidas\}_2$, an.'$_2\{$where $\emptyset\langle a\rangle$ were hidden$\}_2$', to the noun *hiding place*—a very handy and efficient technique when the target lexicon permits it, since a noun is not a clause and hence dispenses with many of the syntactic problems engendered by clauses.

Finally, example (c) is another government case of *procurar* 'try', very much like (12.6) in the source but refashioned quite differently in the target. As may be worked out with the help of the indices, what Rabassa has done here is to Substitute for *encontremos* 'find' a distinct verb *have*, such that the overall message remains roughly the same despite referential role-switching, enabling *try* to construe with a coreferential embedded subject. (Loosely, your⟨a⟩ *having* it⟨b⟩ in better shape will make for our⟨c⟩ *finding* it⟨b⟩ in better shape.) This Substitution is capped off with Diffusion of part of the power of *encontremos* ('find') into the target clause ₂{*when we return*}₂. (Otherwise the relevance to the speaker⟨c⟩| of the addressee's⟨a⟩ *having it in better shape* would be understated in the target version.)

12.4 SITUATIONAL AND STYLISTIC PATTERNS

Up to this point the problems brought into focus by bridge technique have arisen from primarily LINGUISTIC discrepancies between source and target languages. Three cases will now be presented (§12.4.1–§12.4.3) essentially involving SITUATIONAL and STYLISTIC factors.

12.4.1 Spanish versus English Gender

In (12.12s) the conjoined NP *el Cura*⟨a⟩ *y el Barbero*⟨b⟩, an. 'the curate⟨a⟩ and the barber⟨b⟩' has undergone an extended version of Pron (cf.(11.11)), whereby the NP is replaced by a numerical expression agreeing with the replaced NP in relevant features, which in the case of *los dos* ('the two') is manifested through selection of the masculine plural ([+ plural, − feminine]) definite article *los*, as opposed to the feminine plural *las* or the singulars *el*, *la*. In the context of the narrative, moreover, the agreement marked by *los* in *los dos* functions PREG-NANTLY (§2.2), because there is another duo of persons involved in the passage, *su sobrina y su ama*, 'his [Don Quijote's] niece and housekeeper', a purely *feminine* NP which accordingly would have been pronominalized by | + plural, − feminine| *las dos* had Cervantes decided to so phrase the text. Therefore, in the context, which contains only these two sets of persons, the group *los dos* unambiguously references the male set;[7] Cervantes's phrasing is thus SITUATIONALLY (rhetorically) felicitous.

Consider now the English side of the nexus in (12.12t). Unlike Spanish, English numerical pronominalization is not marked for gender, in consequence of which the otherwise Equational rendition *the two* would be ambiguous in reference between *the barber and the curate* and *his niece and housekeeper*, and would accordingly have made for a situationally flawed, albeit grammatically correct, translation. However, Ormsby nicely sidesteps this danger by a sort of negative refashioning: omission of English Pron, whereby the referentially unambiguous NP *the curate and the barber* surfaces as such in the target.

12.4.2 Hebrew versus English Subject Raising

In (12.5) an English example was provided of *Rais*, a rule that takes an embedded clause subject NP up into the matrix clause where it is treated syntactically as object. Though raising processes are quite widespread across languages, specific

(12.12) **s.**

de lo cual recibieron
[el Cura⟨a⟩ y el Barbero⟨b⟩] gran contento

t.

→ from which [the curate⟨a⟩
and the barber⟨b⟩] received great satisfaction

Refashioning: Omission of Pron
(*Other adjustments*, notably
verb Substitution with
argument flip-flop)

b. *Pron* [los dos]⟨a + b⟩
[+ plural, − feminine]

de lo cual recibieron los dos
gran contento (Cervantes:353)

This gave great satisfaction to
the curate and the barber (Ormsby:205)

159

conditions on what raises under what circumstances differ extensively from language to language, and even from dialect to dialect. A Biblical Hebrew example is given in (12.13s), whereby the embedded subject *hɔɔʕɔɔm* 'the people' raises to become the object of the matrix verb *wayyar* 'saw', a role marked by the rule of *Cas* ('Case marking'), which preposes the clitic *ʔɛθ* to the raised constituent. Note also that, unlike the English rule considered in (12.5), where the embedded subject was CHOPPED out of its clause, the Hebrew rule is of a COPYING type (thus *RaisCo*), whereby a pronominal copy of the raised noun, *huu* 'they', is left behind at the extraction site (cf. the discussion of chopping and copying relativization in English and Spanish, (12.7) and (12.11)).

The King James translation of this verse in (12.13t) should impress modern English speakers as quite appropriate and straightforward. Since the verb *see* does not normally trigger (govern) raising, the target derivation contains no analogue of it, and the version that surfaces is stylistically altogether unobtrusive: *and when Moses saw that the people were naked.*

Now consider (12.14). On the Hebrew side, this verse falls out much like (12.13s) except for a few minor differences: movement of the raised constituent prepositively to the verb *rəʔiiθɛm* 'ye have seen';[8] an alternate shape of the clitic, *ʔeθ* instead of *ʔɛθ-*; subject Agr (cf. (11.11),(12.1)) from the pronominal copy *heem⟨a⟩* 'they' onto the verb *rabbuu* 'they⟨a⟩ are many'; and deletion of *heem⟨a⟩*, after it has marked agreement on the verb, by *ProDrop* ('Pronominal Drop'), a rule common to many languages with a rich subject-marking conjugation.

The interesting part of (12.14) is the target version, where the King James translators, in contrast to their treatment of (12.13), have apparently mimicked the Biblical Hebrew syntax by adopting an English raising rule to reconstruct the original text as closely as the target language would allow. (ProDrop could not be introduced, as it is typologically ill-suited). At least for the modern reader, the impact of this ploy by the King James translators is decidedly stylistic. Unlike the everyday English of (12.13t), the translation in (12.14t) has an unmistakably Biblical flavor, a phenomenon that bridge technique quite neatly pinpoints analytically.

12.4.3 NORWEGIAN WORD ORDER VERSUS ENGLISH EXTRAPOSITION

In (12.15) subtle differences between Norwegian and English syntax, of a kind without much impact on cognitive meaning, bothered me as the translator with respect to optimal information flow at this dramatically crucial tail-end to an emotionally wrenching short story. The closest likely counterpart to the original, at the top of the English pylon, not only struck me as somewhat clumsy by virtue of the *there*-construction (which is less used in English than its Norwegian analogue in any event) but more importantly cheated my sense that this important statement should start off on the note of the 'strange feeling'. This was achieved easily enough by the first point of refashioning, as indicated. But this in turn set

(12.13) s.

wayyar Moošεε {kii pɔɔruaʕ hɔɔʕɔɔm⟨a⟩} → and when Moses saw {that the people⟨a⟩
and-saw Moses that naked the-people were naked}

a. *RaisCo,Cas* wayyar Moošεε ʔεθ-hɔɔʕɔɔm⟨a⟩
{kii pɔɔruaʕ huu⟨a⟩} (K:Exodus 32.25) and when Moses saw {that the people ⟨a⟩
an.' and when Moses saw the people⟨a⟩ were naked} (KJ)
{that they⟨a⟩ were naked}

(12.14) s. **t.**

urʔiiθεm {kii- RABB → Ye have seen also {that [the breaches of the
and-ye-have-seen that BE-many city of David ⟨a⟩] BE many}
[bəqiiʕεε ʕiir-Dɔɔwiið⟨a⟩]
breaches-of city-of-David

a. *RaisCo* wəlʔeθ bəqiiʕεε ʕiir-Dɔɔwiið⟨a⟩] Ye have seen also [the breaches…⟨a⟩] **a.** *RaisCo*
rəʔiiθεm {kii-RABB heem⟨a⟩} {that they⟨a⟩ BE many}
c. *Agr* {kii-rabbuu heem⟨a⟩} {that they⟨a⟩ are many} **c.** *Agr*
d. *ProDrop* {kii-rabbuu ∅⟨a⟩}
wəlʔeθ bəqiiʕεε ʕiir-Dɔɔwiið⟨a⟩] Ye have seen also [the breaches of the city of
rəʔiiθεm{kii-rabbuu∅⟨a⟩}(K:Isaiah 22.9) David⟨a⟩] {that they⟨a⟩ are many} (KJ)

up a new problem: I felt that the Norwegian original was dramatically correct in having the phrase referring to the father, *over faren*, directly adjacent to the forms conveying the *specific* emotions affecting him, i.e. 'loneliness, disappointment, and sadness'—an effect blocked in the second-stage English version by the intervening verb *came*. To overcome this I applied the rule of *Extraposition*, which (among other things) allows a group $_{NP}\{$ X $_{PP}\{$ Y $\}_{PP}$ $\}_{NP}$ to separate into $_{NP}\{$ X $\}_{NP}$ and $_{PP}\{$ Y $\}_{PP}$ by 'extraposing' the latter to the back of the sentence. To my sensibilities, this operation had just the right artistic effect.

12.5 DISASSEMBLY AND REASSEMBLY: REPRESENTATIONAL STRATA AND TRAJECTIONS

In this final section we will briefly consider an ancillary tool of bridge technique, DISASSEMBLY AND REASSEMBLY, and conclude with some remarks promised at the beginning of chapter 6 concerning levels of representation and trajections.

It will have been noted throughout the illustration of bridge technique over the course of this chapter that guideline (11.3) has played quite a prominent role: in developing ASRs, substrings functionally apprehendable as sentences (matrix clauses) have for the most part been assimilated to sentences formally as well. It will also have been noted that this formal assimilation was stationary, in the sense that substrings thus rerepresented as matrix clauses retained their surface-structural embedding relations to any other clauses within the same root sentence. This point is schematized in (12.16): taking (a) as an input to guideline (11.3), the result has always been of the form (b), where the original clauselike strings (1',2',3',4') after formal assimilation (1,2,3,4) retain their original mutual embedding properties, rather than being rerepresented as wholly independent clauses (root sentences), as portrayed in (c).

Translational situations frequently arise, however, where for one reason or another the source-text embedding network cannot optimally (or at all) be replicated in the tárget. Furthermore, particularly when dissimilarity between source- and target-language syntax is aggravated by unusual complexity of clause structure in the source text, simple application of Reordering will be defeated (or at least unduly encumbered) by the intricacy of the structures to be addressed.

In cases of this type, a more drastic procedure may be called for, a two-stage subtechnique to be called DISASSEMBLY and REASSEMBLY. Disassembly means no more or less than implementing guideline (11.3) per (12.16a)–(12.16c); and reassembly refers to resynthesizing the clauses into some target-optimal form, such as (12.16c)–(12.16d).

A brief illustration may be provided with the tail end of *Thomas Mann's* sesquipedalian sentence considered earlier in (4.6), repeated and annotated as (12.17s). For convenience, the schemata in (12.16) were tacitly based on this example. As may be seen, (12.17s) has the structure of (12.16a), consisting of a root clause $_1\{$ $\}_1$ containing a succession of three embedded clauses at the first level of depth: $_2\{$ $\}_2$ $_3\{$ $\}\{$ $\}_3$ $_4\{$ $\}_4$.

(12.15) s.

Da falt der $_{NP}${en selsom følelse $_{PP}${av ensomhet, skeffelse og tristhet}$_{PP}$}$_{NP}$ over faren

t.

→ There came $_{NP}${a strange feeling $_{PP}${of loneliness, disappointment and sadness}$_{PP}$}$_{NP}$ over the father

Refashioning I: neutralization of the *there*-construction

$_{NP}${A strange feeling $_{PP}${of loneliness, disappointment and sadness}$_{PP}$}$_{NP}$ came over the father

Refashioning II: Extraposition

$_{NP}${A strange feeling}$_{NP}$ came over the father, $_{PP}${of loneliness, of disappointment and sadness}$_{PP}$ (M1980b:99)

(surface same as ASR) (Mykle:35)

an. 'then fell there $_{NP}${a strange feeling $_{PP}${of loneliness, disappointment and sadness}$_{PP}$}$_{NP}$ over the father'

(12.16) a. 1'{ 2'{ }2' 3'{ }3' 4'{ }4' }1'
b. 1{   2{ }2   3{ }3   4{ }4 }1
c. 1{ }1 , 2{ }2 , 3{ }3 ,4{ }4
d. 1{ 2{ }2 }1   3{ }3   4{ }4

(12.17) (= **tail end of (4.6)**)

s. 1{und mit 2{der⟨b⟩ bald sich nähernden, bald foppend   wieder ins Weite schwindende }2
    and with   the   now approaching   now mockingly again in-the distance disappearing

    Hoffnung⟨b⟩ in 3{einem nachgerade erbitterten}3 Kampfe⟨c⟩ lag,   4{den⟨c⟩ durch
    hope   in an   ever more bitter   struggle was-engaged   which by means of

    einen Gewaltstreich zu beenden er sich neuerdings geneigt zeigte}4}1
    bold action   to end   he was showing himself ever more inclined

disassembled 1{and with 2{ . . . ⟨b⟩ . . . }2 hope⟨b⟩ in 3{ . . . ⟨c⟩ . . . }3 struggle⟨c⟩ was engaged, 4{ . . . ⟨c⟩ . . . }4}
clauses   2{0⟨b⟩ now seemed almost within his grasp, now receded into the distance
                and mocked him there}2

                3{0⟨c⟩ grew daily more embittered}3
                4{he even threatened to end 0⟨c⟩ once and for all by a single bold bid for liberty}4

t. 1{Joachim wrestled⟨c⟩ with these hopes⟨b⟩ of his, 2{that⟨b⟩ now seemed almost within his
    grasp, now receded into the distance and mocked him there}2;3{the struggle⟨c⟩ grew daily
    more embittered}3, 4{he even threatened to end it⟨c⟩ once and for all by
    a single bold bid for liberty}4}1

Disassembly of (12.17s) is given next in the middle of (12.17), which corresponds to (12.16c). Note that root-matrix ₁{ }₁ contains coindexical placeholders of the three disassembled clauses, which are then listed as independent sentences.

Finally, the disassembled clauses are reassembled as (12.17t), with the new organization schematized in (12.16d). Observe the crucial role of coindexing in this connection. If the disassembled clauses were not explicitly tagged for their relations within the original source text, they could not be coherently sewn back together again in a target text purporting to remain (largely) sensically faithful to the source. (Such coindexing is furthermore only a special case of the general requirement that disasembled clauses be somehow tagged for *all* their semantic roles within the original source complex, whether involving coreference or not.)

As a final note in this chapter, let us return to the list of *five factors* given at the outset of chapter 6 (§6.0.(i–v)), which purported to constrain the apparent indeterminacy and arbitrariness to which trajectional analysis is susceptible. The first four of these factors have already been discussed in appropriate sections, leaving just the last for us to consider now: (§6.0.(v)) *Relativization of trajectional analysis to strata of representation.*

Bridge technique affords quite a facile interpretation of this factor, as may be seen in returning to example (12.12) and asking which trajection mediates between the source *los dos* and the target *the curate and the barber*. It will readily be appreciated that if the question is posed relative to a nexus modeled with bridge technique, no genuine response can be given without first answering another question: Which stratum of representation is the truss taken to be? If the truss were taken to be the surface stratum (as for example in the null case from Mykle/M1980b given in §12.1), the answer would be 'Substitution'. But if the truss is taken to be the abstract stratum, as actually portrayed in (12.12), the answer must be 'Equation': *el Cura⟨a⟩ y el Barbero⟨b⟩ → the curate⟨a⟩ and the barber⟨b⟩.* Neither answer is whimsical or arbitrary. Which is apposite will depend on what truss has been determined as optimal for the analysis at large.[9]

NOTES

1. The examples from Tacitus/Grant employed in chapter 11 will be foregone; while suitable for introducing the notion of government and the rudiments of derivational modeling, they are too cumbersome for introducing bridge technique.

2. To say that English and French share these rules is not to say that they are identical, either in point of form or of conditions. Thus here, while the English infinitive is singly marked by the preposition *to*, its French counterpart is marked twice: fore by the preposition *de* and aft by the suffix -er.

3. In addition to (12.6), Máquez/Rabassa evince at least one other similar case of *procurar*, one solved by a different technique than spanning; see (12.11). Even more cases are evinced with the largely synonymous verb *tratar* (at least 125/140, 186/208, 282/313bis, 292/323), most responded to with a span in the target. (I also ran across at least one case in Homer's Iliad, where the Greek verb *peirāi* 'you⟨a⟩try' governs (*hōs ke Trōes⟨b⟩ . . . apolōntai*}'how the Trojans⟨b⟩ might be destroyed' (H i:185[XXI,459]), a nexus that Rouse addresses with the simple expedient of depassivizing the English counterpart of the embedded verb: *∅⟨a⟩ doing your best {∅⟨a⟩ to destroy them⟨b⟩}* (R:252). As will be seen, this solution resembles that used by Rabassa for Spanish *procurar* in (12.11).)

4. Stripped of bridge-technical specifics, refashioning is redolent of Steiner's notion of 'cumlative self-correction' (1975:269).

5. For instance, the Hertfordshire dialect of British English; cf. M1981c:299.

6. This constraint has received much attention by theoreticians over the years, first by Ross (1967) under the rubric of 'Complex NP Constraint'. More recently, attempts have been made to subsume it under the principle of 'Subjacency' (see, e.g., Chomsky (1982), where the difference between the clause-categories *S'* and *S* is also explained).

7. The qualification 'in the context' is necessary, since in Spanish the masculine gender is taxonomically conflative between hyponymic reference to 'male persons' (as here) and generic reference to 'persons regardless of sex' (e.g. masculine *señores* in *Así que mis [señores⟨a + b⟩] Duque⟨a⟩ y Duqueza⟨b⟩, aquí está vuestro gobernador . . .* (Cervantes:624[II,55]), Diffusionally translated by Cohen as *So, my [lord⟨a⟩] Duke⟨a⟩ and my[lady⟨b⟩]Duchess⟨b⟩, here's your governor . . .* (1950:828). Cf. §9.1–§9.2.

8. The [ə] is suppressed upon proclisis of *u-* 'and, also'.

9. There are several precedents in the literature for bridge technique, ranging from general to specific. In the former category are various nontransformational models based on the widespread recognition that translation involves unraveling a source meaning (cf. going up the left pylon, reconstructing it in target terms (crossing the truss), and fitting this result out as an actual target text (coming down the right pylon); cf., e.g., Wilss (1977:49–95) for examples, discussion, and references. Specifically close to bridge technique are Nida and Taber's triad of Analysis-Transfer-Restructuring, and in particular their notions of 'back-transformation' (taking place in the analogue of bridge technique's source pylon) into 'kernel sentences' (cf. bridge technique's disassembly); (Nida and Taber 1974: 33–39). Despite these points of convergence, however, bridge technique is largely an independent development. The seed of the idea goes back to 1961 and my confrontation, as a commercial-legal translator, with two diabolical one-sentence-paragraph source texts, one a Turkish law, the other a German description of an invention. The seed began to germinate a year or so later when I became familiar with some of Sydney Lamb's early work on machine translation; cf. Lamb (1964). (In this connection it is noteworthy that a bridge-technique-like use of transformations has apparently become central in current work on machine translation; cf. Hutchins (1984:97)).

PART THREE

Chapter *13*

PHONETICS, PHONOLOGY, AND POETIC FORM

13. PRELIMINARIES: PHONETIC TRANSCRIPTION

As mentioned in the Introduction (§0.4), the last part of this book will be devoted to consideration of a few types of translational nexus marked by REDUCED SITUATIONAL CONTROL—that is, nexus types where understanding of the extralinguistic components of the source text coupled with knowledge of the target language provides insufficient information for an adequate translation.

By far the most important and most common ingredients to such cases are contributed by CENEMATIC STRUCTURE (§0.2.1), which by its very nature is essentially out of phase both unilinguistically with the plerematic structure of its own language, and translinguistically with the cenematic structure of the paired translational language. Given this primacy of cenematics in the work of this part of the book, fully half of the discussion (this chapter and the next) will be devoted to cenematic structure in its own right, culminating with discussion of a cenematic-geared type of translation called TRANSDUCTION (chapter 14). Chapter 15 will deal with reduced situational control occasioned by a cenematic-plerematic symbiosis called TRANSJACENCE, while chapter 16 will treat control-reduction induced by a largely plerematic phenomenon called PARALLAX.

In view of the cenematic weight of much of the ensuing discussion, it will be useful to provide a simple chart defining the phonetic symbols to be employed. (This chart also serves to define the phonetic transcription employed for certain

C O N S O N A N T S (= [−syllabic])

	[+anterior / −coronal]		[+anterior / +coronal] apical		[−anterior / +coronal]	[−anterior / −coronal]			
	bilab	labden	[−rill]	[+rill]	palatal	velar	uv	phar	glot
stops [−continuant] [−voice]	p		t			k	q		ʔ
stops [−continuant] [+voice]	b		d			g			
affricates [−continuant] [−voice]		pᶠ	c		č				
affricates [−continuant] [+voice]					ǰ				
spirants [+continuant] [−voice]	φ	f	θ	s	š	x		ḥ	h
spirants [+continuant] [+voice]	β	v	ð	z	ž	γ		ʕ	
nasals	m		n			ŋ			
liquids [−lateral]			r						
liquids [+lateral]			l						
glides	w				y				

V O W E L S (= [+syllabic])

	[−back]		[+back]	
	[−round]	[+round]	[−round]	[+round]
high [+tense]	i	ü	ɨ	u
high [−tense]	I	Ü		U
mid [+tense]	e	ö		o
mid [−tense]	ε	ɔ̈	ʌ	ɔ
low	æ		a	

long segments—XX: niṣṣɔɔviim (13.6a), flíisə (13.9)

stress ˈ—(primary) V́ ˌ(secondary) V̌: bráwn # šæ̀gəd (§14.3.2), yəśabbéeʕuu (15.2s)

emphasis (uvularization,pharyngealization)—Ç: niṣṣɔɔviim (13.6a)

palatalization ([+ high, − back])—Ç: s̩Lə́β, glǎað̑ (14.6)

reduction—V̌, ə: wəxii, ʔámɔɔθoo (9.4), s̩Ļə́β (14.6), flíisə (13.9)

fortition—capital C: s̩Ļə́β, kóRax (14.6)

elision—ʾC: ˈmraʔatun (9.4bs)

proclisis—X-X: ʔɛθ-ʕavdoo (9.4as)

nasalization—C̃: áɣoβur (14.6)

Biblical Hebrew ś (cf. M1978): taḥpaśśɛnnɔ

Biblical Hebrew YHWH (the ineffable name of God): (8.25s, 10.4sc)

Sephardic Hebrew à (cf. M1983f): ʔàv (8.13)

languages in earlier sections of the book: Modern Hebrew (8.5), Sephardic Hebrew (8.13), Biblical Hebrew (all Hebrew cases but the preceding: (1.5), (2.9),
etc.); Arabic (9.4); and Yiddish (2.12). For the transcription of other languages,
see §0.4.1).

The symbols and values employed in the chart are largely those prevalent in
American linguistics. (Beyond what will be further specified at pertinent spots
throughout, knowledge of the intrinsic values of the sounds in the chart and the
principles of their classification will not be necessary, but the interested reader is
referred to standard handbooks like Hyman (1975). For the feature [rill], see
M1978a, a publication that also provides the basis for the transcription of Biblical Hebrew employed in this book.

The chart is primarily organized in terms of conventional articulatory classes
(in which vein the following abbreviations on the top row should be noted: *bi-
labi*al, *labio*dental, *uv*ular, *phar*yngeal, *glot*tal), with some cross- and subclassification by features, which will also be required in later contexts (e.g. (13.7),
(13.9), (14.2), (14.7)).

Immediately following the chart is a list of diacritic symbols providing phonetic and phonological information ancillary to the values given in the charts
proper. (A few examples follow the colon in each case.)

Finally, a few special usages from Hebrew are given after the list, symbols
which for one reason or another stand apart but need not be further analyzed for
the purposes at hand (see references if interested).

13.1 CENEMATICS AND ORTHOMETRICS

While cenematic reality subtends all language, its power is manifested differently across text types. This power is probably strongest, and was doubtless even
stronger in earlier days of the human race, in oral text types[2] originally expres-
sive of religion, dance, and music—text types whose classical and modern de-
scendants are largely classified as (if not always felt to be) POETIC.

In what follows, the term 'poetic' will for the most part be avoided as being
unduly connotative of value judgment and will largely be replaced by the term
'orthometric'.[3] A text will be designated as orthometric to the extent that it is
characterized by the special prominence of its cenematic structure, a prominence
frequently but not exclusively symptomized by the presence of one or more
cenematic patterns to be called FIGURAE. Cenematic figurae include but are not
limited to such traditionally recognized forms as meter, rhyme, and alliteration.[4]

With an eye to working up to translational examples from Turkish and Old
Irish to be adduced later, preliminary illustration will be provided with unilinguistic cases from English of both rhyme (13.1) and alliteration (13.2–3). Because poetry in the narrow, formal sense (verse) may first come to mind as the
natural habitat of rhyme and alliteration, examples (13.1–3) have intentionally
been chosen to demonstrate that the pale of orthometric language can be much

wider. The cases in (13.1) comprise a selection of four English-language text types often embellished by rhyme: lyrics of popular songs or folk ballads (a), nursery rhymes (b), aphorisms (c), and one of a variety of styles of Black English adlib dialogue (d).[5] Note in passing that while END RHYME predominates in these examples, (13.1b) contains both that (*lean* and *clean*) and INTERNAL RHYME (*sprat* and *fat*).

The alliterative examples have been chosen to illustrate what I perceive as two salient roles of this figura in the tradition of twentieth-century American English: PLAYFULNESS (13.2, the narrative lines from a cartoon in Herriman (1969:161));[6] and MERISM (13.3), whereby a class of elements is represented through a list of alliterating exemplars that is normally not exhaustive (a) but may be (b). Observe also that while these two functions often overlap, they need not: thus, the topic of (13.3b) is anything but playful.

(13.1) a. Over the [mountains,]
   And over the [waves,]
   Under the [fountains,]
   And under the [graves;]
   Under floods that are [deepest,]
   Which Neptune [obey,]
   Over rocks that are [steepest,]
   Love will find out the [way.] (Anonymous, apud Bartlett: 1013)
 b. Jack [Sprat] could eat no [fat]
   His wife could eat no [[lean]]
   So between them both, you see,
   They licked the platter [[clean]] (Bartlett:1015)
 c. Man [proposes]
   God [disposes] (Thomas À Kempis, apud Bartlett:83)
 d. Off yo' ass an' on yo' [feet]
   The first sergeant wanna see y'all
   On the company [street] (John Delt:p.c.[Fort Benning, Ga, 1958])

(13.2) a. Where 'Train Roik' hurtles with
   immobile speed in *f*atuous *f*ixity along the
   *sh*immering *sh*ore of 'Oljeto' where the
   moon dips its horns—
   A song is *w*arblingly *w*afted to the *w*istful *w*inds
   of *W*unanji.
 b. Continuing the *s*weet *s*inger *p*ersists in his *p*salmody.
 c. With *p*urposeful *p*ursuance the songster *p*ersists in
   *h*is *h*ypothetic *h*ymning with *a*ssiduous
   *i*ndifference and *i*nfelicitous *i*nsistence.
 d. Paff!!! The song is ended. (Herriman 1969:161)

(13.3) **a**. Louis Armstrong, favorite of *p*rincesses,
     *p*residents, and the *p*eople (Commercial aired on radio station
      WNEW-AM, New York City, 14 November 1983)
  b. Dave Marash reporting: A New Gonorrhea . . .
     the *c*auses, the *c*arriers, the *c*ures (*TV Guide*, New York Metropolital
     edition, 27 February–5 March 1982: A-20)

The point just made, that the examples of (13.2–3) are representative of twentieth-century American English, suggests the importance of a distinction that must always be drawn in the study of poetic and literary language: the logical independence of a TRADITION from the LANGUAGE serving as a vehicle to that tradition. Thus, in earlier centuries, an important role of alliteration in English and other North European languages was that of enhancing DRAMATIC CLIMAX, a function that may still be seen in the work of as recent an artist as Edgar Allan Poe; cf. (13.4), the concluding words to a particularly grim tale:

(13.4) 'Here then, at least', I shrieked aloud, 'can I never
    —can I never be mistaken—There arc the full, and the
    black, and the wild eyes—of my *l*ost *l*ove—of the *l*ady—of the
    Lady Ligeia'. (Poe:164)

Looking beyond English, diversity and variability across languages and traditions become even more obvious. Thus, the alliterative function of dramatic climax is still viable in modern Irish prose. This is illustrated with the triplet of adjectives in (13.5s), the climax to an altogether serious and depressing short story. As may be seen in (13.5t), I purposely avoided the alliterative effect in my English translation. To my sensibilities, attempted replication of the alliteration here would have seriously conflicted with the tradition of contemporary American fiction writing. Indeed, it would have incurred the risk of imparting a totally inappropriate aura of playfulness to the sad denouement intended by the author.

(13.5) **s**. Shuigh an bhean ar cholbha na leapan,
    *t*ráite, *t*náite, *t*ugtha. (Ní Shúilleabháin 1976:17)
  t. The woman sat against the bedpost,
    drained, exhausted, spent. (M1980c:31)

Though innumerable examples could be given, just one more illustration will be provided here attesting to the independence of form and function in orthometric figurae across languages and traditions. The device of monothematic end-rhyme extending across large numbers of lines (schematically *aaaaaaa* . . .) is a frequent embellishment to both medieval Hebrew grammatical treatises (13.6a) and contemporary Black American 'rap' poetry (13.6b). Moreover, the kind of rhyme deployed is, as here, often a limiting-case variety involving full morphological repetition: of the plural suffix *-iim* in (13.6a), and of the whole word *bop* in (13.6b).[7]

(**13.6**) **a.** ʔarbaʕ ʔooθooθ nəsuux[iim],
bammiqrɔɔ ʕăruux[iim],
nittan lɔɔhɛɛm mahlǝx[iim],
yɔɔsǝʔuu ʕal šǝnee ðǝrɔɔx[iim],
yɔɔmiin uśmool miθhallǝx[iim],
nɔɔḥăluu šǝnee xǝθɔɔriim tǝmuux[iim],
ʕoomǝðiim niṣṣɔɔviim kimlɔɔx[iim] (Baer and Strack:6)

    an. 'four letters moulded,
set in the Bible,
with their own distribution,
manifested in two ways,
they distribute to the right or the left,
fitted out with crowns,
standing fast like kings' (JM)

    b. Me / I [Bop]
I slide [bop]
band [bop]
saxophone [bop]
radio [bop]
ditty [bop]
no in between bops, you dig
        but
gutter [bop] (Donna Brown:6)

13.2 FEATURE AND SUBSEQUENCE RHYME

Even as there are extreme cases of rhyme of the type illustrated in (13.6), involving fuller matching of paired segments than required for classical English rhyme, so there may be found cases in the opposite direction, manifesting less matching than dictated by classical norms. An example from contemporary rock lyrics is given in (13.7), where the end rhymes of a monothematic quatrain from Bob Dylan's 'Oxford Town' are displayed. Note that only the last two end-words fit the canonical requirements of classical end-rhyme: *come* and *from* = [kʌ́m] and [frʌ́m], whose shared [ʌ́m] fits the general condition for classical English rhyme, which dictates sharing of all units according to the template [V́X#] (the stressed vowel [V́] separated from the end of the word [#] by any or no other segments [X]).

(**13.7**) *Spelling*   *Phonetic transcription*   *Feature analysis*

Spelling	Phonetic transcription	Feature analysis
⟨son⟩	[sʌ́n]	([− low][+ coronal])
⟨bomb⟩	[bám]	([+ low][− coronal])
⟨come⟩	[kʌ́m]	([− low][− coronal])
⟨from⟩	[frʌ́m]	([− low][− coronal])

        (from Bob Dylan's 'Oxford Town', apud Zwicky:678)

There are, to be sure, traditional labels for cataloguing the imperfect end-rhyme of the first two lines of (13.7), as opposed to the canonical pairing [kÁm] and [frÁm] in the last two lines: ASSONANCE and CONSONANCE. Using these notions, one would say that while *son* [sÁn] may not make for full-blown rhyme with [kÁm] and [frÁm], it does assonate with them by virtue of sharing the stressed vowel [Á]. Similarly, *bomb* [bám] would be described as consonating with [kÁm] and [frÁm] by virtue of the shared [m], despite the difference in vocalism ([á] ≠ [Á]).

However, as Arnold Zwicky convincingly documents (1976), the notions of assonance and consonance fail to capture the important regularity of rock lyrics, instantiated in (13.7); lyrically matching words falling short of full rhyme in the classical mode nevertheless normally evidence a specifiable mutual PHONETIC SIMILARITY. Such phonetic similarity, moreover, falls into two general categories, of which that exemplified in (13.7) constitutes what Zwicky calls FEATURE RHYME, according to which matching segments may differ by no more than a specifiably small number of phonetic features (cf. §4.1.1). Thus, the four end-words in (13.7) may not constitute classical full rhyme, but they do pass muster as feature rhyme since [á] ≠ [Á] only by virtue of the single feature disagreement [+low] ≠ [−low], and likewise [n] ≠ [m] by virtue of [+coronal] ≠ [−coronal].

The second category of departure from strict classical rhyme that Zwicky documents for rock lyrics he calls SUBSEQUENCE RHYME, whereby an otherwise matching word may contain a specifiably small number of consonants not shared by its rhyming partner(s). This is illustrated in (13.8), where the [d] of [bɔ́rd] *bored* is discounted, leaving the rhyme to go through by virtue of the shared SUB-SEQUENCE [ɔ́r]:

(13.8) *Spelling*   *Phonetic transcription*
    ⟨bored⟩   [bɔ́rd]
    ⟨war⟩   [wɔ́r]
    ⟨floor⟩   [flɔ́r]
    ⟨before⟩   [bəfɔ́r]
        (from Bob Dylan's 'Highway 61 Revisited', apud Zwicky:680)

Likely testimony to the general validity of Zwicky's formulation of feature and subsequent rhyme is the appearance in other traditions of similar phenomena readily analyzable in accordance with his guidelines. To cite just two cases from German literature, Goethe uses a notable amount of feature rhyme in *Faust* (13.9;[8] and the alliterative set in (13.10) might be interpreted either as feature alliteration—if the initial consonantism of the last two members is analyzed as the unitary affricate [pʲ], differing from the first-member spirant [f] by the feature opposition [−continuant] ≠ [+continuant] respectively; see (13.10a)—or arguably as subsequence alliteration, if the consonantism is analyzed as a cluster [pf] whose [p] is discounted (13.10b).

(13.9) a. Gestärkten Arms hebt er sie hoch[empor]p[εmpɔ́r]([+ mid, + round])
Entführt er sie wohl [gar]   p[gár]   ([− mid, − round])
(Thomas II:88[2,I,6542f])

    an. 'with mighty arm he snatches her up
and straight away abducts her' (JM)

b. Dort! Wie fürchterlich! Ein [Riese]p [ríizə] ([+ voice])
Steht in   Faustens altem [Vliesse]! p[flíisə]([− voice])
(ibid.: 92[2,II,6628f])

    an. 'Look! How frightful! A giant
standing in Faust's old fleece!' p(JM)

c. Doch, ungenügsam wie du [bist]p [bíst]   ([− round])
Empfandest du wohl kein [Gelüst]?p [gəlÜst] ([+ round])
(ibid.:248[2,IV,10132F)

    an. 'But, unsatiable as you are,
didn't you feel any desire?' (JM)

(13.10)   *F*rauen, *Pf*erde und *Pf*eifen (Trautzl:232)
    an. 'women, horses, and pipes' (cf. 'wine, women, and song')
a. [f]   [pᶠ]   [pᶠ]
b. [f]   [pf]   [pf]

13.3 TWO MODES OF LINGUISTIC APPLICATION

The relevance of linguistics to orthometric analysis may be realized in various modes. One such mode has just been illustrated with Zwicky's analysis of rock rhyme, most particularly with his concept of feature rhyme per (13.7). In such situations a class of objects (in this case, rhyming pairs) is preanalytically recognized as having certain properties (in this case, phonetic properties) relevant to their behavior as analytic objects, but the properties in question are not understood clearly enough to predict that behavior—a deficit then removed by the linguistic application in question. Thus, Zwicky has succeeded in applying the theory of phonetic features to the analysis of rock rhyme, thereby revealing that such rhyme is considerably more structured than had previously been recognized.[9]

A second mode of applying linguistic theory turns on discovering (or explicating) that the analytic objects should be viewed from a different perspective than had previously been assumed. In some such cases, moreover, the perspectives themselves may be preanalytically rather well understood, so that perseverance in viewing the analytic objects from the wrong perspective will be of no avail, no matter how thorough one's understanding of that perspective may be. Examples are given in (13.11) and (13.12), which provide additional instances of playful and meristic alliteration, respectively (cf. (13.2–3)). If one approaches

the investigation with the a priori plausible assumption that the fundamental substantive property of contemporary American English alliteration is phonetic,
then cases like (13.11d) and (13.11e) will presumably be analyzed in terms of
feature alliteration. That is, *Chiefly Chopin*, as [čiyfliy] and [šowpæn], would be
analyzed as evidence that homorganic affricates and spirants may match,
waiving the feature distinction [− continuant] ≠ [+ continuant], just as in the
German case of (13.10a); and similarly, *Some Shostakovich*, [sʌm] and
[šastəkowvɪč], might be taken as showing the irrelevance of the opposition
[+ anterior] ≠ [− anterior].

However, such an analysis is almost certainly incorrect, the actual conditions for the alliterability of (13.11d) and (13.11e) following instead from a shift
of perspective: from that of PHONETICS to that of ORTHOGRAPHY, according to
which the examples may be seen to alliterate by virtue of beginning with identical letters (or groups of letters): ⟨Chiefly⟩ and ⟨Chopin⟩; and ⟨Some⟩ and
⟨Shostakovich⟩.

And yet, the hypothesis that contemporary American English alliteration
may be reckoned orthographically cannot be exhaustive, as per cases like
(13.12), which evidences dissimilar initial letters (⟨G⟩ ≠ ⟨J⟩) in the face of phonetic identity ([ǰɛnəsəs] and [ǰækəndaf]). Taking (13.11) and (13.12) together,
an adequate characterization may be phrased along the lines of (13.13).

One may rightfully perceive a resemblance between the dual perspective
(phonetic and orthographic) imputed to linguistic strings by (13.13) and the perspective of STRATA OF REPRESENTATION developed in chapters 11 and 12. The
similarity of the two situations will be developed in the next section.

(13.11) **a**. Predominantly *P*rokofiev
      b. *F*or the Most Part *F*rescobaldi
      c. But a *B*it of *B*izet
      d. *Ch*iefly *Ch*opin
      e. *S*ome *Sh*ostakovich (Michael Winship, apud Collins)

(13.12) western theories of language from *G*enesis to *J*ackendoff (Pratt:14)

(13.13) Contemporary American English alliteration may be
        reckoned either phonetically or orthographically.

13.4 CENEMATIC STRATA AND DERIVATIONS; APRs

If we make the largely uncontroversial assumption that spelling and pronunciation are mediated by a body of conventions popularly called 'spelling rules', we
may organize findings like (13.11–13) into derivations much like those developed in chapters 11 and 12 but differing from the latter in three ways:

      (i) The strata are phonetic and orthographic rather than abstract-syntactic
and surface-syntactic;

(ii) The derivation is driven by spelling rules rather than by syntactic rules;

(iii) A new ingredient is added to the derivation, in the form of an OR-THOMETRIC RULE, in this case (13.13)

An illustrative synthesis is given in (13.14), where the role of orthometric rule (13.13) should be noted. Since the function of a rule of this type is to accept or reject linguistic strings purporting to alliterate in accordance with the canons of some orthometric tradition, we may talk of its operation as INTERFACING two systems: a body of orthometric patterns and a language. The interfacing of (13.13) is portrayed in (13.14) by the slanting arrows in the left margin of the derivation, its effects being marked by underscoring of the initials accepted as alliterative (both [p] and [p] and ⟨P⟩ and ⟨P⟩ in (a), only ⟨Ch⟩ and ⟨Ch⟩ in (b), and only [ǰ] and [ǰ] in (c)).

While orthometric sensitivity to spelling is by no means rare in poetic traditions, it should be noted that most linguists consider orthography to be a paralinguistic accessory to a language rather than a genuine part thereof (cf. §0.2.2). From this point of view, a derivation like (13.14) would be considered heterogeneous, its phonetic input stratum being linguistic but its orthographic output stratum being paralinguistic.

In view of the similarity of (13.14) to the morphosyntactic derivations of chapters 11 and 12, the hybrid nature of (13.14) prompts a question. Since the derivations of chapters 11 and 12 were plerematic and (13.14) is half cenematic, by virtue of its phonetic stratum, might there be such things as fully cenematic derivations?

The answer to this question is decidedly affirmative, and it will be the work of the succeeding pages to demonstrate their usefulness to the analysis of orthometric interfacing, both unilinguistically and translinguistically.

In theoretical linguistics the pertinent area of research is called PHONOLOGY. Fortunately for our purposes, phonology and syntax evince points of similarity in both form and function, so that a good deal of preliminary discussion can be foregone by cross-reference to chapters 11 and 12.

To begin with, even as abstract syntactic representation (ASR) was designed (i) 'to maximize . . . semantic transparency', and (ii) 'as a partial by-product of that, [also to maximize] uniformity of structural modeling' (§11.2), so here AB-STRACT PHONETIC REPRESENTATION (APR)[10] will be designed to maximize transparency of the relation between the sounds of a language ((SURFACE) PHONETIC REPRESENTATION) and the morphosyntactic forms symbolized by those sounds— a design once again enhancing uniformity of structural modeling.

For a simple illustration of these points from English, consider the following pairs of singular-plural nouns: ⟨top, tops; tot, tots; clock, clocks; myth, myths; cliff, cliffs; curb, curbs; card, cards; frog, frogs; pal, pals; pan, pans⟩.

If these nouns are transcribed phonetically, a difference in pronunciation emerges which is disguised by the orthographic homogeneity of the plural suffix ⟨s⟩: While the first five plurals end in the voiceless spirant [s], the last five end in

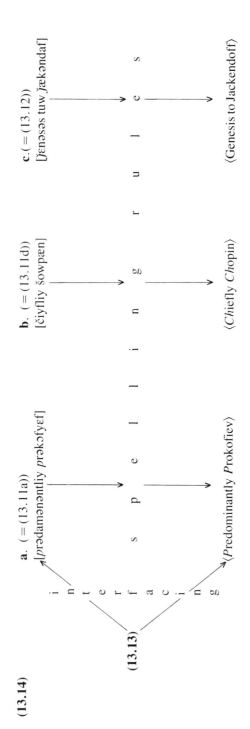

the voiced spirant [z]—[tap, taps; tat, tats; klak, klaks; mIθ, mIθs, kIIf, kIIfs; kərb, kərbz; kard, kardz; pæl, pælz; pæn, pænz].

Moreover, if feature analysis is applied, a pervasive regularity emerges concerning the distribution of [s] and [z]: the voiceless [s] ends nouns whose stems end in a voiceless segment, while the voiced [z] follows voiced segments—[ta   p   s   ], [ta   t   s   ], etc.; [kər   b   z   ], [kar   d   z   ], [− voice] [− voice] [− voice] [− voice] [+ voice] [+ voice] [+ voice] [+ voice] etc.

Now since these relations constitute part of the productive method of forming plural nouns in English, the orderly distribution of the forms and segments in question comprises a pervasive regularity *both* of phonetics (the [− voice]-with-[− voice] and [+ voice]-with-[+ voice] pairings) *and* of morphology (the fact that these pairings serve the same morphological function, pluralization).

This is precisely the sort of dual regularity that phonology is designed to capture, by the twofold procedure of:

(i) rerepresenting the morphological common denominator in a unitary fashion as a PHONOLOGICAL REPRESENTATION (to capture the morphological half of the regularity); and

(ii) relating that phonological representation back to its actual pronunciation by PHONOLOGICAL RULES (to capture the phonetic half of the regularity).

The resemblance of these phonological procedures to those of syntax discussed in chapters 11 and 12 should be obvious, and we shall accordingly exploit that resemblance by formulating a guideline for developing applied-linguistic analogue of phonological representations, ABSTRACT PHONETIC REPRESENTATIONS (APRs):

(13.15) When one morpheme (or other morphosyntactic form) is symbolized by two or more paradigmatically distinct phonetic strings, each such string may be rerepresented in its own syntagmatic context as an abstract phonetic representation (APR) identical in shape for each of the phonetic strings.

As in the case of the ASRs developed in association with bridge technique (chapters 11 and 12), the relation of APRs built up from (13.15) to their corresponding phonetic representations may be portrayed in the form of a derivation mediated by devised analogues of one or more phonological rules.

The procedure is illustrated comprehensively in (13.16) on the basis of two of the English pluralization examples. The two strata of these derivations comprise APRs as input, set off in /   /, and phonetic representations as output, marked by [   ]. In cases (a) and (b), guideline (13.15) is implemented by devising as the APR a string identical to either of the actual phonetic representations, with corresponding selection of an appropriate rule to relate the APR back to its actual pronunciation (respectively Devoicing of /z/ to [s] and Voicing of /s/

(13.16) a.   /tap-z/   /kərb-z/
         Devoicing   s
                            [taps]   [kərbz]
   b.   /tap-s/   /kərb-s/
         Voicing   z
                            [taps]   [kərbz]
   c.   /tap-Σ/   /kərb-Σ/
         Voice Adjustment   s   z
                            [taps]   [kərbz]

to [z]). In case (c), the APR is structured distinctly from either phonetic representation (a result symbolized by the Greek letter Σ), and hence requires a rule to
retrieve both [s] and [z].

As was the case with ASRs in chapters 11 and 12, the researcher should feel
free to experiment with different APRs and rules to obtain an optimal analysis.
As with ASRs too, however, this analytic liberty is best constrained by awareness of the likelihood that the closer one's derivation approaches results con-
firmed by the pure-linguistic enterprise of phonology, the better the chances are
of the technique bearing fruit.[11]

Actual orthometric cases will be considered in the next chapter.

NOTES

1. Stress will be indicated only when germane to the analysis at hand.

2. Cf. note 3 in the Introduction.

3. This term, unearthed from *Roget's Thesaurus* (Mawson 1945), also prevents confusion with novel
senses of other established terms (notably 'metrical' and 'prosodic') recently introduced in phonological theory. Cf., e.g., note 9 below.

4. Some plerematic figurae will be considered in §16.1. (Figurae might also be recognized which are
cenematic-plerematic hybrids; e.g. PARONOMASIA (§15.1).)

5. This was a summons to 'fall in' used by the platoon leader in an all-Black company in the segre-
gated United States Army of the mid 1940s. (Patterns like this are no doubt ancestral to contemporary
'rap'; cf. (13.6b).)

6. The set *persists* and *psalmody* in (13.2b) constitutes ORTHOGRAPHIC ALLITERATION since the initial *p* in *psalmody* is not pronounced; cf. §13.3 below. See also note 3 of chapter 14.

7. Varieties of morphological repetition were also affected by the Romans under the rubric of *anno-
minatio*, a conceit brought to decadent limits in the Middle Ages (Curtius:282f).

8. By itself, the feature-rhyme status of (13.9b) would be open to question since, as Robert Austerlitz and Ernst A. Ebbinghaus kindly point out, in Goethe's native dialect (that of Frankfurt am Main)
both these forms would be pronounced with [s]. However, Goethe deploys several other examples of
[+ voice] and [− voice] feature rhyme throughout *Faust* which are not characteristic of Frankfurt
German: e.g. on [d] and [t] in Kathe*d*er and Pe*t*er, Mo*d*er and To*dt*er, Stau*d*en and Lau*t*en, ba*d*end
and wa*t*end (ibid.: 93[2,II,6649f] 95[2,II,6691f]; 122[2,II,7259f]; 123[2,II,7286f]).

9. Another preeminent case in point is Kiparsky's (1977) reanalysis of classical English meter in terms of METRICAL PHONOLOGY.

10. This use of the abbreviation APR has nothing to do with Jeri J. Jaeger's psycholinguistic APR (Jaeger 1986), though the denotata do evince some overlap. (I did not see Jaeger's article till this book was in production)

11. In this vein, analysis (13.16b) turns out to be untenable. (Some discussion is afforded by Akmajian, et al.:119ff.)

Chapter *14*

TRANSDUCTION

14.1 TURKISH RHYME

Let us return to the Turkish quatrain of (5.1), reproduced in (14.1) and fitted out with an analytic translation:

(14.1)   Dört kitaptan bize haber verildi
Kâmil olan akıl başa derildi
İblis lâin merdud olup sürüldü
Hakkın buyruğundan döneldenberi

an.   'four books-from us-to knowledge give-PASSIVE-PAST
perfect be-ing wisdom head-into gather-PASSIVE-PAST
Satan however rebel be-ing banish-PASSIVE-PAST
God-of command-His-by convert-ing-from-since'

As was briefly discussed in chapter 5, this quatrain evidences a rhyme scheme *aaab*, based on the internal and external symmetry of the verbs ending the first three lines, a symmetry that completely resists Equation into English.

The problem of how this quatrain might be translated will be deferred while we address a fundamental orthometric question not broached at all in chapter 5: Granted that the verbs ending the first three lines of (14.1) may be symmetrically structured, and granted moreover that the first two verbs *verildi* and *derildi* obviously rhyme, yet by what virtue does the third verb, *sürüldü*, fit into the scheme?

In light of the discussion in the preceding chapter, it might seem that FEA-TURE RHYME is involved. Indeed, the relation of *dürüldü* to *verildi* and *derildi* would appear to be virtually the same as the feature-rhyming German pair *Gelüst* and *bist* in (13.9c), since in both cases a high front ($=[-$back]) rounded vowel (*ü*) is being matched with a high front unrounded vowel (*i*), differing only in the value of the one feature [round].[1]

Despite clear resemblances, however, the Turkish case does not constitute feature rhyme. It rather constitutes what might be called PHONOLOGICAL RHYME, a phenomenon than can be neatly captured with the device of cenematic deriva-tion introduced in §13.4. (In what follows, emphasis will be on the mechanics of applying the technique. Arguments for the correctness of the analysis itself, as opposed to one on the basis of feature rhyme, are presented in M1982c.)

The application of guideline (13.15) to the three focal verbs of (14.1) is im-mediately revealing. As shown in their analytic glosses, all three have in com-mon the morphological structure *VB-PASSIVE-PAST*. Moreover, only the verb stem (*VB*) is morphemically distinct across the three cases (*ver* $- \neq der - \neq sür -$), while conversely both the passive-voice suffix and past-tense suffix are morphemically constant across the cases, despite the fact that the first two verbs show one phonetic shape for those suffixes ($[-$il$-]$, $[-$di$]$) and the third verb another ($[-$ül$-]$,$[-$dü$]$). But then, in accordance with guideline (13.15), the pair of morphemically identical but phonetically distinct suffixes $[-$il$-]$ and $[-$ül$-]$ may be rerepresented by one and the same APR, as may the past-tense suffixes $[-$di$]$ and $[-$dü$]$. For reasons unimportant here, the APRs will be con-structed following the general strategy exemplified in (13.16c) and symbolized as $/-$Il$-/$ and $/-$dI/, respectively. Finally, the APRs will be related back to their phonetic representations by the rule given in (14.2), with summary results of the whole synthesis given as the derivation in (14.3).

(14.2) *Vowel Harmony*
An /I/ is replaced by a high vowel whose values for
the features [round] and [back] are identical to
those of the nearest preceding fully specified vowel.

(14.3)   /verIldI/   /derIldI/   /sürIldI/
Vowel Harmony   i   i   i   i   ü   ü
                   [verildi]   [derildi]   [sürüldü]

The derivation of (14.3) now allows a simple resolution to the question of how the three verbs rhyme. They do so not by virtue of similarities on the pho-netic stratum, as would be the case in feature rhyme, but rather by virtue of sharing the identical substring $/-$rIldI/ at the phonological stratum. This regular-ity suggests the rules of orthometric-linguistic interfacing in (14.4–5). Note that the schema in (14.4) requires identity both of the last (. . . #) two vowels (. . . V . . . V . . .) in a word and of any flanking consonants (C_0 . . . C_0 . . . C_0), an identity which, however, must by (14.5) be phonological rather than phonetic.[2]

(14.4) *Basic condition for rhyme in 'Ahi Ali Baba'*
Rhyming words must have identical values of the schema $C_0VC_0VC_0\#$.

(14.5) *Stratum condition for rhyme in 'Ahi Ali Baba'*
Rhyme is reckoned on the phonological stratum.

14.2 ALLITERATION IN OLD IRISH

Alliteration in Old Irish poetry gives a deceptive first-blush impression of being simply a medley of the feature type along the lines of the German example in (13.10a) and the full-segment type requiring phonetic identity of matching initials, similar to the English examples in (13.12–13). To see this, let us consider in a preliminary way the four triplet matches underscored in this phonetically transcribed nature poem (adopted from Lehmann (1982:108), who presents an orthographic version of the poem):

(14.6)   **i.** [s̪Líəβ *kú*ə *kú*ənax *kó*Rax dúβ]
    ii. [*gl*áað̣ *g*áyθ ima γl̥íN̥i]
    iii. [gár̥id̥ ma xlúx̥θe]
    iv. [ḅéeḳið̣ *b*órbð̣am *b*ánoð̣ur]
    v. [iṣin *áγ*oβur *íM̥*e]
    vi. [éeγið̣ kór os a xlúx̥θe]
   an.i. 'mountain *C*ua *w*olf-haunted *r*ugged black
    ii. *c*alls *w*ind around-its *g*lens
    iii. they-sound around-its precincts
    iv. *b*ellows *w*ild-stag *l*ight-brown
    v. *i*n-the Autumn *a*round-it
    vi. cries crane above its precincts'

Taking these four cases at face value as potential alliterative sets, it would appear that only the [k & k & k] of line (i) is of the pure full-segment type, the remaining three cases requiring one or more feature waivers: [g & g & γ] exempts the difference between plain velar stops ([g]) and the palatialized velar spirant ([γ]); [ḅ & b & b] waives the difference between the palatalized [ḅ] and the plain [b]s; and [i & á & í] ignores stress differences and discrepancies in vowel height.

However, it turns out that only the exemption of palatalization constitute true feature alliteration in the Zwickian sense. The vowel set [i & á & í] requires quite another explanation, in terms of three very disparate conditions, two of which are common to various other European alliterative traditions: (i) vowels may alliterate despite color differences (here, height differences); (ii) the restriction that alliteration be limited to initially stressed forms. Accordingly, alliteration on line (v) must, strictly speaking, be limited to the doublet [áγoβur íMe], though it is likely that the unstressed [iṣin] was felt to enhance the euphonic strength of that doublet.[3]

The points just touched on constitute a few of the BASIC CONDITIONS for Old

Irish alliteration, formulated as (14.7). The license for consonants to alliterate ir-respective of palatalization and for vowels to alliterate irrespective of color are given straightforwardly in (14.7b). The stress condition follows from the struc-ture of the template in (a): # (word boundary) is not a segment, so 'the first seg-ment' must be satisfied either by C_0 (a string of zero or more consonants) or by $\acute{V}$ (a stressed vowel).

(14.7) *Some basic conditions for Classical Irish alliteration*
    a. An initial is the first segment in a word satisfying the schema #$C_0\acute{V}$;
    b. For two or more words to alliterate, their initials must agree in relevant features:
       (i) In the case of C, the relevant features are all features except those defining palatalization ([high, back]);
      (ii) In the case of V, the only relevant feature is the defining feature of vowelhood itself, [+ syllabic].

To account for the remaining deviation from full alliteration in the sets of (14.6), the stop-spirant discrepancy of [g & g & γ] on line (ii), we must appeal to the STRATUM CONDITIONS for Classical Irish, an appeal that will also extend to a subtle point not yet broached concerning the set [á & í] on line (v).

A synoptic version of the pertinent stratus conditions appears in (14.8) (for the full analysis, see M1984a, 1986c), with corresponding derivations in (14.9). Both APRs are justified by guideline (13.15), since the phonetic representations [γlíÑe] and [áγoβur] are but paradigmatic allomorphs of other shapes appearing in other syntagmatic contexts, most notably the 'null context' shapes [glíÑe] and [φáγoβur]—shape that are then pressed into service as APRs by the same gen-eral ploy that gave (13.16a–b) (as opposed to (13.16c), which was followed in the Turkish case of (14.3)). The APRs are then derivationally related back to their phonetic forms by the rule of LENITION, which under a variety of morpho-syntactic conditions weakens stem-initial consonants pursuant to their phonetic properties: relevantly here, while stops weaken by spirantizing (/g/ → [γ]), the spirant /φ/ does so by disappearing altogether (/φ/ → [∅]).

Interfacing by the stratum conditions (14.8) operating on (14.9) is indicated by the arrows. Phonological matching is dictated for (14.9a) /g & g & g̯/ by (14.8a), since none of these segments is realized as zero (14.8b). Conversely phonetic matching is indeed dictated for (14.9b) [á & í] by (14.8b), since 'a pho-nological initial' (/φ/) 'is realized phonetically as zero'.

(14.8) *Some stratum conditions for Classical Irish alliteration*
    a. Alliteration is for the most part reckoned on the phonological stratum; but
    b. phonetic stratum reckoning is required under various derivational conditions. Among the latter, if a phonological initial is realized phonetically as zero ([∅]), the entire alliterative set in question must be interfaced on the phonetic stratum.

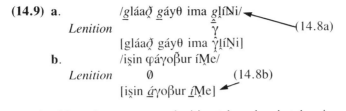

(14.9) a. /g̲láad̪̥ g̲áyθ ima g̲l̪íN̪i/

Lenition γ (14.8a)

[g̲láad̪̥ g̲áyθ ima ɣ̪̂l̪íN̪i]

b. /iṣin φáγoβ̥ur íM̪e/

Lenition ∅ (14.8b)

[iṣin á̲γoβur íM̪e]

At this point, one may legitimately ask what bearing all these arcane-seeming points of Turkish and Irish phonology and orthometrics may have on the question of translating the poems manifesting them. This will be the work of the following sections.[4]

14.3 TRANSDUCTION

Even if one concedes the usefulness of cenematic derivation for revealing and elucidating the orthometric structure of a poem, one's first reaction may be that such a technique is appropriate to unilinguistic literary analysis, rather than to the translinguistic issue of how such poems should be reconstructed in another language. Furthermore, such a reaction tends to be reinforced by the twentieth-century penchant for translating poetry into FREE VERSE, whatever the structure of the original—a procedure that moreover often produces undeniably excellent results. Thus, such an attitude a priori dissociates the unilinguistic work of orthometrically analyzing a poem and the translinguistic work of either translating that poem (operative mode) or of studying the structure of its translation (analytic mode).

However, wholesale endorsement of free-verse translation actually implies a general value judgment that I very much doubt many free-verse translators would consciously or explicitly embrace: that, *a priori, the cenematic patterns of a text are dispensable for translation*. Unilinguistic cenematic analysis is, after all, specifically designed to discover and describe such patterns, notably but not exclusively traditionally recognized figurae such as rhyme and alliteration—even and especially when they are manifested in subtle or exotic forms like those considered in §14.1–§14.2. Accordingly, blanket endorsement of free-verse translation of texts structured with such figurae at best leaves open the possibility that any power conveyed by such figurae may be lost to the target text because of the translator's insufficient awareness of the source text's cenematic structure.

There is also a manner of translation that is diametrical to free verse but in point of fact is often worse than free verse in its disregard of source-text figurae: that of automatic uniform conversion into some orthometric form conventional to the target tradition. An example of a vehicle for such SET-FORM translation from the earlier British-American tradition is end-rhyming iambic pentameter. The fact that in this sort of translation source figurae appear to be answered by target figurae disguises the more important fact that the source and target figurae may be out of phase or even clash. And to make matters worse, this infelicity is often compounded with further insult to the message or beauty of the source text entailed by satisfying the perfunctory dictates of the target figurae comprising the set form.

It is important to clarify that I am not attacking free verse or set-form translation per se but rather the assumption that either or both of these procedures can be employed uncritically. On the other hand, study of the source text may very well convince a translator that free verse or set form is the best response after all; and similarly, an analyst may come away from the study of someone else's free-verse or set-form translation convinced that this was in fact the optimal response. But in neither case can such felicitous results be assured without considering the source text's orthometric structure.

To be sure, many translators do manage to steer quite clear of the limiting-case dangers of free verse and set form, and discussions of their success in so doing are not infrequently encountered in the scholarly and poetic literature. At the same time, however, such results are often so finely geared to the specific source-target nexus in question that the general nature of the procedure does not clearly emerge. Furthermore, the orthometric analysis subtending such results is rarely very explicit and almost never presented with the aid of phonological analysis.

Against this background, I would like to discuss and exemplify an ancillary procedure for orthometric translation which I call TRANSDUCTION. In principle, it is simple to state what transduction consists of. First the analyst studies the orthometric structure of the source text, in particular the nature and disposition of its cenematic figurae. What happens next depends on whether the operative or analytic mode is in play. A translator will attempt to find (or devise) target-tradition figurae similar in function to those of the source, and blend these together into a target version, employing any adjustments and compromises felt necessary to the nexus as a whole. A nontranslator analyst will study the target text for its incidence of figurae and compare them with those of the source text for functional coherence and other points of transtextual integrity.

The rest of this chapter will be devoted to illustration of transduction on the basis of the two cases discussed in the preceding sections: the Turkish religious poem 'Ahi Ali Baba' (§14.1) and the Old Irish nature poem 'Slieve Cua'(§14.2).[5]

14.3.1 'Ahi Ali Baba'.

The first requirement for transduction is a list of source-text figurae, at least of those that are felt to be important enough to transduce. In the case of 'Ahi Ali Baba', this list is easy to compile:[6]

(14.10)   i. Three stanzas, each a quatrain.
   ii. Every line is hendecasyllabic.
   iii. The rhyme scheme for the three stanzas is *abab ccch dddb.*
   iv. Except for the refrain *b*, rhyme is end-rhyme in accordance with basic and stratum conditions (14.4)–(14.5).
   v. The refrain *b* is comprised by the recurrence chain of the suffix *-beri* 'since'.

The first two figurae (14.10i–ii) posed no problem and were simply equated by making the target three stanzas of eleven-syllable quatrains.[7] However, transduction was employed for the remaining three figurae.

To begin with, the final position of the refrain *b* (14.10v) in the rhyme scheme *abab cccb dddb* (iii) runs against the grain of English syntax, where most items of similar function (in this case, the functor *since*) are PREPOSITIVE to their domain, a discrepancy that could undermine the cardinal role played by *−beri* in the rhyme scheme of the poem. Hence, I struck upon a double strategy to transduce some of *−beri*'s refraining power into the English version of the poem: diffusional substitution of the recurrence chain *−beri . . . −beri . . . −beri . . . −beri* both by a chain of variable line-ending alliteration (*all̲urements of l̲ove . . .] l̲abors of l̲ove . . . grac̲e of G̲od . . . unders̲tanding my s̲ins*) and by a line beginning chain of fixed alliteration headed by the participle *being* (*B̲eing b̲ewitched . . . B̲eing b̲eset . . . B̲eing b̲rought . . . B̲eing b̲etter*). The goal of this double transduction was to rescue the integrity of the source rhyme-scheme by maintaining line-ending symmetry and at the same time to replicate some of the specific force of the morpheme *−beri* with a target item similar in sound (dissyllabics in initial [b]) and function (e.g. *being bewitched* = virtually 'Since I have been bewitched') in its normal target-language position (prepositive).

The final point of transduction involves the end-rhyme other than the refrain (14.10iv). Since the overall structure of English would defeat creation of any analogue of Turkish phonological rhyme (14.5) at the outset, it may have been possible to use a kind of set-form strategy and simply back up on full-segment rhyme in the target text. However, to my sensibilities this would have been too stark: Turkish phonological rhyme imparts a MUTED EUPHONY to its patterns which full rhyme would jeopardize with either monotony or blare. Thus, I decided on transduction into Zwickian feature rhyme (§13.2), which shares with phonological rhyme the ruled effect of euphonic matching based on phonetic similarity rather than identity. Hence, the phonologically based [i & i & ü] match in stanza two was transduced into featurally based [I & I & ɛ] and similarly for the other stanzas.

The full translation of stanza two of 'Ahi Ali Baba' is reproduced in (14.11). (The original was given in (14.1)).

(**14.11**) But now rebel Satan from hence is driven
While to us four scrolls of knowledge are given
And into our minds full wisdom from Heaven
Being brought to Truth by the strong grace of God.

14.3.2 'Slieve Cua'

Let us finally consider the transduction of the Old Irish nature poem 'Slieve Cua' (14.6), starting with an inventory of the figurae involved (for the most part based on the synoptic analysis in Lehmann (1982)):[8]

(a) The basic metrical property of a line is its SYLLABLE COUNT, capped off by the STRESS POSITION of the end-word. Lehmann reckons this poem as pervasively heptasyllabic (7), with varying end-word stress positions from the line: ultimate in line (i) (thus 7_1), antepenultimate in line (iv) (7_3), and penultimate in the remaining lines (7_2). However, on the basis of the orthographic text adduced by Lehmann, I get shorter counts in lines (ii) (6_2) and (iii) (5_2) and as will be seen have so responded in my translation.

(b) The analogue of end-rhyme in lines (iii) and (vi) is a full morphological recurrence chain, [[xlúx̰θe] and [xlúx̰θe].

(c) Lines (iv) and (v) are connected by LINKING RHYME (*aicill*), between the end-word of the former [bánoður] and a non-end-word of the letter [áγoβ̃ur]. Moreover, the rhyme used is of a different sort from any considered to this point though sharing with English feature rhyme and Turkish phonological rhyme a toned-down phonetic similarity of matches. The rhyme in question, known as *comhardadh* ('balancing'), does not require identity of posttonic consonants in matching positions but only that such segments belong to the same orthometrically determined EQUIVALENCE CLASS (Zwicky 1976) of the consonant system. Thus here, in addition to the identical word-ending [r & r], both of the word-medial matching pairs [n & γ] and [ð & β̃] are permitted as belonging to the equivalence class comprising voiced lenes (Thurneysen 1949:38).

(d) As was discussed earlier in terms of the basic conditions for Classical Irish alliteration given in (14.7), lines (i), (ii), and (iv) contain consonant-initial alliterative triplets ([k & k & k], [g & g & γ], [b̰ & b & b]), while line (v) contains a vowel-initial doublet [[á & í]).

(e) While the doublet matches phonetically by stratum condition (14.8b), the triplets match phonologically by (14.8a).

Coming now to the discussion of the translation in terms of these points, simple matching could be employed both for the stress properties of end-words (point (a); e.g. ultimate [dúβ] → *bláck*, penultimate [γlíN̰i] → *cányons*, antepenultimate [bánoður] → *brówn-shaggèd*) and for the morphological recurrence chain ending lines (iii) and (vi) (point (c); [xlúx̲θe] & [xlúx̲θe] → *aeries* & *aeries*).

However, unlike the case of the Turkish poem whose eleven-syllable lines (14.10b) were long enough to enable viable English counterparts of equal length, the five-to-seven-syllable length in 'Slieve Cua' (point (a)) does not provide sufficient slack for replication in English, a language whose sentences tend to be longer than those of morphologically denser languages like Irish. Hence, I uniformly transduced the syllable count upward by a factor of two near line: $7_16_25_27_37_27_2 \rightarrow 9_18_27_29_39_29_2$.

Coming to point (c), the Irish *comhardadh* rhyme was transduced similarly to the Turkish phonological rhyme (14.10d) and for the same reason: because classical English full rhyme impressed me as too monotonous or blaring. Hence, I used a medley of Zwickian subsequence and feature rhyme, whereby [bánoður] and [áγoβur] were matched by *brown-shaggèd* and *around the craggèd*.[9] These latter pairs both share a subsequence of segments (viz. those not parenthesized in [(b)rawn#(š)ægəd] and [(ə)rawn(d#ðə#kr)ægəd] and are related by a suprasegmental version of feature rhyme, whereby the primary-secondary stress relations of the two forms are interchanged ([bráwn#šæ̀gəd] and [əràwnd #ðə krǽgəd]).

Coming to the alliteration, the vagaries of available English lexicon permitted me to match only one of the source triplets (point (d)) with a target triplet: [b̲é:k̲ið̲ bórbðam bánoður] → *bull-stag bellows, brown-shaggèd* on line (iv). The remaining two triplets were transduced into pairs of doublets: [kúə kúənax kóRax] → *Craggy Cua, wild . . . wolves* (line (i)), [gláað̲ gáyϑ . . . γlíNi] → *With wind calling . . . canyons* (ii).

Finally, the nature of the Irish stratum conditions for alliteration (point (e)) posed a difficulty resembling that entailed by the Turkish stratum conditions on rhyme (14.4, 14.10d). This resemblance is most straightforward with the phonological alliteration dictated by (14.8a), since in both cases the Irish and Turkish phonetic matches are muted rather than identical. The phonetic alliteration dictated by (14.8b) is subtler, but my feeling was that here too the Irish original evinces a POETIC TENSION (Kiparsky 1977), aesthetically and psychologically akin to euphonic mutedness, by virtue of the discrepancy between the phonetically matching [φáγoβur íM̲e] and its nonmatching APR counterpart /φáγoβur íM̲e/ (14.9b).

I accordingly tried to tone down the alliterative effect on the target side by a pair of transductive strategies: in line (ii), by providing *with* as an unstressed match for *wínd* (contrast (14.7a)) in *With wínd cálling . . . cányons* in response to the phonetic distance of [γ] from [g] in [gláað̲ gáyϑ . . . [γ]l̲íNi]; and in (v), by allowing a quasi-alliteration between *haunts* and *Autumn*, despite the [h] of the former, in *haunts of Autumn,* as a way of responding to the phonological tension between [áγoβur íM̲e] and its discrepant APR /φáγoβur íM̲e/.

The full translation of 'Slieve Cua' is reproduced in (14.12) (cf. references in notes 5 and 8).

(14.12)   **i**. Craggy Cua, wild of wolves, and dark
        ii. With wind calling through its canyons
        iii. And they cry to its aeries
        iv. Where the bull-stag bellows, brown-shaggèd
        v. Around the cragged haunts of Autumn
        vi. The lone crane whoops above its aeries.

NOTES

1. The fact that the German vowels are lax ([− tense] [Ü] and [I] (cf. the chart in §13) is immaterial here.

2. The approach to phonologic-orthometric interfacing illustrated in §14.1 – §14.2 is based on the pioneering work of Kiparsky (1970, 1972), though he must not be held responsible for the various modifications of his model assumed in this book. The notions of 'stratum conditions' and 'basic conditions' used in (14.4 – 5) and below derive from M1984a, where they comprise two of several similar conditions. (For earlier published work in the Kiparskian paradigm, see references in Kiparsky (1970, 1972). Two instances of later work are Chen (1984) for Mandarin Chinese and M1983f for Sephardic Hebrew. In a slightly different vein, cf. Hudak (1985) for Thai.)

3. For further discussion of these two general conditions and various ways of dealing with them, see Kiparsky (1970) and M1984a. It might incidentally be noted that while condition (a) holds for contemporary American English (e.g. the playfully alliterative name *Archibald Oyster* [a] and [ɔy], one of a set with *Abigail Abalone* [æ] and [æ] (Herriman:36)), condition (b) does not (e.g. (13.11c), where the first syllable of *Bizet* is unstressed. (The irrelevance of condition (b) is also demonstrated at several junctures in (13.2), notably with *assiduous indifference and infelicitous insistence* (c), which likewise shows the workings of condition (a) if the initials are pronounced [ǣ] and [I]; and [I] and [I].)

4. The analysis of §14.2 is based on M1984a, with published spin-offs M1985e and M forthcoming.

5. For more on transduction, see M1987b for published applications, in addition to the cases to be discussed below, see M1984b (Babylonian) and the very early-vintage (despite the date) 1983f (Hebrew). It is important to qualify, by the way, that the weight of any claim to originality bespoken by transduction falls to the formal rather than conceptual side. This is so in that the fundamental *idea* of transduction has long been recognized and put into practice. Cf., e.g., Jackson Mathew's statement, 'The translator [of poetry] has to invent formal effects in his own language that give a sense of those produced by the original in its own' (cited in Greene:124). In this vein also, transduction seems closely akin to what Vladimir Nabokov called 'literalist' translation (loc.cit.).

6. The original poem appears in Anonymous (n.d.:76), with translations of the second stanza in M1982c and of the whole poem in M1985f. Some notes on transduction are included in both publications.

7. The term 'equated' is given in lowercase letters because the cenematic nature of the strategy deprives it of full trajectional status; cf. note 5 in chapter 7. This notational distinction will be employed throughout, with capitalization being reserved for plerematic strategies in the translation of a poem.

8. This section is largely based on appendix C of M1984a. A published translation of the poem appears as M1987a with a nontechnical essay on the transduction as M1987b.

9. The grave diacritic on *è* in *brown-shaggèd* represents not stress but syllabicity—thus [šægəd], to rhyme with *cragged* [krægəd]. (The stress of these pairs is important, however, as will be picked up immediately below.)

Chapter *15*

TRANSJACENCE

15.0 PRELIMINARIES

Despite the similarity of the phonological derivations introduced in the last two chapters and the morphosyntactic derivations of chapters 11 and 12, it may have been noticed that the work of bridge technique and transduction does not seem to overlap. This discreteness is merely an artifice of the exposition, however, and should by no means be taken as evidence for a hermetic dissociation of plerematic and cenematic components. For one thing, it is not uncommon for phonology and morphosyntax to interpenetrate in the service of orthometric patterns. Thus, in the first quatrain of stanza XIX from *Don Juan* given in (15.1), Byron implements a special syncope rule to bob normally disyllabic ⟨learnèd⟩ [lə́rnəd] to monosyllabic ⟨learned⟩ [lə́rnd] for the sake of rhyme with ⟨concerned⟩ [kənsə́rnd].[1] Similarly but inversely in (15.2s), the strict morphosyntactic parallelism (cf. §10.1) of the two hemistichs of the Hebrew original of Ezechiel 7.19, whose noun-adverb-verb duplication holds even at the morphemic level (cf. the analytic translation), is enhanced by special *non*application of the phonological rule ULTIMATE JUMP on the verb ending the first hemistich. Had Ultimate Jump applied, as it normally does in similar Biblical contexts lacking the special orthometric pressure, the form of the verb would be [yəśabbəʕúu], which differs from [yəmallée?uu] in both vocalism and stress (M1978:127).

(15.1) He was a mortal of the careless [kind,]
    With no great love for learning, or the [learned,]
  Who chose to go where'er he had a [mind,]
    And never dreamed his lady was [concerned;] (Glover:198)

(15.2)   s. nafšɔ́ɔm lóo yəśabbéeʕuu ‖
      umeeʕeehɛ́ɛm lóo yəmallée?uu (K:Ezechiel 7,19)
  an. 'soul-their not will-satisfy-they ‖
     and-bowels-their not will-fill-they'
   t. they shall not satisfy their souls
     neither fill their bowels (KJ)

15.1 PARONOMASIA AND OTHER CENEMATIC-PLEREMATIC COMPLEXES

To be sure, the phenomenon of cenematic-plerematic intertwining—henceforth to be called TRANSJACENCE—need not directly involve derivations; and in fact, most of the wide variety of transjacent situations that commonly plague translators probably do not usefully lend themselves to derivational modeling.

One sort of transjacence recognized and studied by literary scholars since antiquity is PARONOMASIA, whereby the cenematic form of a word sets up an occasion for plerematic ambiguity or double meaning, usually as an intentional figura on the part of the author. Thus in (15.3s), it is certainly not by a 'slip-of-the-pen' on Shakespeare's part that Sampson chooses the word *maidenheads*, rather than *hymens* or the like, to convey what item of anatomy the *maids* might lose rather than their *heads*. Consideration of the Spanish renditions in (15.3t) will readily underscore the problems typically besetting the translator faced with paronomasia in the source text. Since the Spanish words *doncellas* 'maids' and *cabeza(s)* 'head(s)' simply do not intersect in a third word meaning anything like 'maidenhead', translators cannot be expected to acquit themselves of a passage like this by Equation on plerematic and cenematic strata simultaneously. As may be seen in (ta), Marín comes about as close to that goal as ingenuity and imagination will allow, with *doncellez* (an.'maidenhood'), one of whose senses is in fact 'hymen' and whose cenematic form plainly reprises *doncellas*. Manent, on the other hand (to), loses the paronomasic effect altogether with the cenematically unrelated form *virginidad* (an.'virginity').

The phenomenon of transjacence is by no means limited to paronomasia in the narrow sense but pervades speech and literature in a considerable variety of forms, and almost always portends trouble for the translator. Transjacence was in fact the hub of the difficulty; with the Irish recurrence chain *bhean* 'wife' . . . *bhean* 'woman' considered in (9.13), since it was exactly the Irish-specific cenematic-plerematic disposition of this polyseme that defied Equation into English. Four examples of various transjacent situations will be considered here (§15.1.1–§15.1.4), enough to intimate the diversity of the phenomenon but by

(15.3) **s.** Sampson: I will be cruel with the [maids], and cut off their [heads].
Gregory: The [heads] of the [maids]?
Sampson: Ay, the [heads] of the [maids], or their [[maidenheads]];
take it in what sense thou wilt. (Shakespeare: 882 [Romeo
and Juliet, I, i, 28–31])

    ta. Sansón: seré cruel con las [doncellas]. Les voy a cortar la [cabeza].
Gregorio: ¿la [cabeza] de las [doncellas]?
Sansón: Sí, la [cabeza] de las [doncellas], o su [[doncellez]].
¡Tómalo en el sentido que quieras! (Marín: 17)

    tb. Sansón: seré cruel con las [doncellas]: cortaré sus [cabezas].
Gregorio: ¿La [cabeza] de las [doncellas]?
Sansón: Sí, la [cabeza] de las [doncellas], o su [[virginidad]].
¡Tómalo como quieras! (Manent:16)

no means enough to constitute a representative sample. The examples are approximately ranked from least to most serious, though as will be appreciated, the last three are pretty close in this regard.

15.1.1 Alliterative and Rhyming Binomials

Closely akin to orthometric patterning, and arguably constituting a figura in its own right, is the cenematic enhancement of plerematic sets (§8.1) by devices such as alliteration and rhyme. This phenomenon is rather prominent in Grimm's fairy tales, where the sets affected are commonly BINOMIAL GROUPS (cf. (5.2) in chapter 5) of nouns and verbs. A random sample of eleven cases (from among one hundred or so incidentally noted in reading) is given in (15.4), the breakdown being roughly proportional to the frequency of cenematic embellishment employed: alliteration by itself (a), full rhyme (b), alliteration plus feature rhyme (c).

(15.4)	s(G)	t(HS)
a.	über Stock und Stein (207)	over stock and stone (274)
	auf der ganzen Grenze und Gegend (271)	in any part of the district or country (358)
	ohne Ross und Rinder (487)	without horse or cow (660)
	in Küche oder Keller (555)	in the kitchen or cellar (754)
	ein Geschrei und Gezwitschen (413)	a screaming and twittering (551)
b.	in Saus und Braus (207)	in riot and revel (273)
	unter Dach und Fach (420)	in a house (562)
	Hülle und Fülle (514)	shelter and food (699)
c.	Kisten und Kasten (446)	presses, cupboards (598)
	Knistern und Knastern (509)	crunching and cracking (691)
	schnuppern und schnuffeln (509)	sniff and snuffle (691)

A rough gauge of the largely ornamental function of this type of transjacence may perhaps emerge from the fact that Hunt and Stern have replicated it in their English translation in only four out of the eleven eleven cases, a ratio (36 percent), moreover, that I suspect is higher than that obtaining across the full corpus. As will now be seen, translators cannot so easily evade replication in the remaining three case-types of transjacence to be illustrated.[2]

15.1.2 Mimesis

At times a situational development turns more or less crucially on utterances of one language being incorrectly perceived as utterances of another language, or even on nonhuman sounds being so misunderstood. Thus, the plot of Grimm's fairy tale 'Der gute Handel'/'The Good Bargain' starts off with a peasant's thinking that frogs in a pond croaking [ak ak ak ak . . .] are actually shouting 'eight eight eight eight . . . ', a misperception caused by the fact that the phonetic shape for 'eight' in the North German dialect subtending the tale is passably close to this MIMESIS of a frog's cry: ([ak] or [akt]), Standard German *acht* [axt]). The plot later continues on a similar note, with the peasant perceiving a dog's bark [vas vas vas vas . . .] as the pronoun 'some(thing)', *etwas ~ was* [ɛtvas ~ vas].

Excerpts from this double nexus are presented in (15.5), where it will be seen that Hunt and Stern attempt out-and-out replication only in the first case ((sa-sb), (ta-tb)), where the price for accommodating the stimulus to the English response *eight* [eyt] is to warp the frogs' croak from [ak . . .] to [eyk . . .] ('*Aik, aik, aik, aik*').

At first glance Hunt and Stern appear to have failed altogether to handle the encounter with the dogs ((sc-sd), (tc-td)), since the English bark '*Wow, wow,*

(**15.5**) **sa**. die Frösche riefen: ['Ak, ak, ak, ak'.]
   sb. 'Dummes Vieh, das ihr seid! . . . Sieben Taler sind's,
      und keine [acht]'.
   sc. ein grosser Windhund . . . sprang um das Fleisch,
      schnupperte und bellte: ['Was, was, was, was'.]
   sd. 'Ja, ich merke wohl, du sagst, "Was, was", weil du
      [etwas] von dem Fleisch verlangst . . .' . . . 'Horch,
      jetzt verlangen sie alle [was]' (G:41f)
   ta. the frogs crying: ['Aik, aik, aik, aik']
   tb. 'Stupid animals that you are! . . . It is seven talers
      and not [eight]'.
   tc. a large greyhound . . . jumped at the meat, sniffed at it,
      and barked: ['Wow, wow, wow'.]
   td. 'Yes, yes, I know quite well that you are saying
      "wow, wow, wow", because you want [some] of the meat . . . '
      . . . 'Hark, now they all want [some]'. (HS:51f)

wow' as stimulus lacks any phonetically similar response in the peasant's perception. But in fact the translation of this nexus, though lacking the literary holism of the frog episode, is rescued from out-and-out failure by a PRAGMATIC consideration: the real-world knowledge that a dog barking at a person holding a piece of meat is very likely to be doing so exactly because he wants some of that meat. Accordingly, the target dialogue (tc-td) is understood just as coherently as that of the source (sc-sd), despite the absence of any special cenematic link.[3]

15.1.3 Free Association

In (15.6s) a young Russian officer, Rostov, finds himself dozing off while on night patrol, and as frequently happens to people in such situations, his mind begins to wander over a number of things by the path of FREE ASSOCIATION. Thus, the Russian word for 'patch' *pjatno*⟨a⟩ brings to mind the French equivalent *tache*⟨b⟩ [taš], and when he then concludes he didn't see a patch of snow after all, with the words *ne taš*⟨c⟩, the resemblance in sound leads him to think of his sister *Nataša*⟨d⟩—a name whose diminutive accusative form *Natašku*⟨e⟩ then leads into *tašku*⟨f⟩ 'soldier's belt-pouch'.

This chain continues several lines later with *na tašku*⟨g⟩ 'to the belt-pouch', *nastupit'*⟨h⟩ 'to attack', and *nas tupit*⟨i⟩ 'to knock us down' and then is interrupted by the mini-chain *Gusary*⟨a'⟩ 'hussars' and its follow-up *usy*⟨b'⟩ 'mous-

(15.6) s. 'Dolžno byt', sneg—èto pjatno; pjatno⟨a⟩—*une tache*⟨b⟩—
dumal Rostov.—Vot tebe i ne taš⟨c⟩ . . . 'Nataša⟨d⟩,
sestra, čërnyje glaza. Na—taška . . . (Vot udivitsja,
kogda ej skažu, kak ja uvidal gosudarja!) Natašku⟨e⟩ . . .
tašku⟨f⟩ voz'mi . . .

    . . .

'Da, da! Na tašku⟨g⟩, nastupit'⟨h⟩ . . . nas tupit'⟨i⟩—
Kogo? Gusarov. A gusary⟨a'⟩ i usy⟨b'⟩ . . .

    . . .

'Na—tašku⟨j⟩, nas—tupit'⟨k⟩, da, da, da. Èto xorošo'. (Tolstoy i:263)

  t. 'It must be snow, that patch . . . a patch⟨a⟩—*une tache*⟨b⟩,
he thought half in French, half in Russian. 'There now,
it's no *tache*⟨c⟩ . . . Nat—tash—a⟨d⟩, my sister, black
eyes. Na—tash—a . . . (won't she be surprised when I tell
her I've seen the Emperor!) Na—tash—a⟨e⟩ . . . take my
sabretache⟨f⟩ . . .

    . . .

'Oh yes! Na—tash—a⟨g⟩ . . . *sabretache*⟨h⟩ . . . sabre⟨i⟩ them . . .
Whom? The hussars . . . Ah, the hussars⟨a'⟩ with moustaches⟨b'⟩ . . .

    . . .

'Na—tash—a, *sabretache*⟨j⟩ . . . Ø⟨k⟩ oh yes, yes. That's it'.
(Edmonds i:308)

taches' (the Zwickian subsequence *us . . . y* being contained in the word *Gusary*; see §13.2).

The major chain concludes several lines later with a partial repetition of ⟨g⟩ and ⟨i⟩, *Na—tašku*⟨j⟩ and *nas—tupit'*⟨k⟩.

In view of the capriciousness of the cenematic-plerematic relations throughout these chains, Edmonds's attempt to cope in (15.6t) is admirable indeed. Much of her success derives from carry-over (§1.4.1) both of the name *Nataša* and of the French word *tache* but is helped along by Russian-English etymological relations (*ne* and *no* at ⟨c⟩ and Edmonds's ingenious expropriation of the rare but viable word *sabretache* 'scabbard' as a pragmatically reasonable Substitute for *tašku* 'soldier's pouch' at ⟨f⟩ and ⟨j⟩. Edmonds also helps the target reader by judicious spacing of *Na-tash-a* (⟨d,e,g⟩); by a dominolike Substitution at ⟨g,h,i⟩ highlighted by the use of *sabrel*i⟩ as a verb answering to either or both of *nastupit'*⟨h⟩ and *nas tupit'*⟨i⟩ in the source; and by a wise piece of Reduction at ⟨k⟩.

Her failure to replicate the mini-chain ⟨a',b'⟩ is innocuous at worst, and at best goes partially through anyhow, plerematically, by virtue of the pragmatic datum that hussars did in fact sport moustaches.

15.1.4 Eponymy

The case from the Grimm's fairy tale in (15.7) goes right to the heart of the plerematic-cenematic symbiosis, of which it might be considered a PREGNANT case: two distinct referents (a vegetable and a girl) are magically bonded by sharing the same name (Rapunzel), a phenomenon that may be called EPONYMY.

Such cases can seldom be ignored but very rarely smoothly replicated—an impasse frequently met by GLOSSING (§3.1.1), sometimes in the limiting-case form of footnotes.[4]

Though one may have reservations about the net success of Hunt and Stern's ploy in this case, it is instructive to follow their procedure step by step. They begin with footnote-glossing of the title (ta), then move through on-line glossing (tb) to break the cenematic bond altogether (tc), only to reinstate it at the crucial moment of the naming itself (td).

15.2 SOURCE-TEXT RECURRENCE CHAINS

It may have been noted that all the examples of transjacence in §15.1 were SYNTAGMATIC, in that the plerematic-cenematic connection took place across two or more elements of a text. Moreover, by virtue of their syntagmatic structure, these cases are also RECURRENCE CHAINS, wherein plerematically variable links are cross-associated by cenematic identity or similarity.

It so happens that recurrence chains constitute a general problem for translation even beyond the pale of transjacence in the narrow sense. It will be the work of this section to discuss salient aspects of this problem.[5]

(15.7) **sa**. Rapunzel

sb. Eines Tages, stand die Frau . . . und . . . erblickte ein
Beet, das mit den schönsten [Rapunzeln] bepflanzt war,
und sie sahen so frisch und grün aus, daß sie lüstern
ward und das grösste Verlangen empfand, von den
Rapunzeln zun essen.

sc. 'so will ich dir gestattan, [Rapunzeln] mitzunehmen,
soviel du willst, allein, ich mache eine Bedingung:
Du musst mir das Kind geben, das deine Frau zur Welt
bringen wird . . .'

sd. als die Frau in die Wochen kam, so erschien sogleich
die Zauberin, gab dem Kinde den Namen [Rapunzel]
und nahm es mit sich fort (G:57f)

ta. Rapunzel*

. . .

*Rampion

tb. One day the woman . . . saw a bed which was planted with
the most beautiful [rampion (rapunzel)], and it looked
so fresh and green that she longed for it, and had the
greatest desire to eat some.

tc. 'I will allow you to take away with you as much [rampion]
as you will, only I make one condition, you must give
me the child which your wife will bring into the world . . .'

td. When the woman was brought to bed, the enchantress
appeared at once, gave the child the name of [Rapunzel],
and took it away with her (HS:73f)

Let us begin with consideration of the two-link chains in (15.8), illustrating
a variety of cenematic relations: IDENTICAL LINKS with full repetition of the Norwegian noun *hyssing* 'cord' in (a) (the marking off of the word *tygget* will be discussed later); POLYSEMOUS LINKS, with the Spanish participle *enderezando*, first
in the sense of 'directing' (one's attention and speech to another) and then in the
sense of 'correcting' (a wrong) (b); HOMONYMOUS LINKS, with the Norwegian
verb stems *huske* 'remember' (in *huskelappen*, an. 'remembering list' = 'list of
things to do or purchase') and *huske* 'swing' (c); and of two varieties of CENE-
MATICALLY SIMILAR LINKS, (subsequence) rhyming (d) and alliterative (e).

The chains of (15.8) have two additional facets in common: (i) the repetitions constituting them are likely to be ACCIDENTAL; (ii) their occurrence is partially attributable to something like FREE ASSOCIATION on the author's part—
specifically, by virtue of the first link as a stimulus triggering the second as a
response. None of the particular word-for-word intersections cited in (15.8) follows as an inexorable requirement of the text in question: in each case, either the
event conveyed by one of the two links could have been omitted with no damage

(15.8) as. 'Og så skal jeg klatre opp i taket', sa gutten
og [[tygget]] på en [hyssing]stump.
   . . .
Neste dag, i lunsjpausen, gikk faren inn in en
kolonialforretning for å spørre efter en tomkase. Han
måtte gå i tre forretninger før han fant en kassen
some passet. Han fikk en [hyssing] runt. (Mykle:29f)

bs. Ella, [enderezando] la voz y el rostro a don Quijote,
dijo . . . y vos me habedes prometido de volver por ella,
[enderezándo]le el tuerto que le tienen fecho (Cervantes:606)

cs. Han velgte en tausort på en halv tommes tykkelse, og
forlangte fem meter, efter å ha sett på [huske]lappen.
. . . Det måtte væne kroken som var snodd, som gikk i
spiral ytterst, så taustigen ikke kunne falle av,
selv hvor meget man [husket] i den (Mykle:29)

d. He has to be political, and deal, and [wangle] and
pay off and figure tax [angles] (Bellow:374)

e. *b*eat-up *b*oats spend the winter *b*eached *b*eside houses (Johnston:B6)

(cs); or nonrecurrent synonyms could have been selected (bs, ds, es); or either alternative could have been used (as).

The two parts of this judgment differ in nature and importance. That such accidental chains do occur in source texts, and frequently at that, is an empirical finding that any translator will amply verify from his or her own experience. On the other hand, the judgment that such accidental chains are literally free-associational in origin is speculative on my part, and nothing in the discussion will crucially depend upon its correctness. The important point will only be that recurrence chains frequently do creep into a text without the conscious design of the author, for whatever reason, and that once there, such chains are likely to cause certain difficulties for the translator.

Let us now consider target versions of two of the three examples from (15.8), which are excerpts from works for which published English translations are extant and are given in (15.9bt) and (15.9ct). (The remaining translation, (15.9at), will be considered later.) These two translations in a sense bear formal witness to the respective translators' judgments that the recurrence chains of (15.8bs) and (15.8cs) were in fact accidental, since in neither case is any attempt made to replicate the chain into the source text. Thus, in (15.9bt), Ormsby Diverges the Spanish polyseme *enderezando* into distinct English verbs, according to sense: first the (Diffused) pair *turning . . . and addressing*, then *right*. Similarly, in (15.9ct), I Diverge Mykle's tokens of homonymous *huske* pursuant to sense, first into (Condensed) *list* and then into *swung*.

(15.9) at.   'Then I'm going to climb up to the ceiling!' said the boy[[chewing]]
on a piece of [cord].

. . .

The next day on his lunch hour the father went to a grocery store to
look for an empty wooden crate. He had to go to three grocery stores
before he found one that was just right. He tied a [cord] around
it. (M1980b:96f)

bt.   She then, [turning] to Don Quixote and [addressing] herself to him,
said . . . and you promised me to take her part and [right] the
wrong that has been done her (Ormsby:364)

ct.   He selected a half-inch-thick variety, and after consulting his [list]
asked for six yards . . . They had to be spiral-tipped hooks that
could be screwed in so the rope-ladder wouldn't fall, no matter how
much one [swung] on it. (M1980b:95)

But what if the source repetitions *enderezando* and *huske* in (15.8bs-cs) *had*
been intentional on the part of the authors and had moreover contributed in some
way to the organic structure of the source text? In such a case the translator could
ill afford to lose the effect of the repetitions in the target, as in fact has already
been discussed at some length with a variety of examples in §15.1.1–§15.1.4.

The crux of the problem is now this: *How can a translator know when
source-text repetition is accidental or intentional?* There are no foolproof recipes
for answering this vital question, but several useful rules of thumb will be considered here: symbolism (§15.2.1); situational inducement (§15.2.2); patterned
or arbitrary distribution (§15.2.3); the distance factor (§15.2.4); and author's
proclivity (§15.2.5).

15.2.1   Symbolism

The exercpt from Mykle's Norwegian short story containing the first link of the
accidental recurrence chain *hyssing* . . . *hyssing* 'cord' . . . 'cord' in (15.8as) is
immediately preceded by (15.10s), so that when the two excerpts are taken together another recurrence chain emerges: that of *tygget* . . . *tygget* 'chewed' . . .
'chewed'. However, the repetition of *tygget* is decidedly not accidental but rather
serves as one of at least two SYMBOLIC BONDS between the little boy and the old
sailor whom the father visits for advice on how to build the rope ladder that the
boy wants—symbolic bonds of generational alienation, one of old age and one
of childhood.

Had the chains *hyssing* . . . *hyssing* and *tygget* . . . *tygget* involved polysemous or homonymous repetition rather than that of morphological identity, it
would have been appropriate in the former, accidental case to break the chain in
the English target (as in (15.9ct)), while conversely the latter, symbolic case
would have called for an exercise of ingenuity to somehow replicate the chain in
the target and so maintain its function.[6] However, the fact that these repetitions

(15.10) s. Båtsmannen tok sigaren, brekket et stykke av den og [[tygget]] den. Av en eller annen grunn mislikte faren båtsmannen for det.
Det kom en dag da faren var halvferdig med å surre trinene til taune. (Mykle:31)

t. The old man took a cigar, broke a piece off, and began to [[chew]] it. For some reason or other the father disliked the old man for that.
The day came when the father was half finished with tying the rungs into the ropes. (M1980b:96)

were of the identity type in the source made an easier response possible: both the symbolic and the accidental chain could be replicated on the English side, the function of the former being carried by (the slightly Divergent) *chewing . . . began to chew*, and the latter going harmlessly through as *cord . . . cord*.[7]

To be sure, there can be no advance guarantee that the translator will recognize all the symbolically based repetitions in a source text, let alone manage to replicate them. But in view of the kind of intensive and multiple reading of a source text that normally preconditions a responsible translation, one's chances of grossly overlooking symbolism tend to be much reduced.

15.2.2 ⸱ Situational Inducement

If one were to consider translating the comic-strip dialogue excerpted in (15.11), one might pause on the matter of the alliteration in the fourth turn at (d): *Let's leave a note on the bulletin board about the beer bust*. But even though the generally light nature of comic strips often constitutes a favorable condition for alliteration (§13.1), the likelihood of this instance of the figura being intentional is much weakened by a quirk of situational-linguistic happenstance: if a message is to be synthesized in English concerning bulletin boards and beer busts, the available lexicon virtually forces alliteration, since all the principal straightforward words for the referents in question happen to begin with [b]. Thus, a translator of this strip could pretty confidently forego the attempt to reproduce the alliterative effect in the target.

15.2.3 Patterned or Arbitrary Distribution

Perhaps the surest manifestation of patterned distribution is the incidence of conventionalized figurae in recognized orthometric forms. For example, the occurrences of Turkish rhyme and Irish alliteration in the poems treated in chapter 14

(15.11) a. Cosmo: I got the beer keg in the jeep.
b. Beetle: I rented the pavilion at the lake.
c. Cosmo: How will we get the word out?
d. Beetle: Let's leave a note on the bulletin board about the beer bust.
(Walker 1984)

(**15.12**) **s.** Guth 3: Chun go *d*tabharfaí *t*uairimí
Guth 4: Chun go *g*ceapfaí *c*oiste
Guth 1: Chung go *g*cuirfí an *c*úram chun cinn (Ní Shúilleabbáin 1975:45)
t. 3rd Voice: That *r*eports be *r*eadied
4th Voice: That a *c*ommittee be *c*onvened
1st Voice: That the *m*atter be *m*oved ahead (JM)

embody special cases of source-text recurrence chains whose purposefulness is beyond any question, and which accordingly a translator must at least seriously consider replicating. However, the patterns cuing purposeful repetition need not occur in a conventionalized orthometric context. Such patterns often obtrude on the investigator by virtue of some distributional property specific to the source-text itself. Thus in (15.12), an excerpt from an ultra-modern Irish play evincing virtually no classical ornaments, the intentional nature of the underscored alliterative sets[8] is clinched by the morphosyntactic symmetry of the words hosting them: three tandem cases of two-member sets whose first member is always a verb in the impersonal voice *(dtabharfaí, gceapfaí, gcuirfí)*and whose second member is always an object of that verb *(tuairimí, coiste, cúram)*.[9]

It will be recalled that the heading of this subsection (§15.2.3) mentions not only patterned distribution but also ARBITRARY distribution. This joint classification is not as paradoxical as it may seem, however, when one considers that arbitrariness may cue deviation from normal textual expectations just as effectively as special patterning—a deviation that often bespeaks a hidden factor of importance to the translator or analyst. A case in point was incidentally given with the example of meristic alliteration in (13.12) in chapter 13, *western theories of language from Genesis to Jackendoff*. The arbitrariness involves the specific choice of nouns referencing the book of Genesis and the linguist Ray Jackendoff as end-point exemplars of western-language theorizing. But despite its plerematic whimsicality, the choice is motivated cenematically, just by virtue of the alliteration entailed.[10]

15.2.4   The Distance Factor

All else being equal, the chances of an otherwise unaccounted recurrence chain being accidental decrease with the distance between the links.[11] This rule of thumb gives a gradient of results from strong to weak when applied to the examples of (15.8). The likeliest case is (e), whose alliterating words are adjacent, while case (a) is weakest, with no less than fifteen sentences omitted at the points of suspension. The remaining cases rank (d), with six words intervening, more likely to be accidental than (bs), whose links are separated by a score of words over a sentence break, while (cs) is the weakest of the three, with five intervening sentences.

However, the 'all else being equal' clause prefaced to this rule of thumb must caution that tolerance for close-quarter repetition may differ widely across

(15.13) **as**. Speranskij⟨a⟩, kak v pervoje svidanije c nim u
Kobučeja, tak i potom v seredu doma, gde Speranskij⟨a⟩
s glazu na glaz, prinjav Bolkonskogo, dolgo i
doverčivo govoril s nim, sdelal sil'noje vpečatlenije
na knjazja Andreja (Tolstoy i:426)

    at. As on their first meeting at Kochubey's, Speransky⟨a⟩
produced a strong impression on Prince Andrei on the
Wednesday, when he⟨a⟩ received him *tête-à-tête* at his
own house and talked to him long and confidentially
                                     (Edmonds i:506)

   bs. Do frögt sine Frugge, worumme he se⟨a⟩ nig hädde
middebrocht . . . do gohet se⟨a⟩ dann auck wier hünne (G:391)

   bt. Then the Queen asked why he had not brought their
daughter⟨a⟩ with him . . . Then the King's daughter⟨a⟩
went back again (HS:522)

traditions, genres, and even specific authors similar in other regards.[12] Thus, it is noteworthy that in various passages of Tolstoy's *War and Peace* certain persons are referenced by name with considerably higher frequency than would be tolerated in literary English of an equivalent type. Note for instance (15.13as-at), the first pairs of links in a coreference chain for the character Speransky, extending throughout section II,iii,6 of the novel: while the Russian repeats the name *Speranskij* as the second link (as), the English Diverges to the pronoun *he* (at). The net force of this stylistic difference for the entire section (2 ½ pages long) shows up in the number of tokens of the name *Speranskij/Speransky* in either text: twenty-two in the Russian source but only sixteen in the English target.

    Conversely, some of Grimm's fairy tales are marked by a tendency to launch coreference chains linked by multiply recurrent pronouns. This tendency may be strongest in the dialect tales; cf. the 'Plattdeutsch' snippet in (15.13bs), and note that Hunt and Stern Substitute both tokens of the pronoun *se* 'she' with definite descriptions in their English target.

15.2.5   Author's Proclivity

Though technically this factor is subsumed under various of the preceding points, it deserves special mention because its quirky nature may often beguile people into overlooking it. The fact is, some authors just seem prone to certain kinds of linguistic repetition, for whatever reason; and translators should be on their guard for symptoms of such repetition, so that they can respond appropriately in translating.

    A case in point may incidentally have been given in (15.8e), a patent instance of quadruple alliteration lacking any obvious situational or stylistic basis. On the one hand, even granting the straightforwardness and appropriateness of *boats* and *beached* to the scenario, easy synonyms are available for the remaining members of the alliterative set (e.g. *delapidated*, *next to*). On the other hand, the stylistic function of the alliteration (§13.1) is not obviously of the meristic type, and playfulness is ruled out by the grim tenor of the article from which this is an excerpt: the story of a vicious murder. By itself, failure to isolate some other factor accounting for a recurrence chain would be very weak evidence indeed for hypothesizing an author's proclivity. But it will always be worthwhile to take a second look at the text, in hopes of finding something else that might either strengthen or jeopardize the hypothesis. In this vein, the text containing (15.8e) shows one more patently alliterative string: *Broad Channel's sociable summers, which center around boating, beach bonfires and bait barges* (Johnston:B6). Although the quadruple set of [b]s might be interpreted as meristic alliteration, in the form of an outline of the summer's activities, that account does not easily extend to the triplet of [s]s — and in any event one is struck by the resemblance of this string to that of (15.8e), both of which contain alliterative quadruples on initial [b]. On balance, the chances seem good that the author of this text simply has a weak spot for alliteration, perhaps especially to the tune of [b].[13]

NOTES

1. Such distortion in poetic language has a venerable history in the Occident; ample cases may, for instance, be found in the Homeric ballads, where unusual grammatical or lexical forms are selected to fit the meter; cf. Monro (ii:274,335,372,377).

2. The sort of transjacence illustrated in (15.4) overlaps in various ways with patterns considered earlier, notably in §1.3 (especially example (1.12)), §7.3 (7.6), §8.4 (8.26). Incidentally, an analytic survey of transjacent sets across various languages and traditions would certainly be a worthwhile project, with an eye to typologizing correlations of form and function. To cite just two cases in point involving alliteration: (i) Alliterative sets frequently seem to enhance echoic or onomatopoetic force. Thus, in Gorky's short story "Skuki radi" (1958:386–403), the Russian stem *groxot* [grɔ́xət] is multiply used (e.g. pp.387, 397, 400) to convey the labored chugging of a (nineteenth-century) steam engine, an echoic function magnified in the alliterative set *gluxogo groxota* [glÚxəvə grɔ́xətə] (389), where the lumbering struggle of the train can almost be felt. (Wettlin's rendition as *roar* (1982:196) impresses me as missing the point; something like the analytic translation, 'muffled rumble', would be more like it.) (ii) In at least some Finnish folk poetry, alliteration marks parallelistic forms; for instance, all such forms alliterate in the poem analyzed by Austerlitz (1983:12; cf. also 1965).

3. A similar case involving a frog appears in G:405/HS:541, where the croak is first misunderstood as (dialectal) *wat?*/*what?* and then as *wate!*/*wade!*. The translation of this case is clearly abetted by the etymological affinity of the source and target pairs.

4. This method is, incidentally, pervasive in the Douay translation of the Bible (Douay:passim).

5. Much of this section is based on M1979c.

6. Cf. Lefevere's criticism of breaking the recurrence chain of *Erechtheus* in various English translations of Catullus 64:211 (Lefereve:85).

7. It is striking that ALL AND ONLY the four symbolic recurrence chains in Mykle (1968) are CHIASTI-CALLY DISTRIBUTED throughout the story, viz. *vinket*⟨a⟩(p.26) *hytte*⟨b⟩ (p.28) *et lite hus*⟨c⟩ (p.31) *tygget* ⟨d⟩ (p.31) *tygget* ⟨d⟩ (p.31) *et lite hus*⟨c⟩ (p.31) *hytter*⟨b⟩ (p.32) *à vinke*⟨a⟩ (p.34). The fact that I did not notice this striking distribution until years after my translation was published cheered me; I had only slipped up on chain⟨b⟩: *waved*⟨a⟩ *cottage*⟨b⟩ *a little house*⟨c⟩ *began to chew*⟨d⟩ *chewing*⟨d⟩ *a little house*⟨c⟩ *huts*⟨b⟩ *to wave*⟨a⟩. (M1980b).

8. This is phonological alliteration (§14.2), whereby each verb begins with a voiced stop ([d], [g], [g] spelt ⟨dt⟩, ⟨gc⟩, ⟨gc⟩) deriving from a phonological voiceless stop (/t/, /ķ/, /k/), the match being the transparent voiceless initials of the complement in each case ([t], [k], [k] = /t/, /k/, /k/). (Palatalization of [g] = /ķ/ is waived by (14.7c)).

9. In default of anything more structured, RAW FREQUENCY may sometimes provide a weak (limiting) case of patterned distribution.

10. An interesting special tack on patterned distribution is suggested by O'Connor (1977:17), who notes that in some traditions orthometric patterning may be limited to a subset of the language's phonological system (the case in point being Northwest Semitic alliteration).

11. Cf. also Greenstein (1982:59, 1983:29).

12. Cf. Furneaux on Tacitus's intolerance of repetition and his devices for obviating it (1898:21, 347, 373, 375); and O'Connor's observation that Classical Chinese 'Regulated Verse' disallows morphological repetition altogether. Cf. also Austerlitz (1980).

13. The question of an author's proclivity can assume special urgency in certain case types, such as those of sacred texts, where it is imperative neither to dismiss theologically motivated repetition as accidental nor to interpret quirky repetition as numinous. (Some examples from the Hebrew Bible and the Arabic Qoran are discussed in M1979c:37ff.)

Chapter *16*

PARALLAX

16.0 PRELIMINARIES

As stated at the outset (§13.0.), the fundamental aim of Part Three of this book is to deal with a few areas of translation inherently prone to arbitrariness vis-à-vis the situational components of the text. Since the aspect of language quintessentially constitutive of such arbitrariness is the cenematic structure, the bulk of Part Three has reasonably enough concentrated on cenematics: first in its own right (chapters 13 and 14), and then in its semiotic connection with cenematics under the rubric of transjacence (chapter 15).

This concluding chapter will deal with one manifestation of plerematic arbitrariness, for which I have expropriated the physicist's term PARALLAX ('The apparent displacement or the difference in apparent direction of an object as seen from two different points not on a straight line with the object' (*Webster's* 1961)). In its linguistic sense, parallax will serve as an umbrella concept for a variety of linguistic situations marked by underdetermination or opacity of the morphosyntactic-semantic relation. As will readily be appreciated, this kind of instability is of particular importance for translation, because source-target differences tend to proliferate in parallactic situations, simply as a consequence of the inherent underdetermination.

Six types of parallax will be considered. These will first be briefly characterized with unilinguistic English examples and then discussed in the context of translation: (i) *displacement parallax* (§16.1), (ii) *antipodal parallax*(§16.2); (iii) *macroscopic parallax* (§16.3); (iv) *microscopic parallax* (§16.4); (v) *personalizing parallax* (§16.5); and (vi) *depersonalizing parallax* (§16.6).[1]

(16.1) **a**. Wife: Wait till you hear what he did today! He knocked over a good lamp. He tracked mud all over my clean kitchen floor. And he scared the wig of Mrs. Vanderpew's head!
    b. Husband: Anything else?
    c. Wife: Anything else? Isn't that enough?
    d. Husband: Well, if you think about it . . . This might be one of his more well-behaved days! (Anderson 1981)

(i) *Displacement parallax* occurs when an element semantically construable with another element is morphosyntactically realigned with yet a third element. Thus, in turn (d) of the cartoon excerpted in (16.1) about the shenanigans of the mischievous dog Marmeduke, the adjective *behaved* has been parallactically displaced from an NP denoting Marmaduke to *days*.

(ii) *Antipodal parallax* involves an apparent reversal of expected semantic-morphosyntactic relations. Two examples are given in (16.2): in (a), the gas station attendant speaks of the highway coming along to meet the people in the car, rather than of the people in the car driving to meet the highway; in (b), George Eliot phrases in nineteenth-century British English a message which in twentieth-century American English would normally be phrased as . . . *she had come across the name in her reading*.

(16.2) **a**. Motorist: Pardon me, sir, but how far is it to the interstate?
    Attendant: Well now, buddy-row, lessee . . . Shoot, I reckon I don't rightly know how far a piece it is to the interstate . . . Eight, maybe ten mile . . . But it'll sho'nuff be along direckly! (Marlette 1981)
    b. . . . the name had come across her in her reading (Eliot 1956 [orig.1860]:307)

(iii, iv) *Microscopic and macroscopic parallax* involve providing respectively more and less linguistic information (than dictated by some norm) in the designation of one and the same referent. Thus, in (16.3a) the phrase *Which child*, referring not to a child (John) but rather to the letters that a child has just marked on the blackboard, is macroscopic relative to a linguistically fuller version like *Which child's writing*, or the like. Conversely in (16.3b), *his mind* represents a microscopic way of encoding what normally would be conveyed by the simple pronoun *he*.

(16.3) **a**. 'Which child is that?' She was pointing at the blackboard, at John's letters. (Baldwin:19)
    b. 'Perhaps you had better leave him now, Mrs. Castle. He must not be overtired. His mind does not grasp who you are'. (Lida Bell Hunt:15)

(v, vi) *Personalizing and depersonalizing parallax* involve, on the one hand, the linguistic attribution of a given state or event to a human, animate, or anthropomorphic agent (personalizing); or, on the other hand, the removal or withholding of such attribution (depersonalizing). Thus, the scene in (16.4a) is depersonalizing by virtue of attributing the merits of the drink to the action of delivering the death sentence (*it*) rather than to its agent (*you*). Conversely (16.4b) is personalizing, by virtue of investing the rain disrupting the hobo's park-bench sleep with a malicious humanized agent (*the sonofabitch*).

(16.4) a. 'You delivered the death sentence very deftly', he told them. 'It deserves a drink'. (Simak:417)

   b. 'I thought I'd try the benches, but the sonofabitch started to rain on me.' (Dos Passos:104)

16.1   DISPLACEMENT PARALLAX

As will be noted in several of the examples below, a variety of patterns analyzable as parallactic were classically recognized as literary devices of the general type called FIGURAE in this book (§13.1), this time in the plerematic rather than cenematic mode. In this regard a kind of displacement parallax, whereby an adjective is dislodged from the NP it most straightforwardly modifies, is known to philologists and literary analysts by a variety of names, among them TRANSFERENCE and ENALLAGE. This figura was much affected by numerous authors of classical antiquity, including the Greek playwright Aeschylus and the Roman historian Tacitus. Thus, in the case of the last line (237) of (16.5as), from Aeschylus's play *Agamemnon*, Sidgwick analyzes the adjective *anaudōi* (an.'unspeaking') as an 'epithet transferred from the bound victim to the bonds', and accordingly glosses the line '"With violence and the muffled might of bonds"; a fine phrase for the gag' (1890;18'). Similarly, in (16.5bs) he takes account of the transference of *khamaipetes* 'low-grovelling' from the groveler to the groveler's cry (*boama*), and glosses the whole as '[do not] pour thy low-grovelling clamour in my ears' (1890:47').

   In view of the obvious poetic charge of these lines, Lattimore's English renditions appear to me to be masterful for the way they intimate rather than replicate these displacements in the target. Thus, in (16.5at) the adjective phrase *drowned in strength*, Substituting for *anaudōi* (Sidgwick's 'muffled'), may, but need not be, construed with *bit* (Sidgwick's 'bonds'); and in (bt), the scenario is portrayed in such a way that the cry (Sidgwick's 'clamour') de facto does originate from ground-level (Sidgwick's 'low-grovelling').

   A similar case of displacement parallax from the latin of Tacitus's *Annalia* is given in (16.6as), whereby *veteres populi Romani res*, an. 'early accounts of the Roman people', is considered by Furneaux (361) as an ENALLAGC for 'accounts of the early Roman people'. In (16.6bs) another common displacement-parallactic figura is illustrated with Tacitus: HENDIADYS, whereby an adjective or other nominal modifier is upgraded to a noun in its own right, then taken as one of a bi-

(16.5) as. kataskhein ‖ phthoggon araion oikois ‖ biāi khalimōn
t' anaudōi menei (Aeschylus:ll[lines 235-7])

    at. to check ‖ the curse cried on the house of Atreus ‖
by force of bit and speech drowned in strength (Richard Lattimore,
apud Greene and Lattimore:11)

    bs. Mē . . . ‖ khamaipetes boama proskhaneis emoi (ibid.:33[1.920])

    bt. do not . . . ‖ bow down to earth and with wide mouth cry out
to me (ibid.:33)

nomial pair with the modified noun. Thus, *ex posteritate et infamia*, an. 'of posterity and ill-repute', is a hendiadys for 'of posterity's ill-repute' (Furneaux:19).

Note that unlike Lattimore with Aeschylus, Grant makes no attempt to reconstruct Tacitus's figurae in his English versions (16.6at-bt). I think his failure to do so, here and throughout his translation generally, must be deemed appropriate, given the differences between the Classical Roman and Modern Occidental traditions vis-à-vis literary embellishment of historical writings.

(16.6) as. sed nemo annales nostros cum scriptura eorum
contenderit, qui [veteres populi Romani res]
conposuere (Tacitus:183)

    at. But my chronicle is quite a different matter from [histories of early
Rome] (Grant:172)

    bs. utque pravis dictis factisque [ex posteritate et infamia] metus sit
(ibid.:160)

    bt. to confront evil deeds and words with the fear [of posterity's
denuniciation] (ibid.:150)

16.2 ANTIPODAL PARALLAX

In chapter 7 considerable attention was paid to the German sentence *Er Ließ sich das gefallen* (7.3) in illustration of the notion SPAN, and in the process it was mentioned that the German verb *gefallen* and the English verb *like* 'constitute a PARALLACTIC SET, such that the referents of the subject and object switch places between the two languages while the overall meaning of the two constructions remains more or less constant' (§7.2.1). It may now be seen that specifically ANTIPODAL parallax is involved, whereby semantic-morphosyntactic relations are reversed between the two languages: while with English *like*, the 'liker' is encoded as subject, in the case of German *gefallen* it is rather encoded as (indirect) object; and conversely for the 'liked', which construes as (direct) object in English but as subject in German.

Moreover, antipodal differences of just this sort characterize numerous German-English verb pairs, with the consequence that narrative translated between the two languages will typically involve Reordering, Amplification with spans, and other discourse adjustments of the sort discussed in chapter 7. Just a few more cases in point from the great numbers throughout Grimm's fairy tales are provided in (16.7).

In case (a), the German verb *begegnen* instantiates a case of pure antipodal parallax, whereby one and the same lexeme may contract either of the antipodal sets of relations. In particular here, situationally (narratively) ⟨a⟩:⟨b⟩ = ⟨c⟩:⟨d⟩, since the eldest brother ⟨a⟩ stands in the same meeting-relation to the man⟨b⟩ he encounters on the road, as does the second brother ⟨c⟩ to the man he encounters ⟨d⟩. And yet despite this symmetry, ⟨a⟩ ocurs in the dative case (indirect object) while the narratively isofunctional ⟨c⟩ occurs in the nominative case (subject), with those case roles exactly reversed for ⟨b⟩ and ⟨d⟩, respectively.[2]

Note also in (as) that despite the case discrepancies between the two tokens of *begegnete*, in both instances the brother-referring NP precedes the verb, while the man-referring NP follows it—a discoursal regularity serving exactly the same function as that of *gefallen* in (7.3) of chapter 7, a regularity moreover preserved by Hunt and Stern in (at). The situation of (b) falles out quite similarly, except that *reute* takes the accusative case (direct object) rather than the dative case of the object of the 'repenter'.

Example (c) is a span case quite parallel to that of (7.3), except that the object of the 'liking' is food, so that the German verb is the gustatory *gut schmecken* 'taste good' rather than the all-purpose *gefallen* 'like'.

Finally, though unilinguistically example (d) is a pure-parallactic case much like that of (a), it gives the translinguistic appearance of being quite different because of the syntagmatic Divergence of the one source item *borgen* into two opposed target lexemes, *borrow* and *lend*.

(16.7) **as**. dem ältesten⟨a⟩ [begegnete] ein Mann⟨b⟩ . . . Der
zweite Bruder⟨c⟩ [[begegnete]] einem Mann⟨d⟩ (G:210)

    at. the eldest⟨a⟩ [met] a man⟨b⟩ . . . The second brother ⟨c⟩
[[met]] a man⟨d⟩ (HS:580)

    bs. den⟨a⟩ aber [reute] sein Versprechen⟨b⟩ (ibid.:233)

    bt. he⟨a⟩, however, [repented] of his promise⟨b⟩ (ibid.:119)

    cs. der Fuchs⟨a⟩ [ließ sich]'s⟨b⟩ [gut schmecken] (ibid.:267)

    ct. the fox⟨a⟩ [liked] it⟨b⟩ also (ibid.:353)

    ds. Da [borgte] der Vater⟨a⟩ beim Nachbarn⟨b⟩
eine Axt⟨c⟩ . . . das übrige⟨d⟩ will ich⟨e⟩ Euch⟨f⟩
[[borgen]] (ibid.:345,8)

    dt. The father⟨a⟩ [borrowed] an axe⟨c⟩ of the neighbor⟨b⟩
. . . I⟨e⟩ will [[lend]] you⟨f⟩ the rest⟨d⟩ (ibid.:462)

16.3 MACROSCOPIC PARALLAX

Macroscopic parallax characterizes the Norwegian idiom in (16.8s), compared with the English counterpart in (16.8t): the former, an. 'the boy shone like the sun', provides less detail than the latter as to the locus of the boy's joyful aura.

Viewed parallactically, the terse Latin style of Tacitus's *Annalia* leads to numerous macroscopic constructions, a handful of which are presented in (16.9). Once again (cf. (16.6)), some such cases have been traditionally analyzed as fig-

(**16.8**) **s**. Og [gutten strålte som en sol] da ban hørte
om de nye planene (Mykle:31)

   t. [The boy[[y's face]] lit up like the sun] when he
heard of the new plans (M1980b:97)

urae. In particular here, Furneaux analyzes (a) as ZEUGMA (273), whereby one
verb (*tendens* an.'stretching out') parsimoniously shares two objects (*manus*
an.'hands' and *supplices voces* an.'cries for mercy'), only one of which (*manus*)
is semantically straightforward in the relation so contracted. Note that Grant
undoes the zeugma by Amplification with the verb *cried*, which effectively renders the target text *micro*scopic as compared with the source.

Case (b) instantiates a PREGNANT CONSTRUCTION (Furneaux:20,373), a
brand of macroscopic parallax whereby the (conventional) meaning of a word is
(specially) impregnated with some additional meaning inferrable from the context. Here, *permoveor* an.'I am moved' is enriched to 'I am moved to wonder', a
complex that Grant Reduces to the simplex *wonder* (bt).

Finally in (c), the parallax takes the form of the designation of a person
macroscopically (*Sacrovir*) standing for actions involving that person (Grant's
connivance with Sacrovir (ct), Furneaux' *the doings of Sacrovir* (355).[3]

(**16.9**) **as**. innisusque fratri et manus ac supplices voces
ad Tiberium [tendens] (Tacitus:99)

   at. Leaning on his brother's arm he [stretched out] his
hand to Tiberius and [[cried]] for mercy (Grant:91)

   bs. plerumque [permoveor], num ad ipsum referri
verius sit, saevitiam ac libidinem cum factis promeret,
locis occultantem (ibid.:197)

   bt. I often [wonder] whether it was not really caused by a
desire to hide the cruelty and immorality which actions
made all too conspicuous (ibid.:186)

   cs. conscientia belli [Sacrovir] diu dissimulatus, victoria
per avaritiam foedata et[[uxor Sosia]] (ibid.:177)

   ct. longstanding [[[connivance with]] Sacrovir] and
cognizance of his rebellion; victory ruined by
rapacity; [[failure to check [his wife's] criminal acts]] (ibid.:167)

16.4 MICROSCOPIC PARALLAX

Microscopic parallax often takes the form of an emblematically invested NP
designating the origin of human or anthropomorphic emotions or states. Two examples are provided in (16.10), one from the Greek of the *Iliad* (a) and the other
from the Hebrew of the Bible (b). In the former case, the Goddess Hera does
not simply say that her husband Zeus is *huperphialos* 'overbearing' and *apēnēs*
'harsh', but rather in particular that his *thumos* 'spirit, temper' is. Similarly in
the Hebrew case, the Psalmist does not attribute the Israelites' abhorrence of

meat directly to the individuals themselves but rather mediately to *nafšɔɔm* 'their soul(s)' (cf. Greenstein 1982:49).

Note that in (16.10at) Rouse cleverly sidesteps the problem of replicating the microscopic construction in English by Reordering the emotions to Zeus himself (*the tyrant*) while retaining a disencumbered Match for *thumos* in *temper*. In (16.10bt), on the other hand, the King James translators push the microscopic construction through, thus imparting to the target a characteristic Biblical ring (cf. (12.15)).

(16.10)   **as**.   hoios ekeinou thumos, huperphialos kai apēnēs (H ii:48[XV,94])
     at.   what his temper is, the hard-bearted tyrant (R:176)
     bs.   kɔl-oxɛl təθɔɔʕev nafšɔɔm (K:Psalms 107,18)
     bt.   Their soul abhorreth all manner of meat (KJ)

16.5   PERSONALIZING PARALLAX

Personalizing parallax is one of a number of parallactic situations that tend to crystallize into grammatical patterns explicable by transformational analysis. In this regard, Ancient Greek differs from English in having relatively more adjectives, verbs, and other predicates capable of taking a human subject in the matrix clause while governing an embedded clause with a subject coreferent to that of the matrix. Thus, while English can construe both the impersonal *It is required of him⟨a⟩ {∅⟨a⟩ to take part in mourning}* and the personal *He⟨a⟩ is required {∅⟨a⟩ to take part in mourning}*, only the impersonal construction goes through for *It is beneath his⟨a⟩ dignity {∅⟨a⟩ to take part in mourning}*, while the personal counterpart is ill-formed: **He⟨a⟩ is beneath his⟨a⟩ dignity {∅⟨a⟩ to take part in mourning}*. Greek, on the other hand, has a viable counterpart of the latter, which is used by Aeschylus of the God Apollo in *Agamemnon*; see (16.11as). Moreover, Sidgwick in his commentary recognizes the difficulty of Equating a structure like this into English, which he consequently glosses with the available impersonal construction: 'it beseems him not to be at hand in lamentations' (55'). Relevant also to our purposes is his classification of (16.11as) as an instance of the figura he calls PERSONAL CONSTRUCTION. A similar analysis is proffered for the Homeric line in (16.11bs) by both Monro (281) and Flagg (20), the latter of whom offers the impersonal gloss 'It is hopeless to expect you to comply'.

(16.11)   **as**.   hē d'aute dusphēmousa ton theon kalei ‖ ouden
           prosēkont' en goois parastatein (Aeschylus:39[11.1078f])
     at.   Again, it's a bad omen ‖ She cries for the god who
           wants no part of grief (Fagles:150)
     bs.   amēkhanos essi pararrētoisi pithesthai (H ii:23[XIII,726])
     bt.   you are an obstinate man, you will never
           listen to persuasion (R:161)

s.

(16.12) ouden ∅ PROSĒKEIN {ho⟨a⟩ en goois PARASTATEIN} → it not BEFIT {he⟨a⟩ BE AT HAND in lamentations}

t.

a. *SSRais* ouden ho⟨a⟩ PROSĒKEIN {ho⟨a⟩ en goois PARASTATEIN}
b. *Equi* ouden ho⟨a⟩ PROSĒKEIN {∅⟨a⟩ en goois PARASTATEIN}
c. *Agr* ouden ton⟨a⟩ prosēkont' {∅⟨a⟩ en goois PARASTATEIN}
d. *Inf, ProDrop* ouden ∅⟨a⟩ prosēkont' {∅⟨a⟩ en goois parastatein}

Examples like (16.11as-bs) readily lend themselves to transformational modeling in terms of a raising rule (cf. (12.5) in chapter 12), whereby an embedded subject is lifted into the matrix clause to assume the subject relation to a verb or adjective acting as a governor to the rule, sometimes known as SUBJECT-TO-SUBJECT RAISING (*SSRais*). Greek and English would accordingly differ in the number of verbs or adjectives available as governors to SSRais, Greek having more than English.[4]

The resulting analysis may then be fitted out with bridge technique (chapter 12), along the lines of (16.12), whose right pylon would then be completed pursuant to the ingenuity of the translator and the target language's resources. Returning finally in this vein to the target version given in (16.11at), we see that Eagles has coped by Substituting for *prosēkont'*, which Sidgwick glossed as 'beseems', the passably close *want* (in *wants no part of grief*). Rouse's handling of the Homeric passage in (16.11bt) is a bit more drastic, the hopelessness (Flagg) of the situation being Substituted by its presumed cause, Hector's obstinacy.

16.6 DEPERSONALIZING PARALLAX

Even as Ancient Greek had grammaticized a considerable amount of personalizing parallax, so at least one form of depersonalizing parallax constitutes a virtual grammatical hallmark of Russian. I am referring to the large number of neuter adjectives and impersonal verbs used to convey a person's attitude toward a given state of affairs—adjectives and verbs which, in lieu of contracting a subject relation with the personal NP as English typically does (*she is bored, he felt shy, he was bursting to show*), contract an indirect object relation with that NP in a way largely alien to English (**it is bored to her, *it was shy to him, *it was bursting to him to show*). This phenomenon altogether pervades Tolstoy's *War and Peace*, from which a handful of random examples are given in (16.13). Note that every one of them is Substituted by Edmonds with a personalizing counterpart in her English translation.

16.7 THE FUNCTIONS OF PARALLAX
IN LITERARY LANGUAGE

Though no simple factor is likely to be found as a common functional denominator to all the numerous manifestations of parallax, the general variability inherent in this phenomenon makes it a good candidate as a vehicle for diversifying texts both formally and semantically. This property in turn is most likely to be exploited in literary language, where variety of configuration and message is often prized.

While cases of parallactically induced formal variation are not hard to find,[5] relevant examples introduced in this chapter happen to lend themselves to illustration of semantic variation. This seems particularly true of those from Aeschylus's *Agamemnon*, not a surprising result given the general poetic strength and

(16.13) as. '—I kak ej⟨a⟩ [ne skučno] i [[ne sovestno]] (Tolstoy i:338)

  at. 'How is it she⟨a⟩ [isn't bored to death], why [[has]]
   she⟨a⟩ [[no conscience]]?' (Edmonds i:401)

  bs. Emu⟨a⟩ [sovestno bylo]vyskazivat' vse svoi novyje,
   masonskije mysli . . . vmeste s tem emu⟨a⟩
   [[neuderžimo xotelos']] pokazat' svoemu
   drugu, čto . . . (ibid.:377)

  bt. He⟨a⟩ [felt shy] of coming out with all his new
   masonic ideas . . . at the same time he⟨a⟩ [[was
   bursting]] to show his friend that . . . (ibid.:447)

  cs. 'Nu vot čto, moja duša,' skazal knjaz' Andrej,
   kotoromu⟨a⟩, očevidno, [bylo tože tjaželo i
   stesitel'no] s gostem (ibid.:378)

  ct. 'I know what, my dear fellow', said Prince Andrei,
   who⟨a⟩ apparently also [felt depressed and constrained]
   with his visitor (ibid.:447)

  ds. Rostovu⟨a⟩ [bylo tak nelovko i neprijatno]s Borisom (ibid.:405)

  dt. Rostov⟨a⟩ [felt so ill at ease and uncomfortable]
   with Boris (ibid.:481)

beauty of that play. Thus, the displacements in (16.5) do not simply remove adjectives from the nouns they cognitively modify. In each case the adjective is realigned with another noun with which it bears some other meaningful relation in the scenario: in (as), the effect (*anaudōi* 'unspeaking') is annexed to its cause (*khalinōn . . . menei* 'strength of bonds'), while (bs) expresses the proximity of the cry (*boama*) to the ground (*khamaipetes*) and so enhances the portrait of servility thereby conveyed. The use of the personal construction in (16.11as) arguably transmits a subtextual meaning of a different sort: that Apollo can decide matters of suitability by and for himself. (The forthrightness of the God's power would risk being underplayed by less direct, impersonal phrasing.)

NOTES

1. These six types of parallax represent but a sample of the categories given in M1980d, on which this chapter is largely based. There is, incidentally, considerable overlap between parallax and Vinay and Darbelnet's notion of 'modulation', a similarity that in part extends into the subclassifications: e.g. 'subjectivisme' (cf. personalizing parallax), 'renversement des termes' (cf. antipodal parallax) (1975:205, 235ff). Mention should finally be made of a work that I stumbled across long after the present book had been written: Friedrich (1985). Since I knew nothing at all of Friedrich's work in this area, nor he of mine—he was never a recipient of M1980d or other early manuscripts of mine on parallax—our overlap in this area must instantiate a pure case of scientific convergence.

2. Similarly in Biblical Hebrew, the verb *qɔɔrev* 'approach' may be used either of soldiers entering into battle (e.g. Deuteronomy 20,3), or antipodally of the battle so to speak confronting the soldiers (e.g. I Kings 20,29—KJ: *the battle was joined*).

3. Sometimes macroscopic parallax may be clued grammatically. Thus, in both Spanish and Moabite (a Northwest Semitic language), direct objects that are semantically human are normally marked by prepositions in other respects similar to English *to*, respectively *a* and *l*. But then, if a human noun is used macroscopically for a nonhuman, the preposition should be absent (betraying the nonhuman meaning), and conversely for a nonhuman noun standing in macroscopically for a human. The first case is instantiated in *había llevado . . . un San José de yeso de tamaño natural* (Márquez:274) / *had brought a lifesize plaster Saint Joseph* (Rabassa:308), where in the source *un San José* 'a Saint Joseph' is *not* marked by *a*, as it would be if the referent were a flesh-and-blood saint rather than a plaster figure. The converse situation is instantiated in Moabite, where place names standing for their inhabitants are marked as human by *l* (Blau:153).

4. Such inventories of governors constitute special cases of SETS (chapter 8).

5. Cf. Greenstein (1982:49). Note also the case discussed in M1980d:31f, whereby antipodal-parallactic use of the verb *descend* interacts with chiasmus in one interpretation of Shakespeare's line *Ascend his⟨a⟩ throne⟨b⟩, Ø⟨b⟩ descending now from him⟨a⟩!* (1864:460[King Richard II, iv I lll]).

BIBLIOGRAPHY

A few special symbols and abbreviations should be noted:

In most listed translations, the source author is suffixed with '(s)' and the translator with '(t)'.

AL = Anthropological Linguistics; IJAL = International Journal of American Linguistics; JAOS = Journal of the American Oriental Society; LI = Linguistic Inquiry.

'X' and 'Y' stand for translators left unmentioned in published translations (cf. the last clause in the dedication on p. v).

It will also be useful to list here several points concerning the citation of bibliographical references within the body of the book:

(i) The usual format of such references is (author's name (volume) (year): page(s)), with some exceptions:

(ii) Certain frequently repeated source or target texts are referenced by abbreviations listed in the Bibliography; e.g. 'K' for the edition of the Hebrew Bible used as source text (= Kittel (1937)), and 'KJ' for the King James translation (= King James (1977)).

(iii) Biblical passages are cited by book-chapter-verse rather than page, e.g. (K:Proverbs 8,19) in example (4.1) of chapter 4. Moreover, book-chapter-verse is indicated for Biblical translations only in case of discrepancy from the source (e.g. (9.18)).

(iv) In various other cases, notably those of certain classical authors, source page references are supplemented by another breakdown given in square brackets; e.g., in the case of example (2.2) from Homer's *Iliad*, (Hii:81[XVI 401–404]) = page 81 of the source edition used (volume ii of Monro (1958)), but book XVI verses 401–404 of the *Iliad* itself.

(v) Prime-ticked pagination refers to philological apparatus as opposed to main text; e.g. (Sidgwick :18') in §16.1.

(vi) Occasionally a translational reference is given in the joint format (source/ target); e.g. (G:60/HS:78) in §6.2.1.

(vii) Translations marked (JM) are my own adhoc English renditions; e.g. in (4.5). (Excerpts from full translations by me are given in abbreviated conventional format—cf. (ii) above—as (M year:page(s)).

A = Anonymous (n.d.)

Abe, Kobo. 1962. *Sunna no onna*. Tokyo:Shinchosha.

_____. 1967. *Moetukita tizu*. Tokyo: Shinchosha.

Aeschylus (s). *See* Sidgwick (1890).

Akmajian, A., R. Demers, and R. Harnish. 1984. *Linguistics: an introduction to language and communication*, 2nd ed. Cambridge: MIT.

ʿAlī, M.H. (t). 1951. *The Holy Qurʾān (s)*, 4th ed. Lahore: Aḥmadiyyah Anjuman Ishāʿat Islām.

Alioli, Joseph Franz. 1846. *Die heilige Schrift des alten Testamentes*. New York:William Radde.

Akim, U. Babadir, et al. 1968. *New Redhouse Turkish-English dictionary*. Istanbul: Redhouse Press.

Anderson, Brad. 1981. Marmaduke. *New York Sunday News*, 12 July. (United Feature Syndicate, Inc.)

Anonymous. n.d. *Bektaşi hikâyeleri*. Istanbul(?): Ahmet Sait.

Aronoff, Mark. 1983. A decade of morphology and word formation. *Annual Review of Anthropology* 12:355–75.

Austerlitz, Robert, 1965. Das Ineinandergreifen von Text und Meoldie im Wogulischen Volkslied. *Congressus Secundus Internationalis Fenno-Ugristarum*, Pars II: 94–101.

_____. 1980. Szabad gondolattársítások általában az ismétlődésről, avagy repetitio matrix studiosa. *Ismétlő*dés a Művészetben, ed. I. Horváth and A. Veres. Budapest: Akadémiai Kiadó.

_____. 1984. A Finnish folk poem, its Yakut translation, Goethe, and other personalities. *Journal of Turkish Studies* 8:1–19.

B = Böll (1974).

Baer, S. and H.L. Strack. 1879. *Die Dikduke ha-Tʿamim des Ahron ben Moscheh ben Ascher*. Leopzig: L.Fernau.

Bair, Lowell (t). 1962. François de Voltaire (s). *Candide:* a Bantam dual-language book. New York: Bantam Books.

Baldwin, James. 1952. *Go tell it on the mountain*. New York:Signet Books.

Balzac, Honoré. 1966. *Le lys dans la vallée*, ed. Moïse Yaouanc. Paris: Editions Garnier Frères.

Bartlett, John. 1955. *Familiar quotations*, 13th ed. Boston: Little, Brown & Co.

Bearcan (s). *See* O'Kearney (1969).

Bellow, Saul. 1976. *Herzog*. New York: Avon Books.

Berlin, Isaiah. 1956. *The age of enlightenment*. New York: Mentor Books.

Bjerke, André. 1968. De voksnes fest, in Klouman and Smidt (36–38).

Blau, Joshua. 1979–80. Short philological notes on the inscription of Mešaʿ. *Maarav* 2:145–57.

Bloomfield, Leonard. 1933. *Language*. New York: Holt, Rinehart and Winston.

Böll, Heinrich. 1983. *Billard um halbzehn*. Munich: Deutscher Taschenbuch Verlag.

Brislin, Richard W., ed. 1976. *Translation: applications and research*. New York: Gardner Press.

Britannica. 1911. Encyclopaedia Britannica, vol. XIX. Cambridge, England: Cambridge University Press.

Brown, Cecil A. 1983. Where do cardinal direction terms come from? *AL* 25:121–61.

———. 1984a. Life forms from the perspective of *language and living things*: some doubts about the doubts. American Ethnologist 11:589–93.

———. 1984b. Some speculations on the growth of ethnobiological nomenclature. Unpublished ms., Anthropology Department, Northern Illinois University.

———, et al. 1976. Some principles of biological and non-biological folk classification. *American Ethnologist* 3:73–85.

Brown, D.P., S.R. Driver, and C.A. Briggs. 1978. *The new Brown-Driver-Briggs-Gesenius Hebrew and English lexicon*. Lafayette: Associated Publishers and Authors.

Brown, Donna. 1982. So waddaya wanna do sweetheart? *Stroker* 24:6.

Catford, J.C. 1965. *A linguistic theory of translation*. London: Oxford University Press.

Cervantes, Miguel de. 1959. *El ingenioso hidalgo Don Quijote de la Mancha*. Madrid: Colección Austral.

Chafe, Wallace L. 1970. *A semantically based sketch of Onandaga* = Memoir 25 of *IJAL*.

Chen, Matthew Y. 1984. Abstract symmetry in Chinese verse. *LI* 15:167–70.

Chicago. 1982. *The Chicago manual of style*, 13th ed. Chicago: University of Chicago Press.

Chomsky, Noam. 1982. *Lectures on government and binding*. Dordrecht: Foris.

Chukovsky, Kornei. 1984. *A high art*, translated from Russian by Lauren G. Leighton. Knoxville: University of Tennessee Press.

Cohen, J.M.(t). 1950. Miguel de Cervates (s). *Don Quixote*. New York: Penguin.

Collins, Glenn. 1980. Metropolitan Diary, *New York Times*, 10 September, p. C2.

Colquhoun, Archibald (t). 1951. Alessandro Mansoni (s). *The betrothed*. New York: Dutton.

Conrad, Joseph. 1957. *Victory*. New York: Anchor Books.

Cooper, Jerrold S. 1977. Symmetry and repetition in Akkadian narrative. *JAOS* 97: 508–512.

Curtius, E.P. 1954. *Europäische Literatur und Lateinisches Mittelalter*. Bern: Francke.

De Saussure, Ferdinand. 1962. *Cours de linguistique générale*. Paris: Payot.

Dickens, Charles. 1980. *Bleak house*. New York: New American Library.

Dineen, Patrick S. 1927. *Foclóir Gaedhilge agus Béarla*. Dublin: Irish Texts Society.

Ditlevsen, Tove. 1972. Måden, in Jensen (7–10).

Dorfman, Ariel. 1985. Review of Isaac Goldemberg (s)/ Hardie St. Martin (t), *Play by play* (New York: Persea Books). *New York Times Book Review*, 4 August, p.12.

Dos Passos, John. 1969. *The big money*. New York: Signet Classics.

Douay. n.d. *The Holy Bible containing the Old and New Testaments*, Douay version. Baltimore: John Murphy Company.

Edmonds, Rosemary (t). 1957. L.N. Tolstoy (s). *War and peace*, 2 volumes. Baltimore: Penguin Books.

El Diario-La Prensa. 1977. Mets, Yanquis pierden con Rojos y Orioles. *El Diario-La Prensa*,(New York) 23 May, pp.31,38.

Eliot, George. 1956. *The mill on the floss*. New York: Pocket Books, Inc.

Engelberg, Stephen. 1985. Family with many troubles at center of espionage case. *New York Times*, 10 June, pp.B1, B6.

Fagles, Robert (t). 1982. Aeschylus (s), *The Oresteia*. New York: Bantam Classics.

Flagg, Isaac. 1958. *A Homeric dictionary for schools and colleges*. Norman: University of Oklahoma Press.

Frank, Tamar. 1984. 'Taṣawwuf is . . . ': on a type of mystical aphroism. *JAOS* 104: 73–80.

Frawley, William, ed. 1984. *Translation: literary, linguistic, and philosophical perspectives*. Newark: University of Delaware Press.

Fremantle, Anne. 1955. *The medieval philosophers*. New York: Mentor Books.

Friedrich, Paul. 1985. *The language parallax-linguistic relativism and poetic indeterminacy*. Austin: University of Texas Press.

Fuller, Frederick. 1984. *The translator's handbook*. University Park: Pennsylvania State University Press.

Furneaux, H., ed. 1898. *Cornelii Tacitic annalium* libri I–IV. Oxford: Clarendon Press.

G = Grimm (1983).

Gelb, I.J. and R.M. Whiting. 1980. Evolution of writing systems. *American Academic Encyclopedia*, vol. 20, pp.291–95. Danbury: Grolier.

Glover, A.S.B., ed. 1954. *Byron-selected poems*. Harmondsworth-Penguin Books.

Gorky, Maxim. 1958. *Raskazy*, vol. I. Moscow: Gosudarstvennoe Izdatel'stvo Xudožestvennoj Literatury.

Grant, Michael (t). 1977. Tacitus (s). *The annals of Imperial Rome*. Middlesex: Penguin Books.

Grass, Günter. 1964. *Die Blechtrommel*. Frankfurt am Main: Fischer Bücherei.

Graves, Robert. 1953. *I, Claudius*. Harmondsworth: Penguin Books.

Greene, David and Richard Lattimore, eds. 1960. *Greek tragedies*, volume I. Chicago: University of Chicago Press.

Greene, Tatiana. 1984. Avatars multilingues d'un poème de Verlaine. *Symposium*, Summer issue, 113–26.

Greenstein, Edward L. 1974. Two variations of grammatical parallelism in Canaanite poetry and their psycholinguistic background. *Journal of the Ancient Near East Society of Columbia University* 6:87–105.

———. 1982. How does parallelism mean? A sense of text: the art of language in the study of Biblical literature. *Jewish Quarterly Review* supplement, 41–69.

———. 1983. Theories of modern Bible translation. *Prooftexts* 3:9–39.

Grice, P. 1975. Logic and conversation, in P. Cole, J. Morgan, eds., *Syntax and semantics*, vol. 3. New York: Academic Press.

Grimm, J. and W. 1983. *Die Märchen der Brüder Grimm*, ed. Kurt Waselowsky. Munich: Wilhelm Goldmann.

Guillemin-Flescher, Jacqueline. 1981. *Syntaxe comparée du français et de l'anglais*. Paris: Editions Ophrys.

H = Homer (*see* Monro (1958)).

Harris, Zellig S. 1954. Transfer grammar. *IJAL* 20:259–71.

Hartmann, Hans. 1979. *Synchronische und diachronische Studien zur Syntax des Irischen*. (*Zeitschrift für Celtische Philologie* 37).

Heine. *See* Jones (1916).

Herriman, George. 1969. *Krazy Kat*. New York: Grosset & Dunlap.

Hockett, Charles F. 1954. Translation via immediate constituents, *IJAL* 20:313–15.

———— 1958. *A course in modern linguistics*. New York: Macmillian.

Horn, Laurence R. 1985. Metalinguistic negation and pragmatic ambiguity. *Language* 61:121–74.

HS = Hunt and Stern (1972).

Hudak, Thomas John. 1985. Poetic conventions in Thai *chăn* meters. *JAOS* 105:107–18.

Hunt, Lida Bell. 1984. Another day. *Hoosier Challenger* 15:1.14–15.

Hunt, Margaret and James Stern (t). 1972. J. and W. Grimm (s). *The complete Grimm's fairy tales*. New York: Pantheon Books.

Hutchins, W.J. 1984. Machine translation and machine-aided translation, in Frawley (93–149).

Hutton, Seán. 1976. Radharc-chathair thromluíoch le péileacán ar strae. *Feasta* 29:8–11.

Hyman, Larry M. 1975. *Phonology: theory and analysis*. New York: Holt, Rinehart & Winston.

Jaeger, Jeri J. 1986. "On the acquisition of abstract representations for English vowels," Phonology Yearbook 3.71–97.

Jäger, Gert. 1975. *Translation und Translationslinguistik*. Halle: Max Niemeyer.

Jamiyyaat. 1963. *al-Kitaabu 'l-Muqaddasu*. Beirut: The Bible Society in the Near East.

Jensen, Hans Lyngby, ed. 1972. *Ny dansk prosa*. Copenhagen: Stig Vendelkærs Forlag.

Jerome. *See* Osb (1969).

Jewish Publication Society. 1917. *The Holy Scriptures according to the Masoretic text*. Philadelphia: Jewish Publication Society of America.

Johnston, Laurie. 1979. Token-booth killings echo in Broad Channel. *New York Times*, 21 March, p.B6.

Jones, Howard M.(t). 1916. Heinrich Heine (s). *The North Sea*. Chicago: Open Court.

Jorgenson, T. and P. Galdal. 1955. *Norwegian-English school dictionary*. Lake Mills: St. Olaf College Press.

K = Kittel (1937).

Kade, O. 1968. Zufall und Gestezmässigkeit in der Übersetzung. *Beihefte zur Zeitschrift für Fremdsprachen* 1.

Katsumata, Senkichiro. 1954. *Kenkyusha's New Japanese-English dictionary*. Tokyo: Kenkyusha.

Kerewsky-Halpern, Barbara. 1983. Watch out for snakes! Ethnosemantic misinterpretations and interpretation of a Serbian healing charm. *AL* 25:309–25.

King James. 1977. *The Holy Bible, containing the old and New Testaments in the King James version*. Nashville: Thomas Nelson.

Kiparsky, Paul. 1970. Metrics and morphophonemics in the Kalevala. D.C. Freeman, ed., *Linguistics and literary style*. New York: Holt, Rinehart & Winston.

———— 1972. Metrics and morphophonemics in the Rigveda. M.K. Brame, ed., *Contributions to generative phonology*. Austin: University of Texas Press.

————. 1977. *The rhythmic structure of English verse*. *LI* 8: 189–247.

Kittel, R., ed. 1937. *Biblia Hebraica*. Stuttgart: Württembergische Bibelanstalt.

KJ = King James (1977).

Klouman, S. and A.K. Smidt, eds. 1968. *Moderne norsk litteratur*. Oslo: Universitetsforlaget.

Kroll, Paul W. 1984. The image of the halcyon kingfisher in medieval Chinese poetry. *JAOS* 104:273–51.

Kuno, S. and E. Kaburaki, 1977. Empathy and syntax. *LI* 8:627–72.

Kyookai. 1954–5. *Seisyo*. Tokyo: Japan Bible Society.

Lamb, Sydney M. 1964. Stratificational linguistics as a basis for mechanical translation. Unpublished ms., University of California at Berkeley, Mechanolinguistics Project.

Lefevere, André. 1975. *Translating poetry: seven strategies and a blueprint*. Assen-Amsterdam: Van Goraum.

Lehmann, Ruth P.N.(t). 1982. *Early Irish verse* (s). Austin: University of Texas.

Leonov, Leonid, ed. 1982. *Maxim Gorky: selected stories*. Moscow: Progress Publishers.

Lewis, M.B. 1965. *Teach yourself Malay*. London: English Universities Press.

Lindberger, Ann-Mari (t). 1963. Cora Sandel (s). *Vårt Krångliga Liv*. Stockholm: Forum.

Lowe-Porter, H.T. (t). 1965. Thomas Mann (s). *The magic mountain*. New York: Alfred A. Knopf.

M = Malone, J.

MacNelly, Jeff. 1982. Shoe. *New York Sunday News*, 10 October.

Maillot, Jean. 1979. Anthropoymie et tradution. *Babel* 25:212.

Malkiel, Yakov. 1979. Problems in the diachronic differentiation of near-homophones. *Language* 55:1–36.

Malone, J. 1978a. 'Heavy segments' vs. the paradoxes of segment length: the evidence of Tiberian Hebrew. *Linguistics*, speical issue, 119–58.

———. 1979a. Taxonomies, unmarkedness, and a few other items from the linguist's grab-bag for the translator. Unpublished ms.

———. 1979b. Source language polysemy and problems of translation. *Babel* 25. 207–09.

———. 1979c. Free association as a problem for translation. Unpublished ms.

———. 1980a. Linguistics. *Academic American Encyclopedia*, vol. 12, pp.354–58. Danbury: Grolier.

———. (t). 1980b. Agnar Mykle (s). The rope-ladder. *Scandinavian Review* 68:93–99 (inaugural literary issue).

———. (t). 1980c. Siobhán Ní Shúilleabháin (s). Desertion. *Webster Review* 5:19–31.

———. 1980d. Parallax. Unpublished ms.

———. (t). 1981a. André Bjerke (s). *The grown-ups' party*. Unpublished ms.

———. 1981b. Trajections. Unpublished ms.

———. 1981c. Review of James McCloskey, Transformational syntax and model theoretic semantics (Dordrecht:Reidel). *Studies in Language* 5:293–304.

———. 1982a. False friendship. *Babel* 28:21–25.

———. 1982b. Generative phonology and Early Irish alliteration—a first draft. Unpublished ms.

———. 1982c. Generative phonology and Turkish rhyme. *LI* 13:550–53.

———. (t). 1983a. Seán Hutton (s). A nightmarish city-vision of a wandering pelican. *An Gael*, May issue, 16.

———. (t). 1983b. Siobhán Ní Shúilleabháin (s). What was, what is, and what will be. *Journal of Irish Literature* 11:83–94.

———. (t). 1983c. Cora Sandel (s). Mother. *Webster Review* 8:49–53.

———. (t). 1983d. Siobhán Ní Shúilleabháin (s). Women (a wives' tale). *An Gael*, August issue, 11–13.

———. (t). 1983a. Seán Ua Cearnaigh (s). In memory of Bobby Sands. *The Irish Advocate*, 9 July, p.8.

———. 1983f. Generative phonology and the metrical behavior of *u*- 'and' in the Hebrew poetry of medieval Spain. *JAOS* 103:369–81.

————. 1984a. Generative phonology and Early Irish alliteration, third draft. Unpublished ms.

————. (t). 1984b. Ishtar and the shepherd-man. *Yellow Silk* 13:39–40.

————. 1985a. Bizans. *Pangloss Papers* 4:24–32.

————. (t). 1985b. Tove Ditlevsen (s). The Way. *Webster Review* 10:5–9.

————. 1985c. Classical Mandaic Radical Metatheis, Radical Assimilation and the Devil's Advocate. *General Linguistics* 25:92–122.

————. 1985d. On the feminine pronominalization of Irish and English boat nouns. *General Linguistics* 25:189–98.

————. (t). 1985e. Nuala Ní Dhomhnaill (s). The visitor. *Paintbrush* 11–12.56.

————. (t). 1985f. Ahi Ali Baba. *Paintbrush*. 11–12.57.

————. 1985g. False friendship in international language planning. H. Tonkin and K. Johson-Weiner, eds., Report of the Third Annual Conference of the Center for Research Documentation on World Language Problems.

————. 1986a. Trajectional analysis: five cases in point. *Babel* 32:13–25.

————. 1986b. Talkin' Turkey. *Pangloss Papers* 5:11–13.

————. 1986c. Servo-features, [+distributed], and Old Irish sonorant Lenition. *LI* 17:568–573.

————. (t). 1987a. Slieve Cua, Song 16:36.

————. 1987b. Transduction, Song 16:36-43.

————. forthcoming. On the global-phonologic nature of Classical Irish alliteration. Gregory Stump, ed., Issues in Celtic Grammar Dordrecht:Reidel.

Malone, Pamela Altfeld (t). 1983. Yehuda Yaari (s). Rabbi Nachman of Bratislav's 'The seven beggars', Howard Schwartz, ed., *Gates to the New City*. New York: Avon Books. pp. 547–66.

Manent, A. (t). 1969. William Shakespeare (s). *La tragedia de Romeo y Julieta*. Barcelona: Editorial Juventud.

Manheim, Ralph (t). 1964. Günter Grass (s). *The tin drum*. Greenwich: Crest Reprints.

Mann, Thomas. 1958. *Der Zauberberg*. Berlin: G.B. Fischer.

Manzoni, Alessandro. 1908. *I promessi sposi*. Milan: Ulrico Hoopli.

Marín, Luis Astrana (t). 1980. William Shakespeare (s). *Romeo y Julieta; Julio Cesar*. Barcelona: Editorial Bruguera.

Marlette, Doug. 1981. Kudzu. *New York Sunday News*, 9 August. (Jefferson Communications, Inc.)

Márquez, Gabriel García. 1967. *Cien años de soledad*. Bogotá: La Oveja Negra.

Mawson, C.O.S., ed. 1945. *Roget's international thesaurus of English words and phrases*. New York: Thomas Y. Crowell Co.

McMillan, Eric N. 1982. Two-way translation: is it possible? Unpublished ms., National Resource Center for Translation and Interpretation.

Milner, Jean Claude. 1978. Cyclicité successive, comparatives, et cross-over en français (première partie). *LI* 9:673–79.

Monro, D.B., ed. 1958. *Homer's Iliad*, 2 volumes. Oxford:Clarendon.

Montefiore, D.B. and E. Jakowleff (t). 1905. Maxim Gorky (s). *'The outcasts' and other stories*. London: T. Fisher Unwin.

Mykle, Agnar. 1968. Taustigen, in Klouman and Smidt (26–35).

Nida, Eugene A. 1945. Linguistics and ethnology in translation problems. *Word* 1: 194–208.

————. 1964. *Toward a science of translating: with special reference to principles and procedures involved in Bible translating*. Leiden: E.J. Brill.

————. 1976. A framework for the analysis and evaluation of theories of translation, in Brislin (47–91).

————. and C.R. Taber. 1974. *The theory and practice of translation*. Leiden: E.J. Brill.

Ní Dhomhnaill, Nuala. 1981. An cuairteoir. *Feasta* 34:15.

Ní Shúilleabháin, Siobhán. 1968. Bean ar bhean. *Feasta* 21:5–7.

————. 1975. *Cití*. Dublin: Sáirséal agus Dill.

————. 1976. Tréigean. *Peasta* 29:11–17.

————. 1977. Tá, bhí agus beidh. *An tUltach* 54:3–7.

O'Brien, M.A. 1944. *New English-Russian and Russian-English dictionary*. NY: Dover.

O'Connor, N. 1977. The rhetoric of the Kilamuwa inscription. *Bulletin of the American Schools of Oriental Research* 226:15–29.

————. 1980. *Hebrew verse structure*. Winona Lake: Eisenbrauns.

O'Kearney, Nicholas (t). 1969. *The prophecies of Saints Colum-Cille, Maeltamlacht, Ultan, Senan, Bearcan, and Malachy* (s), new rev. ed. Dublin: John O'Daly.

Ó Muircheartaigh, Pádraig. 1978. Foinsí fuinnimh. *Feasta* 31:5.

Ormsby, John (t). 1952. Miguel de Cervantes (s). *The history of Don Quixote de la Mancha*, R.M. Hutchins, ed. *Great Books of the Western World, vol. 29: Cervantes*. Chicago: Encyclopaedia Britannica.

Osb, Robertus Weber, ed. 1969. *Biblia Sacra iuxta vulgatam versionem*, 2 volumes. Stuttgart: Württembergische Bibelanstalt.

Poe, Edgar Allan. 1952. *Tales, poems, essays*. London: Collins.

Postal, Paul M. and Geoffrey K. Pullum. 1982. The contraction debate. *LI* 13:122–38.

Pratt, Mary Louise. 1981. Review of Roy Harris's *The language makers* (Ithaca: Cornell University Press). *Language* 57:698–701.

Progress. n.d. M. Gorky; *Izbrannje rasskazy na anglijskom jazyke [Selected stories translated into English]*, vol. I. Moscow: Progress Publishers.

Puzo, Mario. 1970. *The dark arena*. New York: Dell Books.

Pynchon, Thomas. 1974. *Gravity's rainbow*. New York: Bantam Books.

Qur'ān. *See* 'Alī (1951).

R = Rouse (1938).

Rabassa, Gregory (t). 1971. Gabriel García Márquez (s). *One hundred years of solitude*. New York: Avon Books.

Rahlfs, Alfred, ed. 1935. *Septuaginta*, 2 volumes. Stuttgart: Württembergische Bibelanstalt.

Ray, Lila. 1976. Multidimensional translation: poetry, in Brislin (261–78).

Robb, Louis A. 1955. *Dictionary of legal terms: Spanish-English and English-Spanish*. New York: John Wiley and Sons.

Rose, Marilyn Gaddis, ed. 1981. *Translation spectrum: essays in theory and practice*. Albany: SUNY Press.

Ross, John R. 1967. *Constraints on variables in syntax*. Bloomington: Indiana University Linguistics Club.

Rouse, W.H.D. (t). 1938. Homer(s). *The Iliad*. New York: Mentor Books.

Sandel, Cora. 1968. Mor, in Klouman and Smidt (1–76).

Santillana, Giorgio de. 1956. *The Renaissance philosophers*. New York: Mentor Books.

Saunders, E. Dale (t). 1964. Kobo Abe (s). *The woman in the dunes*. New York: Vintage Books.

————. (t). 1980. Kobo Abe (s). *The ruined map*. New York: Perigree Books.

Savory, Theodore. 1968. *The art of translation*. Boston: The Writer, Inc.

Schiff, Ronny S., ed. 1976. *Disneyland: the 25th anniversary songbook*. Anaheim: Walt Disney Productions.

Schirmann, Ḥayyim. 1959. *Ha-šira ha-'ivrit bi-Sefarad u-vi-Provans*, 2 volumes. Tel-Aviv: Bialik Institute and Dvir Co.

Schuler, Ruth Wilder. 1985. And birds fly south in winter. *Reflect* 7:13–15, 26–27.

Shakespeare, William. 1864. *The complete works of William Shakespeare*, ed. W.G. Clark and W.A. Wright. New York: Grosset & Dunlap.

Sidgwick, A., ed. 1890. *Aeschylus' Agamemnon*. Oxford: Clarendon.

Simak, Clifford D. 1952. Eternity lost, in John W. Campbell, Jr., ed., *The astounding science fiction anthology*. New York: Simon & Schuster. pp. 415–39.

Skvorecky, Josef. 1985. A translator spills the beans. *New York Times Book Review*, 19 May, pp.1, 34–35.

Steinbach, Renate (t). 1961. Rex Stout (s). *P.H. antwortet nicht*. Frankfurt am Main: Ullstein Bücher.

Steiner, George. 1975. *After Babel*. London: Oxford University Press.

Stockwell, R.P., P. Schachter, and B.H. Partee. 1973. *The major syntactic structures of English*. New York:Holt, Rinehart & Winston.

Stout, Rex. 1956. *Might as well be dead*. New York: Bantam Books.

Tacitus. *See* Furneaux (1898).

Thomas, Calvin, ed. 1912. *Goethe's Faust*, 2 volumes. Boston: D.C. Heath.

Thurneysen, Rudolf. 1949. *Old Irish reader*, tr. P.A. Binchy and Osborn Bergin. Dublin: Dublin Institute for Advanced Studies.

Tolstoy, L.N. 1978. *Vojna i mir*, 2 volumes. Moscow: Xudožestvennaja Literatura.

Trautzl, Viktor. 1928. *Franz Schuberts letzte Liebe*. Reutlingen: Ensslin & laiblin.

T'sou, Benjamin K. 1975. On the linguistic covariants of cultural assimilation. *AL* 17: 445–61.

Ua Cearnaigh, Seán. 1981. I gcuimhne Bobby Sands. *Feasta* 34:18.

Ua Maoileoin, Pádraig. 1978. Fear ag gor. *Feasta* 31:12.

Van Dijk, Teun A., ed. 1985. *Handbook of discourse analysis*, 4 volumes. New York: Academic Press.

Vinay, J.-P. and J. Darbelnet. 1972. *Stylistique comparée du français et de l'anglais: méthode de traduction*. Paris: Didier.

Voegelin, C.F. 1954. Multiple stage translation. *IJAL* 20:271–80.

Voltaire, François de. *See* Bair (1962).

Walker, Mort. 1984. Beetle Bailey. *New York Sunday News*. 1 April. (King Features Syndicate, Inc.)

Waring, James (t). 1901. Honoré Balzac (s). *The lily of the valley*. St. Louis: Thompson Publishing Company.

Webster's. 1961. *Webster's third international dictionary of the English language*, una-bridged,ed. Philip Babcock Gove. Springfield: G. & C. Merriam.

Wettlin, Margaret (t). 1982. Maxim Gorky (s). For want of something better to do, in Leonov (193–212).

White, Morton. 1955. *The age of analysis*. New York: Mentor Books.

Whorf, Benjamin Lee. 1964. *Language, thought, and reality*. Cambridge: MIT.

Wilss, Wolfram. 1977. *Übersetzungswissenschaft: probleme und methode*. Stuttgart: Ernst Flett.

Witkowski, Stanley R. and Cecil H. Brown. 1985. Climate, clothing, and body-part no-menclature. *Ethnology* 24:197–214.

X (t). 1975. Heinrich Böll (s). *Billards at half past nine*. New York: Avon Books.

Y (t). 1876. Alessandro Manzoni (s). *The betrothed*. London: George Bell & Sons.

Yaari, Yehuda. n.d. *Sipure maꟄasiyot mi-Šanim Kadmoniyot*. Jerusalem: Nosad ha-Rav Kool.

Zwicky, Arnold M. 1976. Well, this rock and roll has got to stop. Junior's head is hard as a rock. S.S. Mufwene et al., eds., *Papers from the 12th regional meeting of the Chicago linguistic society*. Chicago: University of Chicago Linguistics Department. pp. 676–97.

INDEX OF PERSONS AND TRANSLATIONAL RESOURCES

[*Note*. Translational resources other than persons (authors, translators) are listed only in cases of anonymous, multiple, or unknown provenence; e.g. *"Bible"*, *"TV Guide"*. (For titles of specific works, see the Bibliography.) Names of source-authors and translators of source-target examples are tagged with "(s)" and "(t)" respectively. The name of a person with credentials in addition to those of author or translator is also tagged with "(a)"; e.g. "Sidgwick, A. (t,a)", since A. Sidgwick is both translator and philological editor.]

INDEX OF
LANGUAGES

[*Note*. A parenthesized specification following an entry means that the specification holds of that entry even when not explicitly indicated in the text. For instance, all references to "Arabic" throughout the book implicitly refer to "Classical Arabic"; thus the entry "Arabic (, Classical)"].

INDEX OF SUBJECTS